THE CONTRAPUNTAL CIVILIZATION

Essays Toward a New Understanding
of the American Experience

I have died
in Viet Nam.

But I have walked
the face of the moon.

I have befouled the waters
and tainted the air of a
magnificent land. But I have
made it safe from disease.

I have flown through the
sky faster than the sun. But I
have idled in streets made
ugly with traffic.

I have littered the land with
garbage. But I have built upon
it a hundred million homes.

I have divided schools with
my prejudice. But I have sent
armies to unite them.

I have beat down my enemies
with clubs. But I have built
courtrooms to keep them free.

I have built a bomb to destroy
the world. But I have used it
to light a light.

I have outraged my brothers
in the alleys of the ghettos.
But I have transplanted a
human heart.

I have scribbled out filth and
pornography. But I have elevated
the philosophy of man.

I have watched children starve
from my golden towers. But I
have fed half of the earth.

I was raised in a grotesque
slum. But I am surfeited by
the silver spoon of opulence.

I live in the greatest country
in the world in the greatest
time in history. But I scorn
the ground I stand upon.

I am ashamed.
But I am proud.
I am an American.

MacManus, John & Adams Inc., Advertising : Bloomfield Hills, New York, Chicago, Los Angeles, Twin Cities, Toronto, Zurich, London

THE CONTRAPUNTAL CIVILIZATION

Essays Toward a New Understanding
of the American Experience

Edited by

MICHAEL KAMMEN
Cornell University

THOMAS Y. CROWELL COMPANY
New York | Established 1834

for Carol—
a promissory note on a very large debt

PREFACE

All of the essays in this collection, despite their diverse subject matter, share a common angle of vision. That vision, or perspective, views the American experience in terms of its paradoxes, its contradictory tendencies, its dualisms, and its polarities. It is certainly true that these anomalous qualities appear universally in many cultures; but it is also true that they have been found extraordinarily meaningful and useful as conceptual tools by students of American civilization. Consequently, I have gathered together these eighteen important and provocative pieces, which have hitherto remained scattered and unrelated to one another in the minds of most readers of American history, literature, and political science. The result, I believe, is a unique and unified anthology of essays which speak eloquently for themselves and, indeed, to each other. Although their intellectual and methodological cohesiveness will be readily apparent, I have written an introductory essay designed to provide both historical and conceptual focus. At the end I have also suggested some varied readings in which more detailed aspects of the contrapuntal civilization may be explored and reflected upon. It is my profound hope that students and scholars alike will find their perspective changed, or at least challenged, by this volume. Perhaps there is something, after all, to that remarkable sign found on the wall of an English inn: "Americans and Australians are requested to turn in before 2 A. M. Germans are requested not to get up before 6 A. M. Italians are requested not to talk or sing after 10 P. M.''

I am especially indebted to friends who have listened to my thoughts on the contrapuntal civilization and have read portions of the interpretive study with which I am still struggling. To Jane and Wendell Garrett, Philip J. Greven, Jr., Joseph F. Kett, Walter LaFeber, and Kenneth A. Lockridge— many thanks. To my students at Cornell, who heard me out and responded thoughtfully—many thanks. To my colleagues at the Columbia University Seminar in Early American History and Culture who showed such interest in my *ballon d'essai* in March 1969—many thanks. To Kenneth Culver, history editor with Crowell, many thanks for his confidence over the years. To Sandy Huttleston, for excellent typing and xeroxing, *merci beaucoup.* And to Linda Lumley, an excellent editor and a very special person, my appreciation for seeing the manuscript through production with so much thoughtfulness.

M. K.

CONTENTS

I
POLARITY AND PARADOX:
A FRAME OF REFERENCE

THE DROPOUTS   By Howard Post

BIFORMITY: A FRAME OF REFERENCE

Michael Kammen

The quest for national characters and cultures plunges us into a tangle of complex historic traditions. "Seminal ideas received in childhood," wrote Edward Eggleston in 1900, "standards of feeling and thinking and living handed down from one overlapping generation to another, make the man English or French or German in the rudimentary outfit of his mind." [1] Nonetheless, those who have sought the root sources of the American national character and culture have usually fallen into over-simplifying and generalizing by stressing the importance of one or two particular factors. Thus we are presented with an enormous catalog of essentially single-factor explanations: the intellectual inheritance of western Europe (Ralph Barton Perry); the English tradition of liberty, which has produced distinctive political institutions (Hans Kohn); the Anglo-Saxon tradition of law, language, religion, and customs (Louis

Source: This essay was written especially for this book.

Michael Kammen (1936–　　), is professor of history at Cornell University. He was educated at George Washington and Harvard universities, and taught at Harvard before coming to Cornell in 1965. He is the author of *A Rope of Sand: The Colonial Agents, British Politics, and the American Revolution* (1968), *Deputyes and Libertyes: The Origins of Representative Government in Colonial America* (1969), *Empire and Interest: The American Colonies and the Politics of Mercantilism* (1970), and editor of *The Glorious Revolution in America: Documents on the Colonial Crisis of 1689* (1964) and *Politics and Society in Colonial America: Democracy or Deference?* (1967).

[1] Edward Eggleston, *The Transit of Civilization from England to America in the Seventeenth Century* (Boston, 1959), p. 1.

B. Wright); the process and psychological impact of immigration (Marcus L.

Hansen, Oscar Handlin, Geoffrey Gorer); the interplay of inheritance and environment (Henry Steele Commager); economic abundance (David Potter); immigration and abundance in tandem (Henry Bamford Parkes); migration and mobility (George W. Pierson); the westward movement of the frontier (Frederick Jackson Turner and Ray Billington); "the American dream"—the desire for liberty, opportunity, and land (James Truslow Adams); the universal passion for physical prosperity (Harold Laski); freedom of enterprise (Louis Hacker); the democratic faith or dogma (Ralph H. Gabriel and Gerald Johnson); "the American conscience"—the dominant body of opinion (Roger Burlingame); our mode of conformity (David Riesman); generosity and the philanthropic impulse (Merle Curti); our modes of child-rearing (Margaret Mead); and the antithesis between highbrow and lowbrow (Van Wyck Brooks), to mention only a few.

One way to reconcile such a bewildering welter of explanations might be to ascertain a style or state of mind common among Americans that takes into consideration all of the above factors, yet has a certain thrust and weight of its own. Erik Erikson, the distinguished psychoanalyst, has pointed the way by suggesting such a state of mind.

> Most [Americans] are faced, in their own lives or within the orbit of their closest relatives, with alternatives presented by such polarities as: open roads of immigration and jealous islands of tradition; outgoing internationalism and defiant isolationism; boisterous competition and self-effacing co-operation; and many others. . . . Thus the functioning American, as the heir of a history of extreme contrasts and abrupt changes, bases his final ego identity on some tentative combination of dynamic polarities such as migratory and sedentary, individualistic and standardized, competitive and co-operative, pious and freethinking, responsible and cynical, etc.[2]

Erikson's schema seems to me far more meaningful and useful than the traditional single-faceted approach to culture

[2] Erik Erikson, *Childhood and Society*, 2d ed. (New York, 1963), pp. 285–86.

and national identity. Moreover, Erikson's insight is reinforced by observations from many fields of study. Ethologists, for example, have recently noted that the existence of opposing impulses does not necessarily cause anxiety or the dissolution of personality, but may instead create a tension which accentuates or strengthens a particular character.[3] Philosophers have shown that "the actual focus of any history is a problem that has been generated by a tension developed between newer and older human ways of acting and believing."[4] Critics of art and taste have piloted the same channel with great success.

> The history of styles as well as the cultural geography of nations can only be successful—that is approach truth—if it is conducted in terms of polarities, that is in pairs of apparently contradictory qualities. English art is Constable and Turner, it is the formal house and the informal, picturesque garden surrounding it. These are polarities evident at one and the same moment. Polarities appearing in two consecutive periods are: the Decorated and the Perpendicular style, Vanbrugh and Lord Burlington, Hogarth and Reynolds.[5]

American historians, however, have been largely blind to this especially European, peculiarly Hegelian, way of perceiving culture and character.[6] Instead they have debated endlessly the relative merits of what they call conflict and consensus historiography, worrying whether our history has been most striking for unity or disunity—whether ours is a country

[3] See Konrad Lorenz, *On Aggression* (New York, 1966).

[4] John Herman Randall, Jr., quoted in Fred Somkin, *Unquiet Eagle: Memory and Desire in the Idea of American Freedom, 1815–1860* (Ithaca, 1967), p. xiv.

[5] Nikolaus Pevsner, *The Englishness of English Art* (London, 1956), p. 18; see also pp. 31, 117.

[6] It is possible to trace this strain of thought through a diverse cluster of Germanic writers. See Georg W. F. Hegel, *The Phenomenology of Mind*, ed. and trans., J. B. Baillie (London, 1910), pp. 117–21 and *passim;* Wilhelm Windelband, *Die Philosophie im Deutschen Geistesleben des XIX. Jahrhunderts* (Tübingen, 1909); Herbert Marcuse, *Reason and Revolution: Hegel and the Rise of Social Theory,* 2d ed. (New York, 1954); and the various nineteenth-century European nationalists who wrote passionately about the creation of ultimate unity through strife.

of contending Jeffersonian and Hamiltonian traditions or harmonious fellow travelers all preferring the back of the church, the front of the bar, and the middle of the road. Disputes about how best to interpret the very real power-struggles between white coats and blue coats, radicals and moderates, conservatives and liberals, have blinded us to the larger, internalized tensions within the society as a whole, as well as within those individuals who comprise it. Since World War II, some brilliant practitioners of the "American Studies" approach to history and literature have tended to explain away friction and uniqueness through the analytical leverage of myth and paradox, thereby minimizing the objective reality of conflict.[7] Somehow we must go beyond as well as get beneath the conflict versus consensus controversy. We must appreciate America's inconsistencies and paradoxes without losing sight of the very real struggles that have taken place.

One obstruction to clearer vision in this matter has been an enduring element of ambiguity in American historical writing—not at all surprising in a culture particularly perplexed by ambivalence and contradictory tendencies. There are superficial ironies that are easily explained, such as the existence of the New Left "Wisconsin School" of diplomatic historians who are highly critical of American foreign policy of the past century, yet developed in a state that as recently as 1924 had a law forbidding the teaching of any historical facts considered unpatriotic by politicians and the people. More perplexing and intriguing are the ambiguities one finds in the writings of Frederick Jackson Turner, Charles A. Beard, Perry Miller, and many others. In Beard's most famous book, *An Economic Interpretation of the Constitution,* for example, it is not at all clear whether he was saying that the Founding Fathers framed the Constitution because they expected to profit by it, or whether the ways in which the Fathers made their profits predisposed them to look at political and constitutional issues from a certain perspective. Beneath this equivocation of Beard's, as Richard Hofstadter has shown, lay a real ambiguity in thought; and both were rooted in a certain dualism in

[7] See David Brion Davis, "Some Recent Directions in American Cultural History," *American Historical Review* 73 (February 1968): 700–703.

Beard's position as scholar and publicist of the Progressive Era.[8]

Curiously enough, then, American historians have been less sensitive to contradictory tendencies in the national style than foreign observers, philosophers and theologians, and scholars of the interdisciplinary American Studies movement have been. The latter group has indeed stressed certain antinomies in the American character, as well as anomalies or dualisms inherent in many American circumstances. But their concern has belletristic origins, has largely located its manifestations in the literary culture, and has been almost exclusively preoccupied with nineteenth- and twentieth-century situations, to the neglect of colonial origins.[9] In contrast, Reinhold Niebuhr has ranged through the length and breadth of our experience in order to depict persuasively the irony of American history. "Our age is involved in irony," he writes, "because so many dreams of our nation have been so cruelly refuted by history. . . . Our idealists are divided between those who would renounce the responsibilities of power for the sake of preserving the purity of our soul and those who are ready to cover every ambiguity of good and evil in our actions by the frantic insistence that any measure taken in a good cause must be unequivocally virtuous."[10]

It is vitally important to recognize, however, that ours is not the only culture characterized by biformity. This condition occurs universally, especially in colonial circumstances. But in diverse cultures the tensions take various forms and are resolved in different ways, if at all. In addition, foreign observers have been noting for generations what Erik Erikson also believes, that "this dynamic country subjects its inhabitants to more extreme contrasts and abrupt changes during a lifetime or a generation than is normally the case with other great

[8] See Lee Benson, *Turner and Beard: American Historical Writing Reconsidered* (New York, 1960), pp. 96–101; Richard Hofstadter, "Beard and the Constitution: The History of an Idea," *American Quarterly* 2 (Fall 1950): 196, 204–8; David A. Hollinger, "Perry Miller and Philosophical History," *History and Theory* 7 (1968): 189–202.

[9] Davis, "Recent Directions in American Cultural History," p. 703.

[10] Reinhold Niebuhr, *The Irony of American History* (New York, 1952), pp. 2, 4.

nations."[11] James Fullarton Muirhead, a Briton who spent the years 1890–93 here preparing *Baedeker's Handbook to the United States,* put it this way:

> It may well be that a long list of inconsistencies might be made out for any country, just as for any individual; but so far as my knowledge goes the United States stands out as preeminently the "Land of Contrasts"—the land of stark, staring, and stimulating inconsistency; at once the home of enlightenment and the happy hunting ground of the charlatan and the quack; a land in which nothing happens but the unexpected; the home of Hyperion, but no less the haunt of the satyr; always the land of promise, but not invariably the land of performance; a land which may be bounded by the aurora borealis, but which has also undeniable acquaintance with the flames of the bottomless pit; a land which is laved at once by the rivers of Paradise and the leaden waters of Acheron.[12]

What we must do, then, is inquire whether these inconsistencies have, in fact, been more pronounced in American history than elsewhere, and inquire as to the precise nature of our paradoxes and their historical sources. In order to do so we must first have some clear notion of "un-American" societies, their uncertainties and biformities. There is no assurance, but when we know what we are not, we may also know better what we are.

Counterpoised tendencies may be found in English life, and have deep historic roots in a country where self-governing, local communities once served as a counterweight to the possibility of absolute and centralized government, and where pugnacity, cruelty, and irritability go hand in glove with gentility, courtesy, and orderliness.[13] In Ireland such pulls have an amusing but also touching quality, for the Irishman is a "shy extrovert." "We drink to loosen our tongues," he will say. He

[11] Erik Erikson, *Childhood and Society,* p. 285.

[12] James Fullarton Muirhead, *The Land of Contrasts: A Briton's View of his American Kin* (Boston, 1898), p. 7.

[13] George L. Haskins, *The Growth of English Representative Government* (Philadelphia, 1948), p. 3; Geoffrey Gorer, *Exploring English Character* (London, 1955), p. 13.

is a supreme individualist but also a great conformist. A quiet, pious, good Catholic in one situation reveals himself at another time to be a Rabelaisian character at heart. Only in Ireland are there so many "married bachelors," men who continue their old patterns of stag friendship and irresponsibility after marriage. And the story is commonly told by Englishmen in Dublin, perhaps puckishly, that "with a little effort you could get an Irish girl to sleep with you, but she would say, 'Now don't be using a contraceptive; I don't want to commit a sin.' "[14]

The real history of Scotland, it has been argued, is compounded of violence and idealism. If the Union of 1707 with Britain made possible a special kind of Scottish national feeling, it also created conditions which restricted its effective working in Scottish culture. The overly elaborate arrangement of simple Scottish airs, as David Daiches has discerningly shown, "was only one aspect of a phenomenon common enough in eighteenth-century Scottish culture—national pride in the native heritage accompanied by a nervous desire to do the genteel thing." The *philosophes* of the Scottish Enlightenment called Edinburgh the Athens of the North. Yet they thought of their country as "North Britain" and tried to be more English than their southern cousins. They exercised themselves over hypothetical or faked primitive Gaelic poetry, while ignoring the genuine Gaelic poetry that was being written by a group of remarkable poets under their very noses! Although Calvinism denied freedom of the will, the special way in which Presbyterianism emerged in Scotland associated it in many quarters with ideas of national freedom and democracy. The paradox of the co-existence of a belief in individual freedom with extreme intolerance crops up at every turning in Scottish ecclesiastical history.[15]

Turning to French history, especially in the early modern

[14] Donald S. Connery, *The Irish* (New York, 1968), pp. 96, 113, 120, 198–200, 207–13.

[15] David Daiches, *The Paradox of Scottish Culture: The Eighteenth-Century Experience* (London, 1964), pp. 8–11, 15, 20–22, 28, 34–36, 41, 47, 55, 65–66, 73, 75, 85, 88–89, 94, 97; Eric Linklater, *The Survival of Scotland* (New York, 1968).

era, we find that its ideas and politics have often been probed in terms of certain symbolic polarities: Voltaire versus Rousseau; Baroque versus Rococo. It has been found that a tension existed between two concepts of humanistic education: the idea of a general moral education and the rather different notion of higher, intensive education designed to produce excellence in political and administrative leadership.[16] François Nourissier suggests that:

> it is awkward to be French because France is now divided between two periods of her history, as she has been, and is divided between her conservative and progressive elements. This double division, this double conflict, is found in individuals, social groups, and ideas. Until quite recently, when one spoke of monarchy and republic, *ancien régime* and revolution, Right and Left, one was alluding to a tension in the nation's life which has proved to be fruitful at some times and paralyzing at others. Today this dual dynamic manifests itself in vacillating ideas.

Not surprisingly, then, in France the common expression is that the more things change the more they stay the same. There, too, Proust made the *homme-femme* a credible figure in French society. Good citizenship in France manages simultaneously to mean respect for the State and scorn for government. Respect for law there is tempered by a predisposition toward anarchy, so that "established disorder" refers to the complex of tensions and tolerances by which an uneasy public peace is maintained.[17]

In Spain the dualisms seem to run ever deeper. Spain has long vacillated between Europe and Africa, between the attractions of the North and the influence of the South, and this hesitant shifting has meant both continuous instability in public affairs and tremendous individuality. In Iberia the only man who walks (and even salutes) with flowers is the most virile of all Spaniards, the matador. Spain has two equally characteris-

---

[16] Irene Q. Brown, "Philippe Ariès on Education and Society in Seventeenth- and Eighteenth-Century France," *History of Education Quarterly* 7 (Fall 1967): 363, 367.

[17] François Nourissier, *The French* (New York, 1968), pp. 13–14, 53, 93, 103–5, 117, 119, 120–21, 247.

tic faces: the elongated visage of the Knight of the Woeful Countenance, and the practical, square head of Sancho. Still, as one Spaniard insisted, Quixote and Sancho are really one identity. "Both of them together form the single unified spirit of Spain. Cervantes divided our spirit into two parts, so that we could see it better. The Spanish spirit is a rich unity, for inside our dry, hard shell, two antithetical forces embrace each other like twin almonds." [18] The Spanish spirit, then, is quixotic-sanchoesque or sancho-quixotic, according to the season. Sometimes one element is dominant, sometimes the other. "But always they are struggling and suffering together." [19]

In Italy, another Latin nation, two sorts of society seem to co-exist within one. One consequence has been that a land notoriously teeming with vigorous and intelligent people often behaves rather erratically in both international relations and domestic politics. Benedetto Croce, the Neapolitan philosopher, was bemused by the contradiction that "those very Italians who, a while earlier, had been accused of being the children of Machiavelli were now thought to be the disciples of . . . the priests." How odd, since Machiavelli was a notorious *mangiapreti,* or priest-eater, an opponent of Vatican policy, and the author of ribald satires against clerical corruption. Nevertheless, ever since the Renaissance, Italians have indeed been disciples of both Machiavelli and the Church. Sicily to the south, of course, is an enigma in its own right. Pirandello, the island's great playwright, put it this way: "In this labyrinth I see a two-headed Hermes which with one face laughs and with the other weeps; it laughs with one face at the other face's weeping." [20]

Turning north to the Teutonic nations, one finds in Ger-

[18] Fernando Diaz-Plaja, *The Spaniard and the Seven Deadly Sins* (New York, 1967), pp. 100, 213.

[19] Nikos Kazantzakis, *Spain* (New York, 1963), pp. 15, 21–22, 28, 44; see also Richard Herr, *The Eighteenth-Century Revolution in Spain* (Princeton, 1958), for the emergence and conflict between progressive anti-clericals and Catholic conservatives.

[20] Luigi Barzini, *The Italians* (New York, 1964), pp. xiii, 88, 234, 312–13; see *The New York Times* editorial on Sicily, January 20, 1968. One is reminded of Richard Strauss's advice to interpret *Der Rosenkavalier* "with one eye weeping and one eye winking."

many a history of extremes. "German" has frequently meant a sentimental, trusting, pious soul, but just as often an unprincipled, degraded brute. Both types of German have existed, not only at the same time, but in the same person. For more than a thousand years, Germans have turned different faces to the East and to the West. Caught between the Roman Empire and French civilization on one side, and "barbarian" Slavs on the other, the German peoples have been anxious to learn from and imitate the West, as well as to exterminate the East. The Germans have become the "civilized barbarians" of Europe, ostensibly the defenders of civilization, occasionally the destroyers of culture. Martin Luther made Germany a nation, but one profoundly in tension. He broke with the medieval dream of universalism, but led Germany into fierce particularism. He taught the Germans to believe in liberty, and taught them also that liberty is to be found only in the service of the prince. "Like the Germans of a thousand years before and of four hundred years after, Luther was the barbarian who looks over the Rhine, at once the most profound expression and the most decisive creator of German dualism." [21]

Scandinavian newspapers provide something of a guide to the style of life in that region. They almost never report divorce actions, rapes, suicides, or family embarrassments. The gossip column is frowned upon. Yet annual listings of taxable income are published from public records so that people can readily find out how much their neighbors make. The Norwegians are said to have an "uneasy self-confidence." They are known as rugged individualists who have, nevertheless, a strong ability to cooperate and a fondness for the welfare state. They are also marked by a kind of worldly provincialism: dedicated homebodies who are renowned as travelers and explorers! The Swedes are still more complex, for as one native journalist remarked, "We like to be alone, but alone together." As the country becomes wealthier, the more it longs for social security and welfare. Alfred Nobel began by inventing dynamite and ended by establishing the world's most famous peace prize. Nor has Sweden's passion for peace prevented her from doing an exceedingly profitable business in

[21] A. J. P. Taylor, *The Course of German History* (London, 1945), pp. 8, 13–15, 21.

armaments. Finland has far more social conflict than her western neighbors because of antagonisms between Finns and Swedish-Finns, between north and south, Left and Right, and within political as well as social organizations. The Finns are fascinating for their strange combination of primitiveness and sophistication, for they cherish the Spartan virtues. Perhaps because of this, they vacillate between deep moodiness and irascibility, and great warmth and generosity.[22]

Peoples to the East have had their fair share of ambivalence too. "I am thus and not thus," writes Yevgeny Yevtushenko, a contemporary Russian poet. "I am industrious and lazy, determined and shiftless. I am . . . shy and impudent, wicked and good; in me is a mixture of everything from the west to the east, from enthusiasm to envy." [23] The average Russian can be plunged for long periods into moods of either pessimism or optimism, apathy or concentrated effort. The icon and the axe which traditionally hang together on the wall of the peasant hut suggest both the visionary and earthy aspects of Russian life. The icon especially was emblematic of cultural counterpoise, for while it gave divine sanction to human authority, it also served to humanize divine authority.[24] In *The First Circle,* Alexander Solzhenitsyn, Russia's greatest living prose writer, suggests a pervasive paradox best seen by his character Gleb Nerzhin: in Stalin's Russia only those in prison were truly free to be honest with one another. "When you've robbed a man of *everything* he's no longer in your power—he's free again."

Like Germany and Russia, Turkey has also faced West and East, and vacillated between dualistic inclinations. Europe has meant democracy, advanced technology, material benefits and intellectual ferment. But to the East lie Turkish roots, societies built on hierarchic aristocracies in which order is more important than economic progress.[25] Persia, through which the Turks migrated to reach Anatolia, has had its enduring polari-

[22] Donald S. Connery, *The Scandinavians* (London, 1966), pp. 19, 26, 30, 32, 58–61, 180–83, 185, 196, 298, 338, 391, 401, 445, 448, 453, 551, 554.

[23] Quoted in Connery, *The Irish,* p. 113.

[24] James H. Billington, *The Icon and the Axe: An Interpretive History of Russian Culture* (New York, 1966), pp. vii–viii, 26, 28, 31.

[25] Kenneth Pearson and Patricia Connor, *The Dorak Affair* (New York, 1968), p. 90.

ties too: warrior bands and sedentary scribes, nomads of the steppes and settled, pastoral peoples.[26]

In Chinese thought, ambiguity runs as a steady undercurrent. Thus their influential *Book of Changes* reveals the dual forces of the cosmos. The God of War is actually the God for the Prevention of War, and therefore really the God of Peace. Where Confucianism has been the religion of an ordered, carefully articulated society, Taoism has been the advocate of anarchy. In Chinese philosophy, constant change in the cosmos results from the interaction of two opposite forces, Yin and Yang. Yin is earth, feminine, negative, passive, dark, weak, even, and moon. Yang is heaven, male, positive, active, light, strong, odd, and sun. Yin contracts and Yang expands, so that the universe "breathes" as it were. Yet Yin and Yang do not divide the world into warring forces, but unite it. Each completes the other. Not surprisingly, the Chinese mind comprehends "antisociety," "unheroes," "uncitizens," "unreason," and "unthink." Contradictory tendencies in the Orient have thus been incorporated into the life style of a civilization.[27]

I remarked earlier that societal tensions and counterpoised inclinations tend to become accentuated or aggravated when transplanted into colonial settings. The reasons for and manifestations of this are important, but not at all obvious. Therefore we should briefly examine the circumstances of New Spain and New France with an eye to our developing frame of reference.

When Spain turned westward at the close of the fifteenth century, her recent unification barely concealed significant sectional differences. Isabella of Castile, the intensely Catholic queen, was deeply concerned about the proper assertion of spiritual authority. Until 1492 the hierarchical Castilian state had directly confronted Moorish Granada, and of necessity retained its medieval orientation. By contrast, Isabella's hus-

[26] Richard N. Frye, *The Heritage of Persia* (Cleveland, 1963). See chap. 1, especially pp. 13–14.

[27] Dennis Bloodworth, *The Chinese Looking Glass* (New York, 1966), pp. 28, 113, 128, 137, 147–48, 155, 190–92, 194–96, 201, 204, 255, 258, 281, 299, 344.

band, Ferdinand of Aragón, who was more oriented to the East and North, was a secular Renaissance ruler. Whereas Isabella presented the unity of spiritually intransigent Christendom to infidel and pagan, Ferdinand was more committed to the shifting, amoral statecraft of competing Christian princes. Managing with sheer personal verve and cunning, he was in every sense Machiavellian.

The point, of course, is that Spanish conquistadors, catechizers, and colonists carried with them to the New World this dual heritage of contemporary tendencies in tension: medieval and Thomistic versus Renaissance and Machiavellian. Consequently the conquest developed as a kind of dual revelation. Richard Morse and Luis Villoro have put it this way: "To the Indian were revealed a triumphant 'universal' Church and its militant temporal agent, the Spanish crown; to Europe were revealed civilizations, fauna, flora and geography of a vast New World, which crumbled agelong sureties and challenged the imagination." [28] One result was that the American Indian was viewed bifocally—through the eyes of the self-assured knight errant, and through those of the inquisitive new humanist. Because of the inevitable myopic ambivalence, there occurred the tragic early fate of the Indian under Spanish dominion.

There was still another but related dualism characteristic of Spain on the eve of colonization. On the one hand, a militant nobility and dependent peasantry shared a common desire for riches by warfare. The aristocracy sought prestige and looted wealth, while the peasants, soldier-cultivators, hoped for land. On the other hand, the town-based bourgeoisie anticipated capital accumulation through commerce and industry. Such entrepreneurs existed in all the Peninsular towns. But only in eastern Spain, especially Catalonia, had they gained sufficient power to restrain the expansionist tendencies of the militants. By 1492 these two Spains were headed for collision, a conflict which might well have altered the face of Spain but for the discovery of America. The New World offered vast expanses of new land, unheard-of wealth, and enormous bri-

[28] Richard M. Morse, "Toward a Theory of Spanish American Government," *Journal of the History of Ideas* 15 (January 1954): 72–77.

gades of disciplined labor. Paradoxically, the new chests of wealth from the Indies would eventually ruin Spanish trade and industry. Ironically also, the new frontier helped to destroy the very class that might have brought a commercial renaissance to Spain. Instead, the merchant-entrepreneur receded into obscurity, while the knight-adventurer, who sought wealth through conquest, gained a new impetus.[29] Thus colonization resolved a major tension in early modern Spain in ways exactly opposite to the pattern in Stuart England, where the bourgeoisie and capitalism flourished in response to the stimulus of overseas expansion.

Once the settlement of New Spain got underway, a fascinating configuration of anomalies and conflicts emerged. The first of these grew simply from the fact that conquerors and colonizers were urban types whose task nevertheless was to make contact with the soil from which all wealth would flow, given the available labor of millions of Africans and American Indians.[30] All too soon the conquistador, on the threshold of capitalism, found himself in a utopia that bore the peculiar marks of a contradiction, caught between past and future. His utopia of gold and freedom was being crushed by opposing forces—the desire for personal aggrandizement and the demands of an increasingly centralized state system under Charles V and Philip II.[31] The tendency of conquistadors to form local enclaves in which they were the elite ran up against the Crown's burgeoning bureaucracy. An irresistible force had met an immovable body. On the one hand, for example, was Don Luis de Velasco, the King's representative, supported by relatives, retainers, and administrative resources of the Mexican colony. On the other, a group of land-owning, strong-willed Creoles, threatened with the loss of their *encomiendas,* who saw in Martín Cortés the defender of their privileges.[32]

Meanwhile the Crown's dual aims of collecting revenue

[29] Eric Wolf, *Sons of the Shaking Earth* (Chicago, 1959), pp. 157–62.

[30] Richard M. Morse, "Latin American Cities: Aspects of Function and Structure," *Comparative Studies in Society and History* 4 (July 1962): 473.

[31] Wolf, *Sons of the Shaking Earth,* pp. 166–67.

[32] Fernando Benítez, *The Century After Cortés* (Chicago, 1965), p. 179; Irving A. Leonard, *Baroque Times in Old Mexico* (Ann Arbor, 1959), chap. 3.

and converting Indians were only theoretically compatible. Bartolomé de Las Casas's awareness of this tension was evident in his appeals (on behalf of the Indian) to both the royal coffers and the royal conscience. Inevitably, however, conflicts grew between the humanitarian compassion of the Spanish administrators and what seemed to be the practical realities and necessities of colonial life. Inexorably the City of Man, peopled by avaricious Spaniards, was trying to destroy the City of God that friars and Indians together were beginning to build.[33]

By the eighteenth century, social tensions in these multiracial societies had begun to reach an explosive level. Local revolts, such as the one at Cochabamba (Upper Peru) in 1730, revealed enormous frustrations and uncertainties that were to destroy the empire in a few more generations. Conflict appeared between new rationalist philosophical ideas and old scholastic traditions, between social hierarchies and ideas of equality, between Europeans and Americans, between regular armies and colonial militia, between monopolistic, grasping treasuries at home and the colonists' desire for economic liberty, and between monarchist absolutism and representation of the people.[34] Because attempts to ease or obviate these polarities during the later eighteenth century were ineffective, they were ultimately resolved only by revolution. Even then, three centuries of colonial uncertainty and anguish were certain to leave their mark. Consequently, Latin American republics since independence have often grafted democratic forms of government on to a social order undemocratic in many ways.[35]

[33] See J. H. Parry, *The Spanish Seaborne Empire* (New York, 1966), pp. 173–91; John Leddy Phelan, *The Millennial Kingdom of the Franciscans in the New World* (Berkeley, 1956), p. 87.

[34] Bartolomé Arzáns de Orsúa y Vela, *Historia de la Villa Imperial de Potosí*, ed. Lewis Hanke and Gunnar Mendoza (Providence, R. I., 1965), 3 vols.; Silvio Zavala "A General View of the Colonial History of the New World," *American Historical Review* 66 (July 1961): 928.

[35] J. Lloyd Mecham, "Latin American Constitutions: Nominal and Real," *The Journal of Politics* 21 (May 1959): 258–75; Kingsley Davis, "Political Ambivalence in Latin America," *Journal of Legal and Political Sociology* 1 (October 1942): 127–50.

Nonetheless scholars have perhaps made overmuch of the apparent paradox of fact and theory, achievement and aspiration in Latin American governments. A recent and important analysis of twenty-seven of the first constitutions written there between 1810 and 1815 demonstrates clear distinctions between Spanish American political thought and ideas allegedly borrowed from western Europe and North America, and therefore suggests an essentially singular tradition in Spanish American politics—a tradition in which theory and practice are often in harmony. It may well be an historical and analytical fallacy to think that Spanish America for the past century and a half has been seeking fruitlessly to fulfill the democratic superstructure it ostensibly adopted in 1810.[36]

Whereas wars of rebellion and independence resolved some of Latin America's colonial contradictions, the English conquest of New France in 1759–60, and her subsequent patterns of administration and control, perpetuated profound dualisms which have persisted in Canadian history and fascinated historians from Parkman's time until our own. Francis Parkman saw in the history of New France a struggle between "barren absolutism" and "a liberty, crude, incoherent, and chaotic, yet full of prolific vitality." As a counter-influence to absolute authority there lay the great interior wilderness. "Rudely and wildly antagonistic," the domain of savage freedom beckoned the "disfranchised, half-starved seigneur, and the discouraged *habitant* who could find no market for his produce." [37]

Like New Spain, New France also had a dual intellectual inheritance. The stronger of the two strains was the Jansenist-inspired pietism of the seventeenth century; the weaker, but nonetheless important, was the libertine and tolerant spirit of the Enlightenment. Pietism won out, yet libertinism would recur repeatedly in French-Canadian literature. The Jansenist

[36] See Glen Dealy, "Prolegomena on the Spanish American Political Tradition," *Hispanic American Historical Review* 48 (February 1968): 40–42, 49.

[37] Wilbur R. Jacobs, ed., *Letters of Francis Parkman* (Norman, Okla., 1960) 1:li; Samuel Eliot Morison, ed., The Parkman Reader (Boston, 1955), pp. 266–67. See also Mason Wade, ed., *Canadian Dualism: Studies of French-English Relations* (Toronto, 1960).

strain appeared in the efforts of French Jesuits to civilize the Indian; but curiously, the religious absolutism of the Jesuits was combined with a surprising sense of cultural relativism. In consequence, the cassocked conquistadors tended to permit the heathens great latitude in the sphere of natural conduct while insisting upon absolute conformity in the realm of religion. Although the Jesuits eventually sanctioned conquest and colonization in the interest of conversion, they objected from time to time to the military and mercantilist concomitants of such programs.[38]

As the fringes of settlement in New France slowly grew, so did the tension between European assumptions or expectations and emerging realities—the conflict between old prescriptions and new imperatives. Even the royal authorities recognized that a vast discrepancy had developed, for example, between the real position of the seigneur and the one ascribed to him. The pressure of new economic necessities was a more powerful determinant of social behavior than the schemes of imperial administrators. Two of them, Beauharnois and Hocquart, noted a sharp contrast between the behavior of Canadians and of young men in the French Antilles.

> [Canadians] prefer voyages and trade, which give them the means of livelihood. It is not surprising that the young men of the Islands seek to fill vacancies for the position of councilor, because not only are their customs different from those of the Canadians, but, having been born with money, they are ambitious only for honors. Poverty reigns in Canada; men seek to escape from it and obtain a little comfort.[39]

The resolution of these problems only began to emerge when what had once been regarded as deviance came to be recognized as in fact the norm. Thus Denonville would eventu-

[38] John C. Rule, "The Old Regime in America: A Review of Recent Interpretations of France in America," *William and Mary Quarterly*, 3d series, 19 (October 1962): 592; J. H. Kennedy, *Jesuit and Savage in New France* (New Haven, 1950), pp. 100—104.

[39] Quoted in Sigmund Diamond, "An Experiment in 'Feudalism': French Canada in the Seventeenth Century," *William and Mary Quarterly*, 3d series, 18 (January 1961): 25—26; Guy Frégault, *La Civilisation de la Nouvelle France* (1713—1744) (Montreal, 1944), pp. 219—20.

ally write Seignelay "that Monseigneur should not determine to cease to give letters of nobility; but that it would be well to give them only to those who will . . . enter into whatever commerce makes a noble in this country." [40] Even so, tensions between feudal rights and royal absolutism continued to cause the same unrest in New France that they did in Europe. Intendants and governors kept up their fierce but subtle enmities in the eighteenth century. And as one would expect, from the conquest of 1759 there emerged two distinct styles of life and taste. One was French, Catholic, conquered, leaderless, and ruled by the law of the Custom of Paris. The other was English, Protestant, vigorous, triumphant, and ruled by the common law tradition. Within this biformity the new French-Canadian, already nascent, would be finally molded. [41]

No one would want to insist, then, that citizens of the United States are uniquely a people of paradox. We have seen that polarities exist in cultures the world over. I have asserted that members of colonial societies are especially susceptible to both the inconsistencies they inherit and those they form anew. Although I have taken New Spain and New France as case studies, one finds similar evidence in Anglo-Dutch South Africa and in Portuguese Brazil. In the formation of Brazilian society, the process of balancing off antagonisms has been central: between the African and the native; between agrarian and pastoral economies; between agrarian and mining regions; between Catholic and heretic; Jesuit and *fazendeiro;* *bandeirante* and plantation owner; *Paulista* and *emboaba,* Pernambucan and *mascate.* [42]

[40] Quoted in Diamond, "An Experiment in 'Feudalism'," pp. 31–32.

[41] Rule, "The Old Regime in America," pp. 590–91, 593; A. R. M. Lower, "Two Ways of Life: The Primary Antithesis of Canadian History," *Canadian Historical Association Report* (1943), pp. 5–18; Lower, "Two Ways of Life: The Spirit of Our Institutions," *Canadian Historical Review* 28 (December 1947): 383–400.

[42] See Charles R. Boxer, *Four Centuries of Portuguese Expansion, 1415–1825: A Succinct Survey* (Johannesburg, 1965), p. 63; Gilberto Freyre, *The Masters and the Slaves: A Study in the Development of Brazilian Civilization,* 1st English ed. (New York, 1946), pp. 7–8, 79–80; Leonard M. Thompson, "The South African Dilemma," in Louis Hartz, ed., *The Founding of New Societies* (New York, 1964), pp. 178–218; Douglas Brown, *Against the World: Attitudes of White South Africa* (New York, 1968).

I have suggested, however, that denizens of these United States and their forebears have been peculiarly and most profoundly perplexed by ambivalence and contradictory pulls. All of the essays in this book are given over to establishing that fact and explaining why it has been so. We must next, at least briefly, indicate some of the dimensions of America's dilemma, its causes and consequences.

The United States is commonly represented by two images or icons. Both are used on posters and in cartoons, though it is not at all clear which is most appropriate to a particular circumstance. One is an extremely tall, thin old man, his beard trimmed to an old-fashioned goatee, his formal suit cut from a Betsy Ross creation. The other is a portly, maternal woman draped in flowing robes of the classical style, crowned with a diadem, and holding a torch aloft in one hand. Uncle Sam symbolizes the government: demanding, negotiating, asking for sacrifices. The Goddess of Liberty, or Columbia, represents the land of freedom and opportunity: America as a bountiful cornucopia. The national iconography seems to be sensitive to what America offers her people and the world, as well as to what the government requires of its citizens.[43]

Symbols such as these have long fascinated foreign observers of the American scene. The most ingenious of them all, Alexis de Tocqueville, recognized that individualism and idealism were somehow just as characteristic of the American style as conformity and materialism. Within the ideal of equality he discerned two tendencies, "the one leading the mind of every man to untried thoughts, the other inclined to prohibit him from thinking at all." If the principle of equality predisposed men to change, it also suggested to them certain interests that could not be satisfied without a settled order of things. "Equality urges them on, but at the same time it holds them back; it spurs them, but fastens them to earth;—it kindles their desires, but limits their powers." Tocqueville admitted to being surprised by two facets of the United States in 1831, "the mutability of the greater part of human actions, and

[43] See Geoffrey Gorer, *The American People: A Study in National Character* (New York, 1948), pp. 50–53.

the singular stability of certain principles." Men were constantly and restlessly in motion; but their minds were fixed. Once an opinion took root, no power on earth might dislodge it.[44]

James Bryce, the perceptive Englishman who visited half a century after Tocqueville, remarked that if Americans were shrewd and tough-minded, they were also very impressionable; that if they were restless and unsettled, they were also rather associative. "Although the atoms are in constant motion, they have a strong attraction for one another." He found them a vacillating people, and again resorted to natural science to make his meaning clear: "They have what chemists call low specific heat; they grow warm suddenly and cool as suddenly." Despite their inclination to change mood and place so readily, Bryce also noted the power of habit, tenacity, and tradition among Americans, and therefore concluded that "it may seem a paradox to add that the Americans are a conservative people."[45]

Students of American culture, much influenced by Bryce and Tocqueville, have occasionally remarked that racial discrimination, civic corruption, and violence are just as much American traditions as equality, morality, and the rule of law. They have noted that Americans tend to be more smug and complacent than other peoples, yet more self-critical and conscience-stricken; that a moral dualism in the United States couples passionate concern for private, material prosperity with a propensity for periodic, public, moral renewal and religious enthusiasm. By constantly breaking with the past and conforming to transitory norms and fashions, the American seems to be both anti-traditionalist and highly conformist. He is also embarrassed by another moral dualism, the conflict between Christian ethical standards and the ethics of the marketplace. Perhaps because of a bad conscience he is extraordinarily generous, yet always afraid of being "played for a sucker." Inevitably the American has been obliged to reconcile

---

[44] Quoted in Richard L. Rapson, ed., *Individualism and Conformity in the American Character* (Boston, 1967), pp. 9–10, 14.

[45] James Bryce, *The American Commonwealth*, 2d ed. (London, 1891) 2:281–83.

morality and expediency. Thus, if generous actions motivated by compassionate considerations are accepted without gratitude, misinterpreted, or unrequited, a cynical repudiation of humanitarianism may follow.[46]

The American has also held conflicting attitudes toward intellectual and manual labor. When the life of the mind has obviously promoted material well-being, it has generally been appreciated and rewarded. But when it has appeared to threaten established norms and comfortable ways of thinking, or the power and influence of entrenched groups, it has been resented and disparaged. Southern ambivalence about labor, leisure, and laziness—beginning with Captain John Smith's jeremiad against "idleness and sloth" at Jamestown—is merely part of a larger configuration of southern images, each of which has its obverse. The other side of chivalry is arrogance, of paternalism, racism. In short, it would seem that the American has been unable to escape his ancient and equivocal tension between authority and the individual.[47]

Some of these insights—to the everlasting credit of American authors—have become staple fare in our literature and formal thought. George Santayana found the American "an idealist working on matter." Van Wyck Brooks, in his first excited report on the condition of American culture, saw a frank acceptance of linked values that no one expected to have anything in common: high ideals and catchpenny realities. "Between university ethics and business ethics, between American culture and American humor, between Good Government and Tammany, between academic pedantry and pavement slang, there is no community, no genial middle ground." Brooks found that colonial literature of the seventeenth cen-

[46] J. R. Pole, "Daniel J. Boorstin," in Marcus Cunliffe and Robin W. Winks, eds., *Pastmasters: Some Essays on American Historians* (New York, 1969), pp. 220–22; Hans Kohn, *American Nationalism: An Interpretive Essay* (New York, 1957), p. 74; Gabriel Almond, *The American People and Foreign Policy* (New York, 1960), pp. 32, 43, 45–46, 52.

[47] Merle Curti, *American Paradox: The Conflict of Thought and Action* (New Brunswick, N. J., 1956), p. viii and *passim;* C. Vann Woodward, "The Southern Ethic in a Puritan World," *William and Mary Quarterly,* 3d series, 25 (July 1968): 343–45, 370; Howard Mumford Jones, *O Strange New World. American Culture: The Formative Years* (New York, 1964), p. 394.

tury was "composed in equal parts . . . of piety and advertise-
ment." Hence from the very beginning there must have been
two main currents running parallel in the American mind: the
transcendental current, elevated by Jonathan Edwards, refined
by Ralph Waldo Emerson; and the practical current that Benjamin Franklin made into a philosophy of common sense and
nineteenth-century humorists raised to a style of entertainment.[48]

In Robert Lowell's recent trilogy, *The Old Glory,* based
upon traditional literary and historic materials, the poet explores certain tensions and antonyms arising from the hidden
painfulness of America's origins. In "Endecott and the Red
Cross," adapted from Hawthorne's story about Massachusetts
Bay during the 1630s, Thomas Morton and Governor Endecott
are set as archetypal American rivals—libertine and Puritan,
Dionysiac and Apollonian, the establishmentarian and the
nonconformist. Lowell has perceived and presented a mov-
ingly poetic (albeit untheatrical) view of the North American
experience and sensibility.[49]

If the insights and reflections of so many observers are
essentially on target, as I believe they are, then we are obliged
to ask three crucial questions: Has America been marked by
more and different biformities than other nations? If so, why?
And what have been the consequences? This entire volume is
devoted to answering these questions. The third one will be
treated at great length in the essays which follow. The first two
may be dealt with, at least summarily, in the remainder of this
one.

Americans and foreigners seem to agree, in varying degrees, with the Italian author Raoul Romoli-Venturi that "all
the tensions of the world have been imported by the United
States." Jacques Maritain, a friendly and philosophical visitor,
put it this way:

[48] Santayana, *Character and Opinion in the United States* (New York,
1920), p. 175; Brooks, *America's Coming of Age* (New York, 1915), pp.
17–20.

[49] Robert Lowell, *The Old Glory* (New York, 1965); see Richard Gilman's
interview with Lowell, described in *The New York Times,* May 5, 1968, sect.
D, pp. 1, 5.

The feelings and instincts of community are much stronger in this country than in Europe . . . the result of which is a tension, perpetually varying in intensity, between the sense of the community and the sense of individual freedom. Such tension, to my mind, is normal and fecund in itself. Of course, it happens to create conflicts, especially when the community feels that it is threatened in its very life, and reacts . . . with "posses" which hunt men who are not necessarily criminals. Then a counteraction follows as a rule, in the name of moral tenets such as individual freedom and civil rights, without which the very existence and unity of the nation cannot hold.[50]

From the very beginning of settlement at Jamestown, Plymouth, Salem, and St. Mary's, there has been contention over the meaning of America. Was it to be a conglomeration of individuals, each going his own way, or a well-ordered society of generally cooperative groups?[51] The very vastness of the landscape made the former almost inevitable, but the latter nearly a necessity. Because the cultural forces of western Europe were transplanted to circumstances of relative isolation, "they reverberated like loud voices in an empty room; and they fell into new relationships." Constance Rourke has said it with admirable grace:

Thus the psychological intensities of Calvinism were greatly deepened in the New England colonies as compared with the practice of Calvinism in English communities, which tended to fringe off into groups of a quite different character and thus to become modified. And these peculiar inner intensities fell into conjunction with wholly primitive influences here. All through the colonial period up to the French and Indian War the colonists fought savage foes and even adopted some of their forms of savagery, against a background of this intricate inner quest. . . . These forces were all but antiphonal, one set completely against the other.[52]

[50] Quoted in *Time,* June 14, 1968, p. 26; Maritain, *Reflections on America* (New York, 1958), pp. 21–22, 163. See also Nourissier, *The French,* p. 123.

[51] See Gerald E. Critolph, "The Contending Americas," in John A. Hague, ed., *American Character and Culture: Some Twentieth-Century Perspectives* (De Land, Fla., 1964), p. 16.

[52] Constance Rourke, *The Roots of American Culture, and Other Essays* (New York, 1942), pp. 54–56.

Our cultural patterns have made the extent of social atomization in the United States perhaps greater than in any other culture. The American is more preoccupied with private or personal values than with societal or political ones. By contrast, in most other cultures there is greater concern with corporate loyalties and more personal involvement in public issues. Because the American is so absorbed in his private values and goals, he is competitive to an extreme degree. Often, as Gabriel Almond suggests, he regards himself and his family as being in direct competition with others for success and achievement. Understandably, then, the American has idealistically subscribed to the perfectibility of man. But all the while, altruistic goals have been cast in materialistic terms, such as raising the standard of living as a means to a better life. Americans have been committed in extraordinary ways to the view that materialistic means are necessary to idealistic ends. Benjamin Franklin caught the essence of it two centuries ago: "An empty sack cannot stand upright." [53]

Why should we be this way? Why should biformity be so pervasive in the American style? There are many reasons. The first in point of time is that England during her great age of colonization and cultural transmission was peculiarly racked by tensions and contradictory tendencies. The conflict of generations in late Elizabethan times, Mary versus Elizabeth, Catholic versus Protestant, Cavalier versus Roundhead, the ambiguous issue of overpopulation, are just a few illustrations.

The second reason rests in the very process of uprooting and immigrating. Many colonists migrated in order to escape certain anxieties at home; but by coming they activated others and created some anew, such as the tension between inherited ideas and environmental realities, which demanded some sort of accommodation.[54]

A third reason also has to do with our being a nation of

---

[53] Almond, *The American People and Foreign Policy,* pp. 48–50; David M. Potter, "The Quest for the National Character," in John Higham, ed., *The Reconstruction of American History* (London, 1962), pp. 198, 207, 212–13, 219.

[54] See Arthur M. Schlesinger, "What Then is the American, This New Man?" *American Historical Review* 48 (January 1943): 225–44.

immigrants. Multiple origins, ethnic diversity, and social heterogeneity have produced discomforting strains. In the guise of
Poor Richard, a certain cosmopolitan provincial publicly ex-
tolled the colonies as places of refuge for Europe's aged, ill,
aliens, and dissenters; but as Benjamin Franklin he privately
expressed his fear of German immigration to Pennsylvania.
The Germans "under-live, and are thereby enabled to under-
work and under-sell the English; who are thereby extremely
incommoded and consequently disgusted." [55] Walt Whitman
would put this problem posed by pluralism most simply a century later in *Leaves of Grass*.

> Do I contradict myself?
> Very well then I contradict myself,
> (I am large, I contain multitudes.)

A fourth factor may be found in the ambivalence of English attitudes toward America and imperial policies during the
colonial era. The provincials were not supposed to deviate, for
example, from institutional norms at home; but neither were
they to imitate the House of Commons too slavishly, or demand its privileges and prerogatives. In consequence, the
meaning of liberty has developed in America not so much in
opposition to force but as a pattern of ways in which force was
to be applied: "The safeguards of liberty lay not in the denial
of the use of force, but in the establishment of appropriate
procedures for its use." [56]

The fifth reason is simply that *America Was Promises,* as
Archibald MacLeish put it thirty years ago. Ever since John
Cotton's 1630 sermon, 'God's Promise to His Plantations," men
have expected much of America: greater freedom, opportunity,
and bounty than was ever offered man in all of known history.
Those are difficult expectations to fulfill consistently, making
frustration inevitable.

The sixth reason is a related one. Our principles and ideals have been so elevated that we have often been unable to

[55] Quoted in Max Savelle, *Seeds of Liberty: The Genesis of the American Mind* (Seattle, 1965), pp. 567–68.
[56] Oscar and Mary Handlin, *The Dimensions of Liberty* (Cambridge, Mass., 1961), pp. 21, 37, 87.

live by them or realize an approximation of them. "American history is a paradox if not a contradiction," writes John W. Caughey. "Ours was the first nation to dedicate itself at the outset to a regime of freedom. . . . Yet as a nation and as a people we have all too often strayed from this path." [57]

The seventh and eighth causes of our biformities are also linked. Rapid physical and social mobility have brought people too quickly from one region to another, from one status to another, and subjected them to unexpected circumstances and unfamiliar strains.[58] The plight of Clyde Griffiths in Dreiser's *American Tragedy,* or of the southern rural Negro transplanted to Chicago's South side, are typical. Meanwhile the intense pace of life and rapidity of change subject Americans to tensions and uncertainties not found elsewhere, or not in the same degree.

The ninth reason has been defined by Perry Miller as "an unreconcilable opposition between Nature and Civilization—which is to say, between forest and town, spontaneity and calculation." Where else is the citizen torn so powerfully between the vastness and beauty of the natural world on one side, and the overwhelming influence of urbanization and technology on the other? [59]

Finally, we have had to reconcile individualism and conformity, and so have developed a very special amalgam, a *collective individualism,* described perfectly by Raph Barton Perry:

> American self-reliance is a plural, collective, self-reliance—not *"I* can," but *"we* can." But it is still individualistic—a togetherness of several and not the isolation of one, or the absorption of all into a higher unity. The appropriate term is not "organism" but "organization"; *ad hoc* organization, extemporized to

[57] John W. Caughey, "Our Chosen Destiny," *Journal of American History* 52 (September 1965): 251.

[58] See George W. Pierson, "Mobility," in C. Vann Woodward, ed., *The Comparative Approach to American History* (New York, 1968), pp. 106–20.

[59] Perry G. Miller, "The Shaping of the American Character," and "The Romantic Dilemma in American Nationalism and the Concept of Nature," in *Nature's Nation* (Cambridge, Mass., 1967), pp. 1–13, 197–207; Leo Marx, *The Machine in the Garden: Technology and the Pastoral Ideal in America* (New York, 1964).

meet emergencies, and multiple organization in which the same individuals join many and surrender themselves to none.[60]

Collective individualism is only one among a cluster of biformities which express the contradictory tendencies of our contrapuntal civilization. There are also the conservative liberalism of our political life, the pragmatic idealism of our cerebral life, the emotional rationalism of our spiritual life, and the godly materialism of our acquisitive life. The English colonies were established by Calvinists who believed that in and of himself man could do little to save his own soul, and that gaining the world conferred no profit; yet Americans have behaved ever since as though he who strives shall indeed gain the world, and save his soul in the bargain. Many of the Founding Fathers believed in national perfectibility despite their deeply pessimistic appraisal of the present state of mankind. Many of the utopian and communitarian experiments of the 1840s were essentially devised as anti-institutional institutions, swerving erratically between the extremes of anarchism and collectivism. The Progressives tried desperately to reconcile within themselves an ethic of communal responsibility with one of unrestrained individualism. And two sorts of liberalism have become solidly entrenched in twentieth-century America: laissez-faire liberalism and welfare-state liberalism. Witness the New Nationalism of Theodore Roosevelt and the New Freedom of Woodrow Wilson; contrast the first and second phases of the New Deal under Franklin Delano Roosevelt. In short, the push-pull of both wanting to belong and seeking to be free has been the ambivalent condition of life in America, the nurture of a contrapuntal civilization.

[60] Ralph Barton Perry, *Characteristically American* (New York, 1949), p. 13.

A CALCULUS FOR POLARITY

Louis W. Norris

Man's chief puzzles arise from the fact that his experience comes full of oppositions, contraries and actual contradictions. He spends his life trying to resolve this condition into meaning and value. His concern with diverse lines of thought and action yields classifications that are found to have some relationships. His crucial choices are made as he tries to locate his actions at the most advantageous point between extremes which are ultimately polar in character. It is essential that he learn to calculate this point reliably.

Consideration of how such calculation may be made is the heart of any philosophy. To show that this is man's ultimate responsibility and how he may go about discharging it are two tasks to be undertaken at the outset.

I

Nature manifests itself as a realm most easily defined by early philosophers in terms of opposites. On earth day and

Source: Louis William Norris, *Polarity: A Philosophy of Tensions Among Values* (Chicago: Henry Regnery Company, 1956), pp. 1–12. Reprinted by permission of the publisher.

Louis W. Norris (1906–   ), is President of Albion College. He was educated at Otterbein College, Boston, Harvard, and the University of Berlin. After serving as a pastor in the Evangelical Congregational Church of Dunstable, Massachusetts, he taught philosophy at Baldwin-Wallace College and DePauw University. From 1952 until 1960 he was President of MacMurray College. In addition to *Polarity: A Philosophy of Tensions Among Values* (1956), he has written *The Good New Days: Moral Hazards of an Executive* (1962).

night bring light and darkness. Summer and winter bring heat and cold. Solids and liquids are dry and wet. The early Ionian physicists found these contrasts structural in nature, for the most matter-of-fact and unreflective mind is impressed by them. As the science of physics advanced it added to this list of cosmic polarities. Cause and effect became effective tools for studying nature, as did stability and change, rest and motion. As quantum mechanics has replaced the classical atomic view of matter, nature has been most fruitfully studied by calculating structures or fields of force which persist intact but yet which emit determinable quantities of force. Atoms remain themselves, yet continuously change by radiation into others beside themselves. With the abandonment of static substances physics has resorted to terms which calculate dynamics and relativities that are meaningful just as they combine contrary, e.g. particle and wave-like, properties.[1]

In the organic world male and female, yang and yin, are the most obvious classifications. The principle of opposition is also found in the fact that organisms live by the death of some other organisms. Men live by eating beef cattle that live by eating grass. The contrary categories of dependence and independence help to understand the cycle of living bodies. A body attains independence just so far as its dependence on its environment yields a given support of its processes. Evolution proceeds as organisms adapt themselves to their environment and adjust their environment to themselves. A living substance itself turns out to be a unity of anabolism and catabolism, the building up of its tissues and breaking down of chemical compounds it appropriates. Cells in the body literally live by dying, as Huxley said. Disturbance to this equilibrium of opposites results in death. Spemann shows how the field of biological forces generating organs of the human body contains polar actions that mutually assist the development of the organ.[2]

Again, man has found himself to be an expression of polar opposites. At least in some sense he is both mind and

[1] J. B. S. Haldane, "Dialectical Materialism and Modern Science: The Unity of Opposites." *Labor Monthly,* 23 (1941), p. 328.

[2] Hans Spemann, *Embryonic Development and Induction* (New Haven: Yale University Press, 1938), pp. 76, 77, 87, 96, 303.

body.[3] Early man discovered there was more to himself than his body as he contemplated death, dreams, illness and its effects upon his power to think. Common experience still reports that mind and body are two different and perhaps opposite phases of reality. The conclusions of materialism and idealism that all is matter or all is mind are *interpretations* of experience after all, and not reports of it. Glandular activities, nerve conduction, blood pressure, or sense impression, are scarcely the same kind of experience as conceiving a poem, solving an equation, or evaluating a type of conduct. In any case, man *experiences* the rock before him to be matter and his mind to be quite other than its object, as Dr. Johnson so vociferously asserted. Berkeley's view, as Johnson saw, was interpretation, not report.

The powers of the mind have shown themselves in many instances to be contraries to each other. Indeed as mind's opposite functions have been employed the management of life has matured. William Blake showed in "The Marriage of Heaven and Hell" that there is a creative factor in human life resulting from opposition. "Attraction and Repulsion, Reason and Energy, Love and Hate, are necessary to human existence. Without contraries there is no progression." [4] Skepticism and doubt have served to help the mind avoid traps of prejudice and illusion, but faith in itself has also been a contrary need to which the mind has had to respond. The premium on "creative thinking" in recent times testifies that this need to trust reason must have its innings.[5] Rationalism and empiricism became classic competitors for acceptance as accounts of the genesis and criterion of knowledge. But Kant showed them to be so involved in each other that they are really polar opposites.

Emotion and reason, faith and reason, as well as sense and reason, have stood often against each other. Focused

[3] Cf. W. H. Sheldon, *America's Progressive Philosophy* (New Haven: Yale University Press, 1944), pp. 29, 41.

[4] Quoted by Geoffrey Sainsbury, *The Theory of Polarity* (London: G. P. Putnam's Sons, 1927), p. 158.

[5] Morris Cohen, *Reason and Nature* (New York: Harcourt, Brace and Company, 1931), p. 59.

upon nature, the mind confronts order and contingency, reason and unreason. The insistence by scientists upon minute observation of fact implies that there always remain phases of nature not captured under the net of rational order.[6] Platonic and Aristotelian efforts at classifying and relating the objects of experience settled down to the nominalist-realist controversy in medieval times. There are individuals and there are universals, and it has often been discussed how the twain do meet.

Another set of contrary relations which man daily confronts is that of fact and value. Facts exist in given times and places. The same values may obtain in different times and at different places. One must know and rely upon specific and concrete facts but possibilities and promised events must also be weighed and some of them avoided while others are repeated. It is necessary to follow an historical sequence of events, yet to rise above this temporal order in the determination of the significance of these events.[7] Facts without values are meaningless, yet values must be checked by the facts also.

In ethics we are beset by the demands of the case where a decision must be made, but we are bound also by loyalty to the principle by which the choice must be guided. The wisdom of man tends to coagulate into absolute rules, such as "Thou shalt not bear false witness." But there is a demand for adjustment in each situation which often suggests the pertinence of an exception to this rule. Mere relativism in morals ends in chaos, while rigid absolutism results in an arid formality which invariably kills goodness itself. The crux of the moral problem lies in selecting the proper function of each of these poles, the relativity and the absoluteness of moral principles. For public morality, responsibility is both individual and collective. Each man is punished or rewarded by his society according to his deed, yet society can never be absolved from its stake in his deed also.

Religion even more commonly involves apparent sets of opposites. In fact, Zoroastrianism was built entirely on the be-

[6] Cf. Cohen, *ibid.*, p. 135.
[7] Cf. Cohen, *ibid.*, p. 385.

lief in strife of opposites in nature and in the ultimate dichotomy of good and evil. Man's human life stands over against the divine. The Catholic doctrine of the *analogia entis* expresses the unity and yet separation which man feels with respect to God.[8] In great religious prophets, notably in Jesus, two natures are said to coexist. Religion arises in "a nice combination of solitariness and of community feeling,"[9] retreat from the crowd and sharing in its burdens. Durkheim, following Comte, has tried to show that religion is primarily a social experience while Whitehead has claimed it to consist in "what a man does with his solitariness." The worshiper vibrates between a sense of sin and one of salvation. He recognizes both "the goodness and severity of God," as St. Paul put it.[10] He is a conserver of established values yet an innovator in search of new ones. He eschews reason for faith, but returns with faith in reason. He waits upon the Lord to renew his strength, yet seeks that he may find.[11] The paradoxes of theology grow out of the diverse ranges of religious life and not out of the alleged class-conscious sophistication of their formulators.

Art thrives on such dichotomies as light and shade, form and content, symmetry and variation, unity and variety, strength and delicacy. Architecture, sculpture, and painting would be nothing without these contrasts. Music abounds in antiphonies, and in fact it is fundamentally constituted of "counterpoint." Literature employs contrasts, counter forces, and paradoxes. Dancing combines pose and movement, established pattern and invention. The creative artist relates the unfamiliar to the familiar, the unconventional to the conventional. Exclusive adherence to the latter would make him monotonous, while total concern with the former would make him unintelligible.

[8] Cf. V. A. Demant, *The Religious Prospect* (London: Frederick Muller, Ltd., 1939), pp. 249–50.

[9] D. Elton Trueblood, *The Logic of Belief* (New York: Harper & Brothers, 1942), p. 15.

[10] Romans 11:22.

[11] Cf. H. F. Rall, *Christianity* (New York: Charles Scribner's Sons, 1941), chap. 3.

Confronted by these oppositions [12] in so many phases of his experience, the metaphysician finds himself occupied with the diremptive character of being itself. The universe is in some sense one whole yet it is obviously full of a number of things. How do the many relate to the one? There is change and even evolution in nature, but these terms would be meaningless without some measure of fixity and permanence. Action never occurs without reaction. Substances are known by functions which are not substantial entities. Like the north and south poles of the earth, or positive and negative poles of a magnet, these diversities are in many cases correlatives and involve each other. Both are true of reality but in different perspectives.[13]

There can be no doubt that a large part of experience occurs in this dichotomous form. The major question is how thought may deal with this contrariety of experience. Whatever ultimate justice there may be in thinking of these differing features of nature, thought, or culture as pairs belonging in some sense together, the fact remains that common experience contains them. Here are logical, epistemological, ethical, metaphysical, physical, psychological, sociological and other oppositions that confront us. To point out that this merely means that reality comes to us in different ways helps little. The significant factor is that there are relationships, complementary kinships, mutual contributions that are discernible among them. Their meaning is tied up in their memberships. Their significance derives from their relations often as much as from their own quality of being.

How does thought go to work on this problem of diversity?

---

[12] Tarde sought to show in *L'Opposition Universelle* that there are oppositions in everything. But his analysis was probably a confusion between internal and external relations. Cf. C. K. Ogden, *Opposition, A Linguistic and Psychological Analysis* (London: Kegan Paul, Trench, Trubner & Co., Ltd., 1932), pp. 24, 32.

[13] Cf. Sheldon, *op. cit.,* p. 46.

2

Whatever else truth-finding may be, it consists at least in assigning experienced data some order so that they yield a meaningful and valuable significance for man's outlook on the world. No doubt there is much uninterpreted, half-interpreted, and misinterpreted experience, but man's problem is to accomplish as relevant interpretations as he can. The oppositions found in experience pose the most serious problems of adjustment. In fact "the human mind has always laboured at this problem of opposites" for "there is at the bottom of our souls a secret conviction that this unconquerable dualism . . . is ultimately conquerable." [14] Mere dualism would not be conquerable, but polarism would be a manageable situation for contraries are then in the same universe of discourse.

As thought sets to work on these oppositions, its distinctively philosophical character appears. "Philosophy may not neglect the multifariousness of the world . . . ," nor be too narrow in the selection of its evidence.[15] The apparent antinomies of the world "always preoccupy the philosophic mind." [16] In fact, as Royce pointed out, the chief difference between common sense and philosophic doctrine is simply that "the philosopher, by his finer analysis, reveals the paradoxes which our everyday consciousness veils by means of a more or less thoughtless traditional phraseology. The philosopher is more frank with his antitheses. He does not invent the paradoxes; he confesses them." [17] If Follett was right in saying that "the core of the . . . experience, growth and progress of humanity, is the confronting and gripping of opposites," [18] philosophy is then working at crucial questions.

[14] Benedetto Croce, *What Is Living and What Is Dead of the Philosophy of Hegel* (tr. Ainslie) (London: Macmillan and Company, Ltd., 1915), pp. 11, 15.

[15] Alfred N. Whitehead, *Process and Reality* (New York: The Macmillan Company, 1929), pp. 512–13.

[16] Henry Bett, *Nicholas of Cusa* (London: Methuen & Co., Ltd., 1932), p. 131.

[17] *Lectures on Modern Idealism* (New Haven: Yale University Press, 1919), p. 93.

[18] M. R. Follett, *Creative Experience* (New York: Longmans, Green & Co., 1924), p. 302.

Aberrations in thought and action have arisen from the absolutizing or positing as reliable some partial perspective or isolated conception apart from opposing views that impinge upon it. Truth holds at various levels and under various conditions but not always in the same sense under different conditions and at different levels of being. It is dogmatism or "anti-philosophy" [19] to let reason become anchored to one point of view with no regard for the play of perspectives that threaten it.

Questions of degree and contrast are fully as relevant to the definition of a term as the differentia and hierarchy of classes to which a term may belong. Serial order is sometimes easier to determine than hierarchical order. The directional base and the degree of opposition are key factors in determining the significance of these contraries. The crucial issue to settle is whether there is a neutral point between the extremes of opposition under consideration. Otherwise there is no opposition, only heterogeneity. The degrees to which one contrary limits, modifies, or otherwise affects the other indicates that some fundamental connection or relevance obtains between them. [20]

Some oppositions found in experience are clearly identifiable as contradictories, where one or the other is to be denied and avoided. The contradictory propositions, "There was a Homer," and "There was no Homer," stand as possibilities only because final evidence, at least in the judgment of some critics, is lacking. But certainly one proposition will go out when evidence beyond any doubt is discovered. Error and truth cannot possibly serve each other, they are mutually exclusive. They may interfuse with each other. The mind does not, however, seek to preserve error, but to escape it. Evil and good are likewise contradictories. The choice of murdering an ill and poverty-stricken man or of giving him food and medical aid is one in which only one alternative can be right. One important service of philosophic thought is the discovery of con-

[19] Cf. Karl Jaspers' discussion of various kinds of "anti-philosophy" in *The Perennial Scope of Philosophy* (translated by Manheim) (New York: The Philosophical Library, 1949), pp. 148–53.

[20] Cf. Ogden, *op. cit.,* pp. 22–28.

tradictories in experience and elimination of erroneous or immoral options.

The more difficult and frequent task concerns those opposites which complement, or as Buckham says, "contraplete" [21] each other. Much thinking is genuinely polar in which concepts stand, not on the relation of duality, for that term suggests hostility and dissidence, but in a relation of mutual fulfillment. "Synthesis" between them is scarcely possible for these poles in thought are not to be united but held in conjunction with each other. Nor are concepts of this type to be considered "correlatives" only. Mere environmental proximity may produce a kind of correlation, as in the case of master and servant. But there is an innate logical consanguinity by which one term necessitates the other for its own validation. The concept of "contrapletion" implies that two poles of thought, while they stand over against one another (*contra*), at the same time fulfill one another (*plere*). "Contrapletion" expresses and conserves both poles of a relationship. It suggests juxtaposition and reciprocity, potential reconciliation and yet supplementary diversity.[22]

This principle of contrapletion not only illuminates the problem of opposites in thought but it could eliminate some of the traditional controversies of philosophy. Thinkers have often taken opposite stands on questions and tried to prove that one side or the other was the truth, without seeing that their differences rested on difficulties and not on contradictions. The greater (though perhaps not the spectacular) part of wisdom lies in getting at these difficulties with a view to determining the extent to which each side of the controversy is justified.[23] Harmony among thinkers is not merely a matter of adopting each other's language, as Emerson said,[24] but of ear-

[21] John W. Buckham, "A Broadening Factor in Logic." *Phil. Rev.,* 40 (1931), 459–68; "Contrapletion: The Values of Synthetic Dialectic." *Personalist,* 26 (1945), pp. 355–66.

[22] John W. Buckham, first article cited, p. 463.

[23] Cohen, *op. cit.,* p. xi. Cf. Wilmon H. Sheldon, *Process and Polarity* (New York: Columbia University Press, 1944), p. xii.

[24] Cf. *Journal,* May 1832, where he says, "To be at perfect agreement with a man of most opposite conclusions you have only to translate your language into his."

nest attention to the possible connection between seemingly contradictory ideas. Profitable communication may still be possible in spite of differing language.

Indeed agreement in thought about basic problems is often not necessary or desirable for linguistic forms fall short of the whole meaning intended. The truth can be stated in differing ways and it is rare, if ever possible at all, that a single proposition states all that can be said of a given state of affairs. Hence uniformity of thought and agreement in language should not be taken as the goal of philosophy. Meaningful reference to differing perspectives, and harmonious relation to all possible points of view must be the aim. Professional philosophers sometimes pridefully set their own views apart from others as an end in itself rather than as an alternative to other meaningful insights.

Fear of paradox must not deter the serious thinker from the problem of opposites. Casserley holds that "to evade the paradox is to lose the truth." [25] He means that since every proposition refers to some feature of the universe in a way that no other does or can, there is something "singular" or unique about its reference. Thinking is bound to be a relating of differing propositions in the mind of a unique thinker. "We are driven to paradox . . . because personal experience is experience of the singular by the singular." [26] Each thinker occupies himself inevitably therefore with propositions at variance with each other. His knowledge of other thinkers' thoughts must be of thoughts necessarily at variance with his own.

This situation does not mean that skepticism must be man's lot. Meanings impinge upon each other and communication still occurs in spite of differences in perspective. Men communicate with each other and with nature (i.e. they grasp meanings in nature shared by others) even though the "singularity" of their perspective remains a fact. Whether this commonly recognized occurrence of communication has implications for the ultimate nature of the universe in which it takes place, need not be discussed here. It suffices to observe that

[25] J. V. Langmead Casserley, *The Christian in Philosophy* (New York: Charles Scribner's Sons, 1951), p. 181, cf. 182.
[26] *Ibid.,* p. 182.

communication takes place else philosophy and culture in general would be a complete illusion.

Some measure of paradox appears unavoidable in critical thought therefore. Instead of trying to refute competing views in philosophy, the thinker would do better to seek the sense in which they contraplete each other. The presence of oppositions in one thinker's thoughts need be no more cause for dismay than the fact that differing thinkers come out with differing perspectives they take to be paramount. Thought reaches in differing directions though it still comes up with meaningful apprehension.

Blades of scissors accomplish the same task by moving in opposite directions. The left and right foot perform opposite functions in the single operation of walking. A pestle and mortar serve in contrary ways to attain the desired end.[27] So the functions of thought need to deal with many phases of reality in "opposite," paradoxical, or polar ways. Such categories as identity and difference, unity and plurality, rest and motion, individuality and universality must always work together though never coalesce, except as they are joined in the same mind of the thinker using them.

One must not agree too easily that polar thinking is needed without observing that the crux of the matter lies in the means by which the role of each term in the contrapletal relation may be determined. It is common knowledge that a man lost in the woods may walk in a circle rather than a given direction because one leg takes a different stride than the other. So one pole in thought may exert such tension on the other as to distort the proper function of each. An easy-going middle-of-the-road type of thought leaves us liable to this disaster. The too facile identification of opposing alternatives, such as saying that idealism is *actually* realism, or that subjectivity is *really* objectivity, reveals that no serious attention has been given to calculating the ratio between these poles of thought. In short, what is needed is a calculus for polarity, a means of assurance that each term will contribute its proportionate share in the whole truth which includes these dual phases.

[27] Cf. Cohen, *op. cit.,* p. 165.

W. H. Sheldon's definition of polarity may be taken as basic. He says it is a relation between opposites, each having "a partly independent status, asymmetrical and productive because of their cooperation, and also just because each has already a being, power and efficacy of its own which enables it to contribute something in the cooperation." [28] Polarity as a term referring to opposed principles of any sort came into general use about 1810. Its earlier application to the extremities of the earth's axis and to opposing surfaces of a magnet seems to have been expanded to this more general use by the time of Coleridge. By 1818 he spoke of a "law of polarity" that reigns throughout nature. Whewell referred to "the general notion of polarity" in his *Philosophy of the Inductive Sciences* published in 1840. Emerson also used the term "polarity" in 1840 as a condition of action and reaction which "we meet in every part of nature." [29]

Thought deals constantly with diversities, contraries, and polarities. Its most fruitful activities consist in consideration of polar relations for they provide a range of reference that gives thought the most adequate method of dealing with reality. It is not presupposed here that polar method serves thought better than others. Choice of it as the superior method grows out of the evidence both that experience comes heavily freighted with oppositions and that thought by its nature performs to some extent a paradoxical function. It is a method that identifies diversities but seeks above all to find how they intensify, limit, modify or qualify each other. This is the most inclusive method of procedure available. It gives standing room to others but gathers them in to itself ultimately.

Bahm has recently developed an analysis of "existence and its polarities." [30] He has rightly seen that the polar condition of reality implies some kind of "organicism" to account for this impingement of opposites on each other. However, his identification of "poles" in being often leaves one mystified as

[28] *Process and Polarity* (New York: Columbia University Press, 1944), p. 108. Cf. a similar definition in Archie Bahm, *Philosophy* (New York: John Wiley & Sons, Inc., 1953), p. 241; also Ogden, *op. cit.,* p. 56.

[29] Ogden, *op. cit.,* pp. 56–58.

[30] Archie Bahm, "Existence and Its Polarities." *Jour. Phil.,* 46 (1949), pp. 629–37. See also Bahm's *Philosophy* cited above, chap. 20.

to how they are involved in their opposites. For example, "being" and "non-being," taken by Bahm to be polar opposites, are logical opposites or contradictions, but it is not clear how they fructify each other. Nor does Bahm supply what we need most, a calculus for polarity, i.e. a means of weighing the function of each pole.[31] Like the work of Cohen, Sheldon, and Whitehead, we are left with an analysis of the polar condition of existence but without means to determine how these poles involve and complete each other.

[31] For further criticism of this position see the present writer's article, "Existence and Its Polarities—Revision and Supplement." *Jour. Phil.,* 47 (1950), 96–99.

REFLECTIONS ON THE AMERICAN IDENTITY

Erik H. Erikson

Polarities

It is a commonplace to state that whatever one may come to consider a truly American trait can be shown to have its equally characteristic opposite. This, one suspects, is true of all "national characters," or (as I would prefer to call them) national identities—so true, in fact that one may begin rather than end with the proposition that a nation's identity is derived from the ways in which history has, as it were, counterpointed certain opposite potentialities; the ways in which it lifts this counterpoint to a unique style of civilization, or lets it disintegrate into mere contradiction.

This dynamic country subjects its inhabitants to more extreme contrasts and abrupt changes during a lifetime or a generation than is normally the case with other great nations.

Source: Erik Erikson, *Childhood and Society*, 2d ed. rev. (New York: W. W. Norton and Company, Inc., 1963), pp. 285–96. Copyright © 1950, 1963 by W. W. Norton and Company, Inc. Reprinted by permission.

Erik H. Erikson (1902–   ), is professor of human development and lecturer in psychiatry at Harvard University. He was born in Germany, educated in Denmark and Vienna, and came to the United States in 1933. He has taught at the Harvard, Yale, and Pittsburgh medical schools, the University of California at Berkeley, and served as a staff member at the Austen Riggs Center in Stockbridge, Massachusetts. In addition to *Childhood and Society* (1950), he has written *Young Man Luther* (1958), *Identity: Youth and Crisis* (1968), *Insight and Responsibility: Lectures on the Ethical Implications of Psychoanalytic Insight* (1964), and *Gandhi's Truth: On the Origins of Militant Nonviolence* (1969).

Most of her inhabitants are faced, in their own lives or within the orbit of their closest relatives, with alternatives presented by such polarities as: open roads of immigration and jealous islands of tradition; outgoing internationalism and defiant isolationism; boisterous competition and self-effacing co-operation; and many others. The influence of the resulting contradictory slogans on the development of an individual ego probably depends on the coincidence of nuclear ego stages with critical changes in the family's geographic and economic vicissitudes.

The process of American identity formation seems to support an individual's ego identity as long as he can preserve a certain element of deliberate tentativeness of autonomous choice. The individual must be able to convince himself that the next step is up to him and that no matter where he is staying or going he always has the choice of leaving or turning in the opposite direction if he chooses to do so. In this country the migrant does not want to be told to move on, nor the sedentary man to stay where he is; for the life style (and the family history) of each contains the opposite element as a potential alternative which he wishes to consider his most private and individual decision.

Thus the functioning American, as the heir of a history of extreme contrasts and abrupt changes, bases his final ego identity on some tentative combination of dynamic polarities such as migratory and sedentary, individualistic and standardized, competitive and co-operative, pious and freethinking, responsible and cynical, etc.

While we see extreme elaborations of one or the other of these poles in regional, occupational, and characterological types, analysis reveals that this extremeness (of rigidity or of vacillation) contains an inner defense against the always implied, deeply feared, or secretly hoped-for opposite extreme.

To leave his choices open, the American, on the whole, lives with two sets of "truths": a set of religious principles or religiously pronounced political principles of a highly puritan quality, and a set of shifting slogans, which indicate what, at a given time, one may get away with on the basis of not more than a hunch, a mood, or a notion. Thus, the same child may have been exposed in succession or alternately to sudden decisions expressing the slogans "Let's get the hell out of here" and again, "Let's stay and keep the bastards out"—to mention only two of the most sweeping ones. Without any pretense of logic or principle, slogans are convincing enough to those involved to justify action whether within or just outside of the lofty law (insofar as it happens to be enforced or forgotten, according to changing local climate). Seemingly shiftless slogans contain time and space perspectives as ingrained as those elaborated in the Sioux or Yurok system; they are experiments in collective time-space to which individual ego defenses are co-ordinated. But they change, often radically, during one and the same childhood.

A true history of the American identity would have to correlate Parrington's observations on the continuity of formulated thought with the rich history of discontinuous American slogans which pervade public opinion in corner stores and in studies, in the courts and in the daily press. For in principles and concepts too, an invigorating polarity seems to exist on the one hand between the intellectual and political aristocracy which, always mindful of precedent, guards a measure of coherent thought and indestructible spirit, and, on the other hand, a powerful mobocracy which seems to prefer changing slogans to self-perpetuating principles. This native polarity of aristocracy and mobocracy (so admirably synthesized in Franklin D. Roosevelt) pervades American democracy more effectively than the advocates and the critics of the great American middle class seem to realize. This American middle class, decried by some as embodying an ossification of all that is mercenary and philistine in this country, may represent only a transitory series of overcompensatory attempts at settling tentatively around some Main Street, fireplace, bank account, and make of car; it does not, as a class should, preclude high mobility and a cultural potential unsure of its final identity. Status expresses a different relativity in a more mobile society: it resembles an escalator more than a platform; it is a vehicle, rather than a goal.

All countries, and especially large one, complicate their own progress in their own way with the very premises of their beginnings. We must try to formulate the way in which self-contradictions in American history may expose her youth to an emotional and political short circuit and thus endanger her dynamic potential.

"Mom"

In recent years the observations and warnings of the psychiatric workers of this country have more and more converged on two concepts: the "schizoid personality" and "maternal rejection." Essentially this means not only that many people fall by the wayside as a result of psychotic disengagements from reality, but also that all too many people, while not overtly sick, nevertheless seem to lack a certain ego tonus and a certain mutuality in social intercourse. One may laugh at this suggestion and point to the spirit of individualism and to the gestures of animation and of jovial friendliness characterizing much of the social life in this country; but the psychiatrists (especially after the shocking experience during the last war, of being forced to reject or to send home hundreds of thousands of "psychoneurotics") see it differently. The streamlined smile within the perfectly tuned countenance and within the standardized ways of exhibiting self-control does not always harbor that true spontaneity which alone would keep the personality intact and flexible enough to make it a going concern.

For this the psychiatrists tend to blame "Mom." Case history after case history states that the patient had a cold mother, a dominant mother, a rejecting mother—or a hyper-possessive, over-protective one. They imply that the patient, as a baby, was not made to feel at home in this world except under the condition that he behave himself in certain definite ways, which were inconsistent with the timetable of an infant's needs and potentialities, and contradictory in themselves. They imply that the mother dominated the father, and that while the father offered more tenderness and understanding to the children than the mother did, he disappointed his children in the end because of what he "took" from the mother. Gradually what had begun as a spontaneous movement in thousands of clinical files has become a manifest literary sport in books decrying the mothers of this country as "Moms" and as a "generation of vipers."

Who is this "Mom?" How did she lose her good, her simple name? How could she become an excuse for all that is rotten in the state of the nation and a subject of literary temper tantrums? *Is* Mom really to blame?

In a clinical sense, of course, to blame may mean just to point to what the informed workers sincerely considers the primary cause of the calamity. But there is in much of our psychiatric work an undertone of revengeful triumph, as if a villain had been spotted and cornered. The blame attached to the mothers in this country (namely, that they are frigid sexually, rejective of their children, and unduly dominant in their homes) has in itself a specific moralistic punitiveness. No doubt both patients and psychiatric workers were blamed too much when they were children; now they blame all mothers, because all causality has become linked with blame.

It was, of course, a vindictive injustice to give the name of "Mom" to a certain dangerous type of mother, a type apparently characterized by a number of fatal contradictions in her motherhood. Such injustice can only be explained and justified by the journalistic habit of sensational contraposition—a part of the publicist folkways of our day. It is true that where the "psychoneurotic" American soldier felt inadequately prepared for life, he often implicitly and more often unconsciously blamed his mother; and that the expert felt compelled to agree with him. But it is also true that the road from Main Street to the foxhole was longer—geographically, culturally, and psychologically—than was the road to the front lines from the home towns of nations which were open to attack and had been attacked, or which had prepared themselves to attack other people's homelands and now feared for their own. It seems senseless to blame the American family for the failures, but to deny it credit for the gigantic human achievement of overcoming that distance.

"Mom," then, like similar prototypes in other countries— see the "German father," to be discussed in the next chapter —is a composite image of traits, none of which could be present all at once in one single living woman. No woman consciously aspires to be such a "Mom," and yet she may find that her experience converges on this Gestalt, as if she were forced to assume a role. To the clinical worker, "Mom" is something comparable to a "classical" psychiatric syndrome which you come to use as a yardstick although you have never seen it in pure form. In cartoons she becomes a caricature, immediately convincing to all. Before analyzing "Mom," then, as a historical phenomenon, let us focus on her from the point of view of the pathogenic demands which she makes on her children and by which we recognize her presence in our clinical work:

1. "Mom" is the unquestioned authority in matters of mores and morals in her home, and (through clubs) in the community; yet she permits herself to remain, in her own way, vain in her appearance, egotistical in her demands, and infantile in her emotions.

2. In any situation in which this discrepancy clashes with the respect which she demands from her children, she blames her children; she never blames herself.

3. She thus artificially maintains what Ruth Benedict would call the discontinuity between the child's and the adult's status without endowing this differentiation with the higher meaning emanating from superior example.

4. She shows a determined hostility to any free expression of the most naïve forms of sensual and sexual pleasure on the part of her children, and she makes it clear enough that the father, when sexually demanding, is a bore. Yet as she grows older she seems unwilling to sacrifice such external signs of sexual competition as too youthful dresses, frills of exhibitionism, and "make-up." In addition, she is avidly addicted to sexual display in books, movies, and gossip.

5. She teaches self-restraint and self-control, but she is unable to restrict her intake of calories in order to remain within the bounds of the dresses she prefers.

6. She expects her children to be hard on themselves, but she is hypochondriacally concerned with her own well-being.

7. She stands for the superior values of tradition, yet she herself does not want to become "old." In fact, she is mortally

afraid of that status which in the past was the fruit of a rich life, namely the status of the grandmother.

This will be sufficient to indicate that "Mom" is a woman in whose life cycle remnants of infantility join advanced senility to crowd out the middle range of mature womanhood, which thus becomes self-absorbed and stagnant. In fact, she mistrusts her own feelings as a woman and mother. Even her overconcern does not provide trust, but lasting mistrust. But let it be said that this "Mom"—or better: any woman who reminds herself and others of the stereotype Mom—is not happy; she does not like herself; she is ridden by the anxiety that her life was a waste. She knows that her children do not genuinely love her, despite Mother's Day offerings. "Mom" is a victim, not a victor.

Assuming, then, that this is a "type," a composite image of sufficient relevance for the epidemiology of neurotic conflict in this country: to explain it would obviously call for the collaboration of historian, sociologist, and psychologist, and for a new kind of history, a kind which at the moment is admittedly in its impressionistic and sensational stages. "Mom," of course, is only a stereotyped caricature of existing contradictions which have emerged from intense, rapid, and as yet unintegrated changes in American history. To find its beginning, one would probably have to retrace this history back to the time when it was up to the American woman to evolve one common tradition, on the basis of many imported traditions, and to base on it the education of her children and the style of her home life; when it was up to her to establish new habits of sedentary life on a continent originally populated by men who in their countries of origin, for one reason or another, had not wanted to be "fenced in." Now, in fear of ever again acquiescing to an outer or inner autocracy, these men insisted on keeping their new cultural identity tentative to a point where women had to become autocratic in their demands for some order.

The American woman in frontier communities was the object of intense rivalries on the part of tough and often desperate men. At the same time, she had to become the cultural censor, the religious conscience, the aesthetic arbiter, and the teacher. In that early rough economy hewn out of hard nature it was she who contributed the finer graces of living and that spirituality without which the community falls apart. In her children she saw future men and women who would face contrasts of rigid sedentary and shifting migratory life. They must be prepared for any number of extreme opposites in milieu, and always ready to seek new goals and to fight for them in merciless competition. For, after all, worse than a sinner was a sucker.

We suggested that the mothers of the Sioux and of the Yurok were endowed with an instinctive power of adaptation which permitted them to develop child-training methods appropriate for the production of hunters and hunters' wives in a nomadic society, and of fishermen and acorn gatherers in a sedentary valley society. The American mother, I believe, reacted to the historical situation on this continent with similar unconscious adjustment when she further developed Anglo-Saxon patterns of child training which would avoid weakening potential frontiersmen by protective maternalism. In other words, I consider what is now called the American woman's "rejective" attitude a modern fault based on a historical virtue designed for a vast new country, in which the most dominant fact was the frontier, whether you sought it, or avoided it, or tried to live it down.

From the frontier, my historian-sociologist and I would have to turn to puritanism as a decisive force in the creation of American motherhood and its modern caricature, "Mom." This much-maligned puritanism, we should remember, was once a system of values designed to check men and women of eruptive vitality, of strong appetites, as well as of strong individuality. In connection with primitive cultures we have discussed the fact that a living culture has its own balances which make it durable and bearable to the majority of its members. But changing history endangers the balance. During the short course of American history rapid developments fused with puritanism in such a way that they contributed to the emotional tension of mother and child. Among these were the continued migration of the native population, unchecked immigration, industrialization, urbanization, class stratification, and female emancipation. These are some of the influences which put puritanism on the defensive—and a system is apt to become rigid when it becomes defensive. Puritanism, beyond defining sexual sin for full-blooded and strong-willed people, gradually extended itself to the total sphere of bodily living, compromising all sensuality—including marital relationships —and spreading its frigidity over the tasks of pregnancy, childbirth, nursing, and training. The result was that men were born who failed to learn from their mothers to love the goodness of sensuality before they learned to hate its sinful uses. Instead of hating sin, they learned to mistrust life. Many became puritans without faith or zest.

The frontier, of course, remained the decisive influence which served to establish in the American identity the extreme polarization which characterizes it. The original polarity was the cultivation of the sedentary and migratory poles. For the same families, the same mothers, were forced to prepare men and women who would take root in the community life and the gradual class stratification of the new villages and towns and at the same time to prepare these children for the possible physical hardships of homesteading on the frontiers. Towns, too, developed their sedentary existence and oriented their inward life to work bench and writing desk, fireplace and altar, while through them, on the roads and rails, strangers passed bragging of God knows what greener pastures. You had either to follow—or to stay behind and brag louder. The point is that the call of the frontier, the temptation to move on, forced those who stayed to become defensively sedentary, and defensively proud. In a world which developed the slogan, "If you can see your neighbor's chimney, it is time to move on," mothers had to raise sons and daughters who would be determined to ignore the call of the frontier—but who would go with equal determination once they were forced or chose to go. When they became too old, however, there was no choosing, and they remained to support the most sectarian, the most standardized adhesiveness. I think that it was the fear of becoming too old to choose which gave old age and death a bad name in this country. (Only recently have old couples found a solution, the national trailer system, which permits them to settle down to perpetual traveling and to die on wheels.)

We know how the problems of the immigrant and of the migrant, of the émigré and of the refugee, became superimposed on one another, as large areas became settled and began to have a past. To the new American, with a regional tradition of stratification, newcomers increasingly came to be characterized by the fact that they had escaped from something or other, rather than by the common values they sought; and then there were also the masses of ignorant and deceived chattels of the expanding industrial labor market. For and against all of these latter Americans, American mothers had to establish new moral standards and rigid tests of social ascendancy.

As America became the proverbial melting pot, it was the Anglo-Saxon woman's determination which assured that of all the ingredients mixed, puritanism—such as it then was— would be the most pervasive streak. The older, Anglo-Saxon type became ever more rigid, though at the same time decent and kind in its way. But the daughters of immigrants, too, frantically tried to emulate standards of conduct which they had not learned as small children. It is here, I think, that the self-made personality originated as the female counterpart of the self-made man; it is here that we find the origin of the popular American concept of a fashionable and vain "ego" which is its own originator and arbiter. In fact, the psychoanalysis of the children of immigrants clearly reveals to what extent they, as the first real Americans in their family, become their parents' cultural parents.

This idea of a self-made ego was in turn reinforced and yet modified by industrialization and by class stratification. Industrialization, for example, brought with it mechanical child training. It was as if this new man-made world of machines, which was to replace the "segments of nature" and the "beasts of prey," offered its mastery only to those who would become like it, as the Sioux "became" buffalo, the Yurok salmon. Thus, a movement in child training began which tended to adjust the human organism from the very start to clocklike punctuality in order to make it a standardized appendix of the industrial world. This movement is by no means at an end either in this country or in countries which for the sake of industrial production want to become like us. In the pursuit of the adjustment to and mastery over the machine, American mothers (especially of the middle class) found themselves standardizing and overadjusting children who later were expected to personify that very virile individuality which in the past had been one of the outstanding characteristics of the American. The resulting danger was that of creating, instead of individualism, a mass-produced mask of individuality.

As if this were not enough, the increasing class differentiation in some not large but influential classes and regions combined with leftovers of European aristocratic models to create the ideal of the lady, the woman who not only does not need to work, but who, in fact, is much too childlike and too determinedly uninformed to even comprehend what work is all about. This image, in most parts of the country, except the South, was soon challenged by the ideal of the emancipated woman. This new ideal seemed to call for equality of opportunity; but it is well known how it came, instead, to represent often enough a pretense of sameness in equipment, a right to mannish behavior.

In her original attributes, then, the American woman was a fitting and heroic companion to the post-revolutionary man, who was possessed with the idea of freedom from any man's autocracy and haunted by the fear that the nostalgia for some homeland and the surrender to some king could ever make him give in to political slavery. Mother became "Mom" only when Father became "Pop" under the impact of the identical historical discontinuities. For, if you come down to it, Momism is only misplaced paternalism. American mothers stepped into the role of the grandfathers as the fathers abdicated their dominant place in the family, in the field of education, and in cultural life. The post-revolutionary descendants of the Founding Fathers forced their women to be mothers *and* fathers, while they continued to cultivate the role of freeborn sons.

I cannot try to appraise the quantity of emotional disturbance in this country. Mere statistics on severe mental disorders do not help. Our improved methods of detection and our missionary zeal expand together as we become aware of the problem, so that it would be hard to say whether today this country has bigger and better neuroses, or bigger and better ways of spotlighting them—or both. But I would, from my clinical experience, dare to formulate a specific *quality* in those who are disturbed. I would say that underneath his proud sense of autonomy and his exuberant sense of initiative the troubled American (who often looks the least troubled) blames his mother for having let him down. His father, so he claims, had not much to do with it—except in those rare cases where the father was an extraordinarily stern man on the surface, an old-fashioned individualist, a foreign paternalist, or a native "boss." In the psychoanalysis of an American man it usually takes considerable time to break through to the insight that there was a period early in life when the father did seem bigger and threatening. Even then, there is at first little sense of that specific rivalry for the mother as stereotyped in the oedipus complex. It is as if the mother had ceased to be an object of nostalgia and sensual attachment before the general development of initiative led to a rivalry with the "old man." Behind a fragmentary "oedipus complex," then, appears that deep-seated sense of having been abandoned and let down by the mother, which is the silent complaint behind schizoid withdrawal. The small child felt, it seems, that there was no use regressing, because there was nobody to regress to, no use investing feelings because the response was so uncertain. What remained was action and motion right up to the breaking point. Where action, too, failed, there was only withdrawal and the standardized smile, and later, psychosomatic disturbance. But wherever our methods permit us to look deeper, we find at the bottom of it all the conviction, the mortal self-accusation, that it was *the child who abandoned the mother,* because he had been in such a hurry to become independent.

PARADOX AND DREAM

John Steinbeck

One of the generalities most often noted about Americans is that we are a restless, a dissatisfied, a searching people. We bridle and buck under failure, and we go mad with dissatisfaction in the face of success. We spend our time searching for security, and hate it when we get it. For the most part we are an intemperate people: we eat too much when we can, drink too much, indulge our senses too much. Even in our so-called virtues we are intemperate: a teetotaler is not content not to drink—he must stop all the drinking in the world; a vegetarian among us would outlaw the eating of meat. We work too hard, and many die under the strain; and then to make up for that we play with a violence as suicidal.

The result is that we seem to be in a state of turmoil all the time, both physically and mentally. We are able to believe

Source: John Steinbeck, *America and Americans* (New York: Viking Press, 1966), pp. 29–34. Copyright © 1966 by John Steinbeck. All Rights Reserved. Reprinted by permission of The Viking Press, Inc.

John Steinbeck (1902–1969), won the Nobel Prize for literature in 1962 and the Pulitzer Prize in 1940. He was educated at Salinas, California, at Stanford University, as a reporter, and "on the road." In addition to *America and the Americans* (1966), he wrote *Cup of Gold* (1929), *Pastures of Heaven* (1932), *To a God Unknown* (1933), *Tortilla Flat* (1935), *In Dubious Battle* (1936), *Of Mice and Men* (1937), *The Grapes of Wrath* (1939), *The Moon Is Down* (1942), *Cannery Row* (1945), *The Wayward Bus* (1947), *A Russian Journal* (1948), *The Log from the Sea of Cortez* (1951), *East of Eden* (1952), *Sweet Thursday* (1954), *The Short Reign of Pippin IV* (1957), *Once There Was a War* (1958), *The Winter of Our Discontent* (1961), and *Travels with Charley* (1962).

that our government is weak, stupid, overbearing, dishonest, and inefficient, and at the same time we are deeply convinced that it is the best government in the world, and we would like to impose it upon everyone else. We speak of the American Way of Life as though it involved the ground rules for the governance of heaven. A man hungry and unemployed through his own stupidity and that of others, a man beaten by a brutal policeman, a woman forced into prostitution by her own laziness, high prices, availability, and despair—all bow with reverence toward the American Way of Life, although each one would look puzzled and angry if he were asked to define it. We scramble and scrabble up the stony path toward the pot of gold we have taken to mean security. We trample friends, relatives, and strangers who get in the way of our achieving it; and once we get it we shower it on psychoanalysts to try to find out why we are unhappy, and finally—if we have enough of the gold—we contribute it back to the nation in the form of foundations and charities.

We fight our way in, and try to buy our way out. We are alert, curious, hopeful, and we take more drugs designed to make us unaware than any other people. We are self-reliant and at the same time completely dependent. We are aggressive, and defenseless. Americans overindulge their children and do not like them; the children in turn are overly dependent and full of hate for their parents. We are complacent in our possessions, in our houses, in our education; but it is hard to find a man or woman who does not want something better for the next generation. Americans are remarkably kind and hospitable and open with both guests and strangers; and yet they will make a wide circle around the man dying on the pavement. Fortunes are spent getting cats out of trees and dogs out of sewer pipes; but a girl screaming for help in the street draws only slammed doors, closed windows, and silence.

Now there is a set of generalities for you, each one of them canceled out by another generality. Americans seem to live and breathe and function by paradox; but in nothing are we so paradoxical as in our passionate belief in our own myths. We truly believe ourselves to be natural-born mechanics and do-it-yourself-ers. We spend our lives in motor cars, yet most of us—a great many of us at least—do not know enough about a car to look in the gas tank when the motor fails. Our lives as we live them would not function without electricity, but it is a rare man or woman who, when the power goes off, knows how to look for a burned-out fuse and replace it. We believe implicitly that we are the heirs of the pioneers; that we have inherited self-sufficiency and the ability to take care of ourselves, particularly in relation to nature. There isn't a man among us in ten thousand who knows how to butcher a cow or a pig and cut it up for eating, let alone a wild animal. By natural endowment, we are great rifle shots and great hunters—but when hunting season opens there is a slaughter of farm animals and humans by men and women who couldn't hit a real target if they could see it. Americans treasure the knowledge that they live close to nature, but fewer and fewer farmers feed more and more people; and as soon as we can afford to we eat out of cans, buy frozen TV dinners, and haunt the delicatessens. Affluence means moving to the suburbs, but the American suburbanite sees, if anything, less of the country than the city apartment dweller with his window boxes and his African violets carefully tended under lights. In no country are more seeds and plants and equipment purchased, and less vegetables and flowers raised.

The paradoxes are everywhere: We shout that we are a nation of laws, not men—and then proceed to break every law we can if we can get away with it. We proudly insist that we base our political positions on the issues—and we will vote against a man because of his religion, his name, or the shape of his nose.

Sometimes we seem to be a nation of public puritans and private profligates. There surely can be no excesses like those committed by good family men away from home at a convention. We believe in the manliness of our men and the womanliness of our women, but we go to extremes of expense and discomfort to cover any natural evidence that we are either. From puberty we are preoccupied with sex; but our courts, our counselors, and our psychiatrists are dealing constantly with cases of sexual failure or charges of frigidity or impotence. A small failure in business can quite normally make a man sexually impotent.

We fancy ourselves as hard-headed realists, but we will buy anything we see advertised, particularly on television; and we buy it not with reference to the quality or the value of the product, but directly as a result of the number of times we have heard it mentioned. The most arrant nonsense about a product is never questioned. We are afraid to be awake, afraid to be alone, afraid to be a moment without the noise and confusion we call entertainment. We boast of our dislike of high-brow art and music, and we have more and better-attended symphonies, art galleries, and theaters than any country in the world. We detest abstract art and produce more of it than all the rest of the world put together.

One of the characteristics most puzzling to a foreign observer is the strong and imperishable dream the American carries. On inspection, it is found that the dream has little to do with reality in American life. Consider the dream of and the hunger for home. The very word can reduce nearly all of my compatriots to tears. Builders and developers never build houses—they build homes. The dream home is either in a small town or in a suburban area where grass and trees simulate the country. This dream home is a permanent seat, not rented but owned. It is a center where a man and his wife grow graciously old, warmed by the radiance of well-washed children and grandchildren. Many thousands of these homes are built every year; built, planted, advertised, and sold—and yet, the American family rarely stays in one place for more than five years. The home and its equipment are purchased on time and are heavily mortgaged. The earning power of the father is almost always over-extended, so that after a few years he is not able to keep up the payments on his loans. That is on the losing side. But suppose the earner is successful and his income increases. Right away the house is not big enough, or in the proper neighborhood. Or perhaps suburban life palls, and the family moves to the city, where excitement and convenience beckon.

Some of these movements back and forth seem to me a

result of just pure restlessness, pure nervousness. We do hear, of course, of people who keep the same job for twenty years, or thirty years, or forty years, and get a gold watch for it; but the numbers of these old and faithful employees are decreasing all the time. Part of the movement has to do with the nature of business itself. Work in factories, in supermarkets, for contractors on the construction of houses, bridges, public buildings, or more factories is often temporary; the job gets done, or local taxes or wage increases or falling sales may cause a place of business to move to a new area. In addition, many of the great corporations have a policy of moving employees from one of their many branches to another. The employee with the home dream finds that with every removal he loses money. The sellers of homes make their profit on the down payment and on the interest on the loan; but the private owner who wants to turn over his dream home and move on to another finds that he always takes a loss. However, the dream does not die—it just takes another form.

Today, with the ancient American tendency to look for greener pastures still very much alive, the mobile home has become the new dream. It is not a trailer; it is a house, long and narrow in shape, and equipped with wheels so that it can, if necessary, be transported over the highway to a new area. In a mobile home, a man doesn't have to take a loss when he moves; his home goes with him. Until recently, when the local authorities have set about finding means of making Mr. Mobile pay his way, a mobile home owner living in a rented space in a trailer park could avoid local taxes and local duties while making use of the public schools and all the other facilities American towns set up for their people. The mobile way of life is not a new thing in the world, of course. It is more than probable that humans lived this way for hundreds of thousands of years before they ever conceived of settling down—the herdsmen followed the herds, the hunters followed the game, and everybody ran from the weather. The Tartars moved whole villages on wheels, and the die-hard gypsies have never left their caravans. No, people go back to mobility with enthusiasm for something they recognize, and if they can double the dream —have a symbol home and mobility at the same time—they have it made. And now there are huge settlements of these metal houses clustered on the edges of our cities. Plots of grass and shrubs are planted, awnings stretched out, and garden chairs appear. A community life soon springs up—a life having all the signs of status, the standards of success or failure that exist elsewhere in America.

There is no question that American life is in the process of changing, but, as always in human history, it carries some of the past along with it; and the mobile home has one old trap built into it. Automobile manufacturers discovered and developed the American yearning for status. By changing the appliances and gadgetry on each new model, they could make the car owner feel that his perfectly good automobile was old-fashioned and therefore undesirable. His children were afraid to be seen in it; and, since a family's image of success in the world, or status, is to a certain extent dependent on the kind of a car the man drives, he was forced to buy a new one whether he needed it or not. Outdated mobile homes carry the same stigma. Every year new models appear, costing from five thousand to fifty thousand dollars, with new fixtures, colors— new, and therefore desirable. A family with an old model, no matter how comfortable and sound, soon feels *déclassé*. Thus the turnover in mobile houses is enormous, and thus the social strata re-establish themselves: the top people have the newest models, and lesser folk buy the used homes turned in as down payments on the newer ones. And the trailer cities have neighborhoods as fiendishly snobbish as have any other suburban developments—each one has its Sugar Hill, its upper-middle-class area, and its slums. The pattern has not changed; and none of this has in any way affected the American dream of home, which remains part Grandma Moses and part split-level ranch house in an area where to keep a cow or a pen of chickens is to break the law.

Of course, the home dream can be acted out almost anywhere. A number of years ago, when I lived on East 51st Street in New York City, I saw an instance of it every day on my morning walk, near Third Avenue, where great numbers of old red brick buildings were the small, walk-up cold-water flats in which so many New Yorkers lived. Every summer morning about nine o'clock a stout and benign-looking lady came down the stairs from her flat to the pavement carrying the great outdoors in her arms. She set out a canvas deck chair, and over it mounted a beach umbrella—one of the kind which has a little cocktail table around it—and then, smiling happily, this benign and robust woman rolled out a little lawn made of green raffia in front of her chair, set out two pots of red geraniums and an artificial palm, brought a little cabinet with cold drinks —Coca-Cola, Pepsi-Cola—in a small icebox; she laid her folded copy of the *Daily News* on the table, arranged her equipment, and sank back into the chair—and she was in the country. She nodded and smiled to everyone who went by, and somehow she conveyed her dream to everyone who saw her, and everyone who saw her was delighted with her. For some reason I was overwhelmed with a desire to contribute to this sylvan retreat, and so one day when she had stepped inside for a moment, I deposited on her table a potted fern and a little bowl with two goldfish; and the next morning, I was pleased to see that these had been added to the permanent equipment. Every day through that summer the fern and the goldfish were part of the scene.

The home dream is only one of the deepset American illusions which, since they can't be changed, function as cohesive principles to bind the nation together and make it different from all other nations. It occurs to me that all dreams, waking and sleeping, are powerful and prominent memories of something real, of something that really happened. I believe these memories—some of them, at least—can be inherited; our generalized dreams of water and warmth, of falling, of monsters, of danger and premonitions may have been pre-recorded on some kind of genetic tape in the species out of which we evolved or mutated, just as some of our organs which no longer function seem to be physical memories of other, earlier processes. The national dream of Americans is a whole pattern of thinking and feeling and may well be a historic memory surprisingly little distorted. Furthermore, the participators in the dream need not have descended physically from the people to whom the reality happened. This pattern of thought and conduct which is the national character is absorbed even by the children of immigrants born in America, but it never comes to the immigrants themselves, no matter how they may wish it; birth on American soil seems to be required.

I have spoken of the dream of home that persists in a time when home is neither required nor wanted. Until very recently home was a real word, and in the English tongue it is a magic word. The ancient root word *ham,* from which our word "home" came, meant the triangle where two rivers meet which, with a short wall, can be defended. At first the word "home" meant safety, then gradually comfort. In the immediate American past, the home meant just those two things; the log houses, even the sod houses, were havens of safety, of defense, warmth, food, and comfort. Outside were hostile Indians and dangerous animals, crippling cold and starvation. Many houses, including the one where President Johnson was born, built only a few generations back, have thick walls and gunslits for defense, a great hearth for cooking and for heat, a cellar under the floor and an attic for the storage of food, and sometimes even an interior well in case of siege. A home was a place where women and children could be reasonably safe, a place to which a man could return with joy and slough off his weariness and his fears. This symbol of safety and comfort is so recent in our history that it is no wonder that to all of us it remains dear and desirable.

It is an American dream that we are great hunters, trackers, woodsmen, deadshots with a rifle or a shotgun; and this dream is deeply held by Americans who have never fired a gun or hunted anything larger or more dangerous than a cockroach. But I wonder whether our deep connection with firearms is not indeed a national potential; not long ago we had to be good hunters or we starved, good shots or our lives were in danger. Can this have carried over? Early in World War II, I worked for the Training Command of the Air Force, and spent a good deal of time at the schools for aerial gunnery. The British, having been in the war for a long time, sent teams of instructors to teach our newly inducted men to handle the tail and ball-turret guns in our B-17 bombers, but the instruction began with small arms, since all shooting is pretty much the same. I remember an Englishman saying to me, "It is amazing how quickly these men learn. Some of them have never handled a weapon, and yet it seems to come to them as though they knew it; they pick it up much faster than the English lads do. Maybe they're just born with the knack."

I suggested, "Think of the time of Crécy and Agincourt, when the longbow dominated battlefields. Now, the yew of the longbows was not English, it was Spanish. The French had access to the longbow and surely they knew its effectiveness, and still they never used it."

"That's right," he said. "Our lads had the knack, didn't they? But also they had practice and habit; the bow was in their blood. Maybe they were bowmen before they ever handled a bow, because it was expected of them. You may have genes of firearms in your systems."

The inventiveness once necessary for survival may also be a part of the national dream. Who among us has not bought for a song an ancient junked car, and with parts from other junked cars put together something that would run? This is not lost; American kids are still doing it. The dreams of a people either create folk literature or find their way into it; and folk literature, again, is always based on something that happened. Our most persistent folk tales—constantly retold in books, movies, and television shows—concern cowboys, gunslinging sheriffs, and Indian fighters. These folk figures existed— perhaps not quite as they are recalled nor in the numbers indicated, but they did exist; and his dream also persists. Even businessmen in Texas wear the high-heeled boots and big hats, though they ride in air-conditioned Cadillacs and have forgotten the reason for the high heels. All our children play cowboy and Indian; the brave and honest sheriff who with courage and a six-gun brings law and order and civic virtue to a Western community is perhaps our most familiar hero, no doubt descended from the brave mailed knight of chivalry who battled and overcame evil with lance and sword. Even the recognition signals are the same: white hat, white armor— black hat, black shield. And in these moral tales, so deepset in us, virtue does not arise out of reason or orderly process of law—it is imposed and maintained by violence.

I wonder whether this folk wisdom is the story of our capability. Are these stories permanent because we know within ourselves that only the threat of violence makes it possible for us to live together in peace? I think that surviving folk tales are directly based on memory. There must have been a leader like King Arthur; although there is no historical record to prove it, the very strength of the story presumes his existence. We know there were gunslinging sheriffs—not many, but some; but if they had not existed, our need for them would have created them. It interests me that the youthful gangs in our cities, engaging in their "rumbles" which are really wars, and doing so in direct and overt disobedience of law and of all the pressures the police can apply—that these gangs take noble names, and within their organizations are said to maintain a code of behavior and responsibility toward one another and an obedience to their leaders very like that of the tight-knit chivalric code of feudal Europe; the very activities and attitudes which raise the hand of the law against these gangs would, if the nation needed them, be the diagnostics of heroes. And indeed, they must be heroes to themselves.

A national dream need not, indeed may not be clear-cut and exact. Consider the dream of France, based on a memory and fired in the furnace of defeat and occupation, followed by the frustration of a many-branched crossroads until Charles-*le-plus-Magne* [1] polished up the old word "glory" and made it shine. *La Gloire* brightened French eyes; defensive arrogance hardened and even the philosophically hopeless were glorious and possessive in their hopelessness, and the dark deposits of centuries were washed from the glorious buildings in Paris. When this inspired people looked for examples of glory they remembered the Sun King, who left them bankrupt, and the Emperor Napoleon, whose legacy was defeat and semi-anarchy; but glory was in both men and both times—and France needed it, for glory is a little like dignity: only those who do not have it feel the need for it.

For Americans too the wide and general dream has a

[1] [Charles de Gaulle—Ed.]

name. It is called "the American Way of Life." No one can define it or point to any one person or group who lives it, but it is very real nevertheless, perhaps more real than that equally remote dream the Russians call Communism. These dreams describe our vague yearnings toward what we wish were and hope we may be: wise, just, compassionate, and noble. The fact that we have this dream at all is perhaps an indication of its possibility.

II
BIFOCALISM AND DOUBLE-CONSCIOUSNESS: THE AMERICAN VISION

THE LAND OF CONTRASTS

James Fullarton Muirhead

When I first thought of writing about the United States at all, I soon come to the conclusion that no title could better than the above express the general impression left on my mind by my experiences in the Great Republic. It may well be that a long list of inconsistencies might be made out for any country, just as for any individual; but so far as my knowledge goes the United States stands out as preëminently the "Land of Contrasts"—the land of stark, staring, and stimulating inconsistency; at once the home of enlightenment and the happy hunting ground of the charlatan and the quack; a land in which nothing happens but the unexpected; the home of Hyperion, but no less the haunt of the satyr; always the land of promise, but not invariably the land of performance; a land which may be bounded by the aurora borealis, but which has also undeniable acquaintance with the flames of the bottom-

Source: James Fullarton Muirhead, The Land of Contrasts: A Briton's View of His American Kin (London: John Lane, 1898), pp. 7–23.

James Fullarton Muirhead (1853–1934), was an Englishman assigned by Karl Baedeker, publishers in Leipzig, Germany, to the task of providing a handbook for English-speaking travelers to the United States. He began in 1890, published his guide in 1893, married a Boston woman, and used his travel notebooks to write a second volume—more literary and impressionistic—built upon the many contradictions he had encountered. In addition to The Land of Contrasts: A Briton's View of His American Kin (1898), and The United States, With an Excursion Into Mexico: Handbook for Travellers (1893), he wrote Great Britain: Handbook for Travellers (1910), and A Wayfarer in Switzerland (1926).

less pit; a land which is laved at once by the rivers of Paradise and the leaden waters of Acheron.

If I proceed to enumerate a few of the actual contrasts that struck me, in matters both weighty and trivial, it is not merely as an exercise in antithesis, but because I hope it will show how easy it would be to pass an entirely and even ridiculously untrue judgment upon the United States by having an eye only for one series of the startling opposites. It should show in a very concrete way one of the most fertile sources of those unfair international judgments which led the French Academician Joüy to the statement: "Plus on réfléchit et plus on observe, plus on se convainct de la fausseté de la plupart de ces jugements portés sur un nation entière par quelques ecrivains et adoptés sans examen par les autres." The Americans themselves can hardly take umbrage at the label, if Mr. Howells truly represents them when he makes one of the characters in "A Traveller from Altruria" assert that they pride themselves even on the size of their inconsistencies. The extraordinary clashes that occur in the United States are doubtless largely due to the extraordinary mixture of youth and age in the character of the country. If ever an old head was set upon young shoulders, it was in this case of the United States —this "Strange New World, thet yit was never young." While it is easy, in a study of the United States, to see the essential truth of the analogy between the youth of an individual and the youth of a State, we must also remember that America was in many respects born full-grown, like Athena from the brain of Zeus, and coördinates in the most extraordinary way the shrewdness of the sage with the naïveté of the child. Those who criticise the United States because, with the experience of all the ages behind her, she is in some points vastly defective as compared with the nations of Europe are as much mistaken as those who look to her for the fresh ingenuousness of youth unmarred by any trace of age's weakness. It is simply inevitable that she should share the vices as well as the virtues of both. Mr. Freeman has well pointed out how natural it is that a colony should rush ahead of the mother country in some things and lag behind it in others; and that just as you have to go to French Canada if you want to see Old France, so, for many things, if you wish to see Old England you must go to New England.

Thus America may easily be abreast or ahead of us in such matters as the latest applications of electricity, while retaining in its legal uses certain cumbersome devices that we have long since discarded. Americans still have "Courts of Oyer and Terminer" and still insist on the unanimity of the jury, though their judges wear no robes and their counsel apply to the cuspidor as often as to the code. So, too, the extension of municipal powers accomplished in Great Britain still seems a formidable innovation in the United States.

The general feeling of power and scope is probably another fruitful source of the inconsistencies of American life. Emerson has well said that consistency is the hobgoblin of little minds; and no doubt the largeness, the illimitable outlook, of the national mind of the United States makes it disregard surface discrepancies that would grate horribly on a more conventional community. The confident belief that all will come out right in the end, and that harmony can be attained when time is taken to consider it, carries one triumphantly over the roughest places of inconsistency. It is easy to drink our champagne from tin cans, when we know that it is merely a sense of hurry that prevents us fetching the chased silver goblets waiting for our use.

This, I fancy, is the explanation of one series of contrasts which strikes an Englishman at once. America claims to be the land of liberty *par excellence,* and in a wholesale way this may be true in spite of the gap between the noble sentiments of the Declaration of Independence and the actual treatment of the negro and the Chinaman. But in what may be called the retail traffic of life the American puts up with innumerable restrictions of his personal liberty. Max O'Rell has expatiated with scarcely an exaggeration on the wondrous sight of a powerful millionaire standing meekly at the door of a hotel dining-room until the consequential head-waiter (very possibly a coloured gentleman) condescends to point out to him the seat he may occupy. So, too, such petty officials as policemen and railway conductors are generally treated rather as the masters than as the servants of the public. The ordinary American citizen accepts a long delay on the railway or an interminable "wait" at the theatre as a direct visitation of Providence, against which it would be useless folly to direct cat-calls, grumbles, or letters to the *Times*. Americans invented the slang word "kicker," but so far as I could see their vocabulary is here miles ahead of their practice; they dream noble deeds, but do not do them; Englishmen "kick" much better, without having a name for it. The right of the individual to do as he will is respected to such an extent that an entire company will put up with inconvenience rather than infringe it. A coal-carter will calmly keep a tramway-car waiting several minutes until he finishes his unloading. The conduct of the train-boy . . . would infallibly lead to assault and battery in England, but hardly elicits an objurgation in America, where the right of one sinner to bang a door outweighs the desire of twenty just persons for a quiet nap. On the other hand, the old Puritan spirit of interference with individual liberty sometimes crops out in America in a way that would be impossible in this country. An inscription in one of the large mills at Lawrence, Mass., informs the employees (or did so some years ago) that "regular attendance at some place of worship and a proper observance of the Sabbath will be expected of every person employed." So, too, the young women of certain districts impose on their admirers such restrictions in the use of liquor and tobacco that any less patient animal than the native American would infallibly kick over the traces.

In spite of their acknowledged nervous energy and excitability, Americans often show a good deal of a quality that rivals the phlegm of the Dutch. Their above-mentioned patience during railway or other delays is an instance of this. . . . Boston men of business, after being whisked by the electric car from their suburban residences to the city at the rate of twelve miles an hour, sit stoically still while the congested traffic makes the car take twenty minutes to pass the most crowded section of Washington street,—a walk of barely five minutes.[1]

Even in the matter of what Mr. Ambassador Bayard has styled "that form of Socialism, Protection," it seems to me that

[1] The Boston Subway, opened in 1898, has impaired the truth of this sentence.

we can find traces of this contradictory tendency. Americans consider their country as emphatically the land of protection, and attribute most of their prosperity to their inhospitable customs barriers. This may be so; but where else in the world will you find such a volume and expanse of free trade as in these same United States? We find here a huge section of the world's surface, 3,000 miles long and 1,500 miles wide, occupied by about fifty practically independent States, containing seventy millions of inhabitants, producing a very large proportion of all the necessities and many of the luxuries of life, and all enjoying the freest of free trade with each other. Few of these States are as small as Great Britain, and many of them are immensely larger. Collectively they contain nearly half the railway mileage of the globe, besides an incomparable series of inland waterways. Over all these is continually passing an immense amount of goods. The San Francisco *News Letter,* a well-known weekly journal, points out that of the 1,400,000,000 tons of goods carried for 100 miles or upwards on the railways of the world in 1895, no less than 800,000,000 were carried in the United States. Even if we add the 140,000,000 carried by sea-going ships, there remains a balance of 60,000,000 tons in favor of the United States as against the rest of the world. It is, perhaps, impossible to ascertain whether or not the actual value of the goods carried would be in the same proportion; but it seems probable that the value of the 800,000,000 tons of the home trade of America must considerably exceed that of the *free* portion of the trade of the British Empire, *i.e.,* practically the whole of its import trade and that portion of its export trade carried on with free-trade countries or colonies. The internal commerce of the United States makes it the most wonderful market on the globe; and Brother Jonathan, the rampant Protectionist, stands convicted as the greatest Cobdenite of them all!

We are all, it is said, apt to "slip up" on our strongest points. Perhaps this is why one of the leading writers of the American democracy is able to assert that "there is no country in the world where the separation of the classes is so absolute as ours," and to quote a Russian revolutionist, who lived in exile all over Europe and nowhere found such want of sympathy between the rich and poor as in America. If this were true it would certainly form a startling contrast to the general kind-heartedness of the American. But I fancy it rather points to the condition of greater relative equality. Our Russian friend was accustomed to the patronising kindness of the superior to the inferior, of the master to the servant. It is easy, on an empyrean rock, to be "kind" to the mortals toiling helplessly down below. It costs little, to use Mr. Bellamy's parable, for those securely seated on the top of the coach to subscribe for salve to alleviate the chafed wounds of those who drag it. In America there is less need and less use of this patronising kindness; there is less kindness from class to class simply because the conscious realisation of "class" is non-existent in thousands of cases where it would be to the fore in Europe. As for the first statement quoted at the head of this paragraph, I find it very hard of belief. It is true that there are exclusive *circles,* to which, for instance, Buffalo Bill would not have the entrée, but the principle of exclusion is on the whole analogous to that by which we select our intimate personal friends. No man in America, who is personally fitted to adorn it, need feel that he is *automatically* shut out (as he might well be in England) from a really congenial social sphere.

Another of America's strong points is its sense of practical comfort and convenience. It is scarcely open to denial that the laying of too great stress on material comfort is one of the rocks ahead which the American vessel will need careful steering to avoid; and it is certain that Americans lead us in countless little points of household comfort and labour-saving ingenuity. But here, too, the exception that proves the rule is not too coy for our discovery. The terrible roads and the atrociously kept streets are amongst the most vociferous instances of this. It is one of the inexplicable mysteries of American civilisation that a young municipality,—or even, sometimes, an old one,—with a million dollars to spend, will choose to spend it in erecting a most unnecessarily gorgeous town-hall rather than in making the street in front of it passable for the ordinarily shod pedestrian. In New York itself the hilarious stockbroker returning at night to his palace often finds the pavement between his house and his carriage more difficult to negotiate than even the hole for his latch-key; and I have more than once been absolutely compelled to make a détour from Broadway in order to find a crossing where the icy slush would not come over the tops of my boots.[2] The American taste for luxury sometimes insists on gratification even at the expense of the ordinary decencies of life. It was an American who said, "Give me the luxuries of life and I will not ask for the necessities"; and there is more truth in this epigram, as characteristic of the American point of view, than its author intended or would, perhaps, allow. In private life this is seen in the preference shown for diamond earrings and Paris toilettes over neat and effective household service. The contrast between the slatternly, unkempt maid-servant who opens the door to you and the general luxury of the house itself is sometimes of the most startling, not to say appalling, description. It is not a sufficient answer to say that good servants are not so easily obtained in America as in England. This is true; but a slight rearrangement of expenditure would secure much better service than is now seen. To the English eye the cart in this matter often seems put before the horse; and the combination of excellent waiting with a modest table equipage is frequent enough in the United States to prove its perfect feasibility.

In American hotels we are often overwhelmed with "all the discomforts that money can procure," while unable to obtain some of those things which we have been brought up to believe among the prime necessaries of existence. It is significant that in the printed directions governing the use of the electric bell in one's bedroom, I never found an instance in which the harmless necessary bath could be ordered with fewer than nine pressures of the button, while the fragrant cocktail or some other equally fascinating but dangerous luxury might often be summoned by three or four. The most elaborate dinner, served in the most gorgeous china, is sometimes spoiled by the Draconian regulation that it must be devoured between the unholy hours of twelve and two, or have all its courses brought on the table at once. Though the Americans invent the most delicate forms of machinery, their hoop-iron

[2] It is only fair to say that this was originally written in 1893, and that matters have been greatly improved since then.

knives, silver plated for facility in cleaning, are hardly calculated to tackle anything harder than butter, and compel the beef-eater to return to the tearing methods of his remotest ancestors. The waiter sometimes rivals the hotel clerk himself in the splendour of his attire, but this does not render more appetising the spectacle of his thumb in the soup. The furniture of your bedroom would not have disgraced the Tuileries in their palmiest days, but, alas, you are parboiled by a diabolic chevaux-de-frise of steam-pipes which refuse to be turned off, and insist on accompanying your troubled slumbers by an intermittent series of bubbles, squeaks, and hisses. The mirror opposite which you brush your hair is enshrined in the heaviest of gilt frames and is large enough for a Brobdignagian, but the basin in which you wash your hands is little larger than a sugar-bowl; and when you emerge from your nine-times-summoned bath you find you have to dry your sacred person with six little towels, none larger than a snuff-taker's handkerchief. There is no carafe of water in the room; and after countless experiments you are reduced to the blood-curdling belief that the American tourist brushes his teeth with ice-water, the musical tinkling of which in the corridors is the most characteristic sound of the American caravanserai.

If there is anything the Americans pride themselves on— and justly—it is their handsome treatment of woman. You will not meet five Americans without hearing ten times that a lone woman can traverse the length and breadth of the United States without fear of insult; every traveller reports that the United States is the Paradise of women. Special entrances are reserved for them at hotels, so that they need not risk contamination with the tobacco-defiled floors of the public office; they are not expected to join the patient file of room-seekers before the hotel clerk's desk, but wait comfortably in the reception-room while an employee secures their number and key. There is no recorded instance of the justifiable homicide of an American girl in her theatre hat. Man meekly submits to be the hewer of wood, the drawer of water, and the beast of burden for the superior sex. But even this gorgeous medal has its reverse side. Few things provided for a class well able to pay for comfort are more uncomfortable and indecent than the arrangements for ladies on board the sleeping cars. Their dressing accommodation is of the most limited description; their berths are not segregated at one end of the car, but are scattered above and below those of the male passengers; it is considered *tolerable* that they should lie with the legs of a strange, disrobing man dangling within a foot of their noses.

Another curious contrast to the practical, material, matter-of-fact side of the American is his intense interest in the supernatural, the spiritualistic, the superstitious. Boston, of all places in the world, is, perhaps, the happiest hunting ground for the spiritualist medium, the faith healer, and the mind curer. You will find there the most advanced emancipation from theological superstition combined in the most extraordinary way with a more than half belief in the incoherences of a spiritualistic séance. The Boston Christian Scientists have just erected a handsome stone church, with chime of bells, organ, and choir of the most approved ecclesiastical cut; and, greatest marvel of all, have actually had to return a surplus of $50,000 (£10,000) that was subscribed for its building. There are two pulpits, one occupied by a man who expounds the Bible, while in the other a woman responds with the grandiloquent platitudes of Mrs. Eddy. In other parts of the country this desire to pry into the Book of Fate assumes grosser forms. Mr. Bryce tells us that Western newspapers devote a special column to the advertisements of astrologers and soothsayers, and assures us that this profession is as much recognised in the California of to-day as in the Greece of Homer.

It seems to me that I have met in America the nearest approaches to my ideals of a *Bayard sans peur et sans reproche;* and it is in this same America that I have met flagrant examples of the being wittily described as *sans père et sans proche* —utterly without the responsibility of background and entirely unacquainted with the obligation of *noblesse.* The superficial observer in the United States might conceivably imagine the characteristic national trait to be self-sufficiency or vanity (this mistake *has,* I believe, been made), and his opinion might be strengthened should he find, as I did, in an arithmetic published at Richmond during the late Civil War, such a modest example as the following: "If one Confederate soldier can whip seven Yankees, how many Confederate soldiers will it take to whip forty-nine Yankees?" America has been likened to a self-made man, hugging her conditions because she has made them, and considering them divine because they have grown up with the country. Another observer might quite as easily come to the conclusion that diffidence and self-distrust are the true American characteristics. Certainly Americans often show a saving consciousness of their faults, and lash themselves with biting satire. There are even Americans whose very attitude is an apology—wholly unnecessary—for the Great Republic, and who seem to despise any native product until it has received the hall-mark of London or of Paris. In the new world that has produced the new book, of the exquisite delicacy and insight of which Mr. Henry James and Mr. Howells may be taken as typical exponents, it seems to me that there are more than the usual proportion of critics who prefer to it what Colonel Higginson has well called "the brutalities of Haggard and the garlic-flavors of Kipling." While, perhaps, the characteristic charm of the American girl is her thorough-going individuality and the undaunted courage of her opinions, which leads her to say frankly, if she think so, that Martin Tupper is a greater poet than Shakespeare, yet I have, on the other hand, met a young American matron who confessed to me with bated breath that she and her sister, for the first time in their lives, had gone unescorted to a concert the night before last, and, *mirabile dictu,* no harm had come of it! It is in America that I have over and over again heard language to which the calling a spade a spade would seem the most delicate allusiveness; but it is also in America that I have summoned a blush to the cheek of conscious sixty-six by an incautious though innocent reference to the temperature of my morning tub. In that country I have seen the devotion of Sir Walter Raleigh to his queen rivalled again and again by the ordinary American man to the ordinary American woman (if there be an *ordinary* American woman), and in the same country I have myself been scoffed at and made game of because I opened the window of a railway carriage for a girl in whose delicate veins flowed a few drops of coloured blood. In Washington I met Miss Susan B. Anthony, and realised, to some extent at least, all she stands for. In Boston and other places I find there is actually an organised opposition on the part of the ladies themselves to the extension of the franchise to women. I have hailed with delight the democratic spirit displayed in the greeting of my friend and myself by the porter of a hotel as "You fellows," and then had the cup of pleasure dashed from my lips by being told by the same porter that "the other *gentleman* would attend to my baggage!" I have been parboiled with salamanders who seemed to find no inconvenience in a room-temperature of eighty degrees, and have been nigh frozen to death in open-air drives in which the same individuals seemed perfectly comfortable. Men appear at the theatre in orthodox evening dress, while the tall and exasperating hats of the ladies who accompany them would seem to indicate a theory of street toilette. From New York to Buffalo I am whisked through the air at the rate of fifty or sixty miles an hour; in California I travelled on a train on which the engineer shot rabbits from the locomotive, and the fireman picked them up in time to jump on the baggage-car at the rear end of the train. At Santa Barbara I visited an old mission church and convent which vied in quaint picturesqueness with anything in Europe; but, alas! the old monk who showed us round, though wearing the regulation gown and knotted cord, had replaced his sandals by elastic-sided boots and covered his tonsure with a common chummy.[3]

Few things in the United States are more pleasing than the widespread habits of kindness to animals (most American whips are, as far as punishment to the horse is concerned, a mere farce). Yet no American seems to have any scruple about adding an extra hundred weight or two to an already villainously overloaded horse-car; and I have seen a score of American ladies sit serenely watching the frantic straining of

[3] This may be paralleled in Europe: "The Franciscan monks of Bosnia wear long black robes, with rope, black 'bowler hats,' and long and heavy military moustachios (by special permission of the Pope)."—*Daily Chronicle,* Oct. 5, 1895.

two poor animals to get a derailed car on to the track again, when I knew that in "brutal" Old England every one of them would have been out on the sidewalk to lighten the load.

In England that admirable body of men popularly known as Quakers are indissolubly associated in the public mind with a pristine simplicity of life and conversation. My amazement, therefore, may easily be imagined, when I found that an entertainment given by a young member of the Society of Friends in one of the great cities of the Eastern States turned out to be the most elaborate and beautiful private ball I ever attended, with about eight hundred guests dressed in the height of fashion, while the daily papers (if I remember rightly) estimated its expense as reaching a total of some thousands of pounds. Here the natural expansive liberality of the American man proved stronger than the traditional limitations of a religious society. But the opposite art of cheese-paring is by no means unknown in the United States. Perhaps not even canny Scotland can parallel the record of certain districts in New England, which actually elected their parish paupers to the State Legislature to keep them off the rates. Let the opponents of paid members of the House of Commons take notice!

Amid the little band of tourists in whose company I happened to enter the Yosemite Valley was a San Francisco youth with a delightful baritone voice, who entertained the guests in the hotel parlour at Wawona by a good-natured series of songs. No one in the room except myself seemed to find it in the least incongruous or funny that he sandwiched "Nearer, my God, to thee" between "The man who broke the bank at Monto Carlo" and "Her golden hair was hanging down her back," or that he jumped at once from the pathetic solemnity of "I know that my Redeemer liveth" to the jingle of "Little Annie Rooney." The name Wawona reminds me how American weather plays its part in the game of contrasts. When we visited the Grove of Big Trees near Wawona on May 21, it was in the midst of a driving snow-storm, with the thermometer standing at 36 degrees Fahrenheit. Next day, as we drove into Raymond, less than forty miles to the west, the sun was beating down on our backs, and the thermometer marked 80 degrees in the shade.

There is probably no country in the world where, at times, letters of introduction are more fully honoured than in the United States. The recipient does not content himself with inviting you to call or even to dinner. He invites you to make his house your home; he invites all his friends to meet you; he leaves his business to show you the lions of the town or to drive you about the country; he puts you up at his club; he sends you off provided with letters to ten other men like himself, only more so. On the other hand, there is probably no country in the world where a letter of introduction from a man quite entitled to give it could be wholly ignored as it sometimes is in the United States. The writer has had experience of both results. No more fundamental contrast can well be imagined than that between the noisy, rough, crude, and callous street-life of some Western towns and the quiet, reticence, delicacy, spirituality, and refinement of many of the adjacent interiors.

The table manners of the less-educated American classes are hardly of the best, but where but in America will you find eleven hundred charity-school boys sit down daily to dinner, each with his own table napkin, as they do at Girard College, Philadelphia? And where except at that same institute will you find a man leaving millions for a charity, with the stipulation that no parson of any creed shall ever be allowed to enter its precincts?

In concluding this chapter, let me say that its object, as indeed the object of this whole book, will have been achieved if it convinces a few Britons of the futility of generalising on the complex organism of American society from inductions that would not justify an opinion about the habits of a piece of protoplasm.[4]

[4] In the just-ended war with Spain, the United States did not fail to justify its character as the Land of Contrasts. From the wealthy and enlightened United States we should certainly have expected all that money and science could afford in the shape of superior weapons and efficiency of commissariat and medical service, while we could have easily pardoned a little unsteadiness in civilians suddenly turned into soldiers. As a matter of fact, the poverty-stricken Spaniards had better rifles than the Americans; the Commissariat and Medical Departments are alleged to have broken down in the most disgraceful way; the citizen-soldiers behaved like veterans.

THE SOULS OF BLACK FOLK

W. E. Burghardt Du Bois

Of Our Spiritual Strivings

O water, voice of my heart, crying in the sand,
   All night long crying with a mournful cry,
As I lie and listen, and cannot understand
      The voice of my heart in my side or the voice of the sea,
   O water, crying for rest, is it I, is it I?
   All night long the water is crying to me.

Unresting water, there shall never be rest
   Till the last moon droop and the last tide fail,
And the fire of the end begin to burn in the west;
      And the heart shall be weary and wonder and cry like the sea,
   All life long crying without avail,
      As the water all night long is crying to me.

Arthur Symons

Source: W. E. Burghardt Du Bois, *The Souls of Black Folk: Essays and Sketches* (Chicago: A. C. McClurg & Co., 1903), pp. 1–12. Reprinted by permission of Shirley Graham Du Bois. All Rights Reserved.

William Edward Burghardt Du Bois (1868–1963), was educated at Fisk, Harvard, and the University of Berlin, and taught at Wilberforce, Pennsylvania, and Atlanta universities. One of the founders of the NAACP, founder of *Crisis* magazine, and of the *Phylon Quarterly Review*, a founder of the Pan-African Congress, he also authored many works of history, sociology, and literature. In addition to *The Souls of Black Folk* (1903), his books include *The Suppression of the African Slave Trade* (1896), *The Philadelphia Negro* (1899), *John Brown* (1909), *Quest of the Silver Fleece,* a novel (1911), *The Negro* (1915), *Darkwater* (1920), *The Gift of Black Folk* (1924), *Dark Princess,* a novel (1928), *Black Reconstruction* (1935), *Black Folk, Then and*

Between me and the other world there is ever an unasked question: unasked by some through feelings of delicacy; by others through the difficulty of rightly framing it. All, nevertheless, flutter round it. They approach me in a half-hesitant sort of way, eye me curiously or compassionately, and then, instead of saying directly, How does it feel to be a problem? they say, I know an excellent colored man in my town; or, I fought at Mechanicsville; or, Do not these Southern outrages make your blood boil? At these I smile, or am interested, or reduce the boiling to a simmer, as the occasion may require. To the real question, How does it feel to be a problem? I answer seldom a word.

And yet, being a problem is a strange experience,— peculiar even for one who has never been anything else, save perhaps in babyhood and in Europe. It is in the early days of rollicking boyhood that the revelation first bursts upon one, all in a day, as it were. I remember well when the shadow swept across me. I was a little thing, away up in the hills of New England, where the dark Housatonic winds between Hoosac and Taghkanic to the sea. In a wee wooden schoolhouse, something put it into the boys' and girls' heads to buy gorgeous visiting-cards—ten cents a package—and exchange. The exchange was merry, till one girl, a tall newcomer, refused my card,—refused it peremptorily, with a glance. Then it dawned upon me with a certain suddenness that I was different from the others; or like, mayhap, in heart and life and longing, but shut out from their world by a vast veil. I had thereafter no desire to tear down that veil, to creep through; I held all beyond it in common contempt, and lived above it in a region of blue sky and great wandering shadows. That sky was bluest when I could beat my mates at examination-time, or beat them at a foot-race, or even beat their stringy heads. Alas, with the years all this fine contempt began to fade; for the worlds I longed for, and all their dazzling opportunities, were theirs, not mine. But they should not keep these prizes, I said; some, all, I

Now (1939), *Dusk of Dawn* (1940), *Color and Democracy* (1945), *The World and Africa* (1947), *The Black Flame, A Trilogy* (1957–61), *Worlds of Color* (1961), and *The Autobiography of W. E. B. Du Bois* (1968).

would wrest from them. Just how I would do it I could never decide: by reading law, by healing the sick, by telling the wonderful tales that swam in my head,—some way. With other black boys the strife was not so fiercely sunny: their youth shrunk into tasteless sycophancy, or into silent hatred of the pale world about them and mocking distrust of everything white; or wasted itself in a bitter cry, Why did God make me an outcast and a stranger in mine own house? The shades of the prison-house closed round about us all: walls strait and stubborn to the whitest, but relentlessly narrow, tall, and unscalable to sons of night who must plod darkly on in resignation, or beat unavailing palms against the stone, or steadily, half hopelessly, watch the streak of blue above.

After the Egyptian and Indian, the Greek and Roman, the Teuton and Mongolian, the Negro is a sort of seventh son, born with a veil, and gifted with second-sight in this American world,—a world which yields him no true self-consciousness, but only lets him see himself through the revelation of the other world. It is a peculiar sensation, this double-consciousness, this sense of always looking at one's self through the eyes of others, of measuring one's soul by the tape of a world that looks on in amused contempt and pity. One ever feels his two-ness,—an American, a Negro; two souls, two thoughts, two unreconciled strivings; two warring ideals in one dark body, whose dogged strength alone keeps it from being torn asunder.

The history of the American Negro is the history of this strife,—this longing to attain self-conscious manhood, to merge his double self into a better and truer self. In this merging he wishes neither of the older selves to be lost. He would not Africanize America, for America has too much to teach the world and Africa. He would not bleach his Negro soul in a flood of white Americanism, for he knows that Negro blood has a message for the world. He simply wishes to make it possible for a man to be both a Negro and an American, without being cursed and spit upon by his fellows, without having the doors of Opportunity closed roughly in his face.

This, then, is the end of his striving: to be a coworker in the kingdom of culture, to escape both death and isolation, to husband and use his best powers and his latent genius. These powers of body and mind have in the past been strangely wasted, dispersed, or forgotten. The shadow of a mighty Negro past flits through the tale of Ethiopia the Shadowy and of Egypt the Sphinx. Throughout history, the powers of single black men flash here and there like falling stars, and die sometimes before the world has rightly gauged their brightness. Here in America, in the few days since Emancipation, the black man's turning hither and thither in hesitant and doubtful striving has often made his very strength to lose effectiveness, to seem like absence of power, like weakness. And yet it is not weakness,—it is the contradiction of double aims. The double-aimed struggle of the black artisan—on the one hand to escape white contempt for a nation of mere hewers of wood and drawers of water, and on the other hand to plough and nail and dig for a poverty-stricken horde—could only result in making him a poor craftsman, for he had but half a heart in either cause. By the poverty and ignorance of his people, the Negro minister or doctor was tempted toward quackery and demagogy; and by the criticism of the other world, toward ideals that made him ashamed of his lowly tasks. The would-be black *savant* was confronted by the paradox that the knowledge his people needed was a twice-told tale to his white neighbors, while the knowledge which would teach the white world was Greek to his own flesh and blood. The innate love of harmony and beauty that set the ruder souls of his people a-dancing and a-singing raised but confusion and doubt in the soul of the black artist; for the beauty revealed to him was the soul-beauty of a race which his larger audience despised, and he could not articulate the message of another people. This waste of double aims, this seeking to satisfy two unreconciled ideals, has wrought sad havoc with the courage and faith and deeds of ten thousand thousand people, —has sent them often wooing false gods and invoking false means of salvation, and at times has even seemed about to make them ashamed of themselves.

Away back in the days of bondage they thought to see in one divine event the end of all doubt and disappointment; few men ever worshipped Freedom with half such unquestioning faith as did the American Negro for two centuries. To him, so far as he thought and dreamed, slavery was indeed the sum of all villainies, the cause of all sorrow, the root of all prejudice; Emancipation was the key to a promised land of sweeter beauty than ever stretched before the eyes of wearied Israel-ites. In song and exhortation swelled one refrain—Liberty; in his tears and curses the God he implored had Freedom in his right hand. At last it came,—suddenly, fearfully, like a dream. With one wild carnival of blood and passion came the mes-sage in his own plaintive cadences:—

> Shout, O children!
> Shout, you're free!
> For God has bought your liberty!

Years have passed away since then,—ten, twenty, forty; forty years of national life, forty years of renewal and develop-ment, and yet the swarthy spectre sits in its accustomed seat at the Nation's feast. In vain do we cry to this our vastest social problem:—

> Take any shape but that, and my firm nerves
> Shall never tremble!

The Nation has not yet found peace from its sins; the freed-man has not yet found in freedom his promised land. Whatever of good may have come in these years of change, the shadow of a deep disappointment rests upon the Negro people,—a dis-appointment all the more bitter because the unattained ideal was unbounded save by the simple ignorance of a lowly peo-ple.

The first decade was merely a prolongation of the vain search for freedom, the boon that seemed ever barely to elude their grasp,—like a tantalizing will-o'-the-wisp, maddening and misleading the headless host. The holocaust of war, the terrors of the Ku-Klux Klan, the lies of carpet-baggers, the disorganization of industry, and the contradictory advice of friends and foes, left the bewildered serf with no new watch-word beyond the old cry for freedom. As the time flew, how-ever, he began to grasp a new idea. The ideal of liberty de-manded for its attainment powerful means, and these the

Fifteenth Amendment gave him. The ballot, which before he had looked upon as a visible sign of freedom, he now regarded as the chief means of gaining and perfecting the liberty with which war had partially endowed him. And why not? Had not votes made war and emancipated millions? Had not votes enfranchised the freedmen? Was anything impossible to a power that had done all this? A million black men started with renewed zeal to vote themselves into the kingdom. So the decade flew away, the revolution of 1876 came, and left the half-free serf weary, wondering, but still inspired. Slowly but steadily, in the following years, a new vision began gradually to replace the dream of political power,—a powerful movement, the rise of another ideal to guide the unguided, another pillar of fire by night after a clouded day. It was the ideal of "book-learning"; the curiosity, born of compulsory ignorance, to know and test the power of the cabalistic letters of the white man, the longing to know. Here at last seemed to have been discovered the mountain path to Canaan; longer than the highway of Emancipation and law, steep and rugged, but straight, leading to heights high enough to overlook life.

Up the new path the advance guard toiled, slowly, heavily, doggedly; only those who have watched and guided the faltering feet, the misty minds, the dull understandings, of the dark pupils of these schools know how faithfully, how piteously, this people strove to learn. It was weary work. The cold statistician wrote down the inches of progress here and there, noted also where here and there a foot had slipped or some one had fallen. To the tired climbers, the horizon was ever dark, the mists were often cold, the Canaan was always dim and far away. If, however, the vistas disclosed as yet no goal, no resting-place, little but flattery and criticism, the journey at least gave leisure for reflection and self-examination; it changed the child of Emancipation to the youth with dawning self-consciousness, self-realization, self-respect. In those sombre forests of his striving his own soul rose before him, and he saw himself,—darkly as through a veil; and yet he saw in himself some faint revelation of his power, of his mission. He began to have a dim feeling that, to attain his place in the world, he must be himself, and not another. For the first time he sought to analyze the burden he bore upon his back, that dead-weight of social degradation partially masked behind a half-named Negro problem. He felt his poverty; without a cent, without a home, without land, tools, or savings, he had entered into competition with rich, landed, skilled neighbors. To be a poor man is hard, but to be a poor race in a land of dollars is the very bottom of hardships. He felt the weight of his ignorance,—not simply of letters, but of life, of business, of the humanities; the accumulated sloth and shirking and awkwardness of decades and centuries shackled his hands and feet. Nor was his burden all poverty and ignorance. The red stain of bastardy, which two centuries of systematic legal defilement of Negro women had stamped upon his race, meant not only the loss of ancient African chastity, but also the hereditary weight of a mass of corruption from white adulterers, threatening almost the obliteration of the Negro home.

A people thus handicapped ought not to be asked to race with the world, but rather allowed to give all its time and thought to its own social problems. But alas! while sociologists gleefully count his bastards and his prostitutes, the very soul of the toiling, sweating black man is darkened by the shadow of a vast despair. Men call the shadow prejudice, and learnedly explain it as the natural defence of culture against barbarism, learning against ignorance, purity against crime, the "higher" against the "lower" races. To which the Negro cries Amen! and swears that to so much of this strange prejudice as is founded on just homage to civilization, culture, righteousness, and progress, he humbly bows and meekly does obeisance. But before that nameless prejudice that leaps beyond all this he stands helpless, dismayed, and well-nigh speechless; before that personal disrespect and mockery, the ridicule and systematic humiliation, the distortion of fact and wanton license of fancy, the cynical ignoring of the better and the boisterous welcoming of the worse, the all-pervading desire to inculcate disdain for everything black, from Toussaint to the devil,—before this there rises a sickening despair that would disarm and discourage any nation save that black host to whom "discouragement" is an unwritten word.

But the facing of so vast a prejudice could not but bring

the inevitable self-questioning, self-disparagement, and lowering of ideals which ever accompany repression and breed in an atmosphere of contempt and hate. Whisperings and portents came borne upon the four winds: Lo! we are diseased and dying, cried the dark hosts; we cannot write, our voting is vain; what need of education, since we must always cook and serve? And the Nation echoed and enforced this self-criticism, saying: Be content to be servants, and nothing more; what need of higher culture for half-men? Away with the black man's ballot, by force or fraud,—and behold the suicide of a race! Nevertheless, out of the evil came something of good,— the more careful adjustment of education to real life, the clearer perception of the Negroes' social responsibilities, and the sobering realization of the meaning of progress.

So dawned the time of *Sturm und Drang:* storm and stress to-day rocks our little boat on the mad waters of the world-sea; there is within and without the sound of conflict, the burning of body and rending of soul; inspiration strives with doubt, and faith with vain questionings. The bright ideals of the past, —physical freedom, political power, the training of brains and the training of hands,—all these in turn have waxed and waned, until even the last grows dim and overcast. Are they all wrong,—all false? No, not that, but each alone was over-simple and incomplete,—the dreams of a credulous race-childhood, or the fond imaginings of the other world which does not know and does not want to know our power. To be really true, all these ideals must be melted and welded into one. The training of the schools we need to-day more than ever,—the training of deft hands, quick eyes and ears, and above all the broader, deeper, higher culture of gifted minds and pure hearts. The power of the ballot we need in sheer self-defence, —else what shall save us from a second slavery? Freedom, too, the long-sought, we still seek,—the freedom of life and limb, the freedom to work and think, the freedom to love and aspire. Work, culture, liberty,—all these we need, not singly but together, not successively but together, each growing and aiding each, and all striving toward that vaster ideal that swims before the Negro people, the ideal of human brotherhood, gained through the unifying ideal of Race; the ideal of fostering and developing the traits and talents of the Negro, not in opposition to or contempt for other races, but rather in large conformity to the greater ideals of the American Republic, in order that some day on American soil two world-races may give each to each those characteristics both so sadly lack. We the darker ones come even now not altogether empty-handed: there are to-day no truer exponents of the pure human spirit of the Declaration of Independence than the American Negroes; there is no true American music but the wild sweet melodies of the Negro slave; the American fairy tales and folk-lore are Indian and African; and, all in all, we black men seem the sole oasis of simple faith and reverence in a dusty desert of dollars and smartness. Will America be poorer if she replace her brutal dyspeptic blundering with light-hearted but determined Negro humility? or her coarse and cruel wit with loving jovial good-humor? or her vulgar music with the soul of the Sorrow Songs?

Merely a concrete test of the underlying principles of the great republic is the Negro Problem, and the spiritual striving of the freedmen's sons is the travail of souls whose burden is almost beyond the measure of their strength, but who bear it in the name of an historic race, in the name of this the land of their fathers' fathers, and in the name of human opportunity.

THE AMERICAN CAST OF MIND

Ralph Barton Perry

1

There is no more teasing and baffling task than the definition of national characteristics. Just as we love to talk over our
friends, whether in a kindly or in a malicious spirit, and put
their indescribable peculiarities into words, so we turn again
and again to such complex and unanswerable questions as,
"What is the distinctive genius of the Englishman?" "What is
particularly French about Frenchmen?" "What are those German traits which have brought disaster to Europe?" "What is
that dark Russian soul on which the future of mankind so
largely depends?" These are delightful subjects for discussion
because almost anybody can have an opinion without imper-
tinence. There are no experts who have the answers.

Source: Ralph Barton Perry, *Characteristically American* (New York:
Alfred A. Knopf, Inc., 1949), pp. 3–20. Copyright © 1949 by The Regents of
the University of Michigan. Reprinted by permission of Alfred A. Knopf, Inc.
  Ralph Barton Perry (1876–1957), was educated at Princeton and Harvard
universities, and taught philosophy at Harvard from 1902 until 1946. In addition to *Characteristically American* (1949), he wrote *The Approach to Philosophy* (1905), *The Moral Economy* (1909), *Present Philosophical Tendencies*
(1912), *The Free Man and the Soldier* (1916), *The Present Conflict of Ideals*
(1918), *Philosophy of the Recent Past* (1926), *General Theory of Value*
(1926), *A Defense of Philosophy* (1931), *The Thought and Character of William James* (1935), *Shall Not Perish from the Earth* (1940), *On All Fronts*
(1941), *Plea for an Age Movement* (1942), *Our Side is Right* (1942), *Puritanism and Democracy* (1944), *One World in the Making* (1945), *The Citizen
Decides* (1951), *Realms of Value* (1954), and *The Humanity of Man* (1956).

What of ourselves? What is it to be American—in thought and deed and feeling? The fascination of such questions lies not only in the uncertainty of the answer, but in its paradoxes. Each nation appears to be a compound not only of many characteristics, but of opposite characteristics. Start with any formula and you will shortly be reminded not only that it is incomplete, but that it is contradicted by what it omits. The Englishman "muddles," but he "muddles *through*"; that is, he gets results. The Frenchman is logical, but he is obsessed with *"l'amour."* The German appears to be a mysterious blend of romanticism and technology, of kindliness and cruelty. The Russian is both autocratic and socialistic. And, similarly, America is, in the same curious fashion, both harshly competitive and humanely idealistic. What is needed, then, is some idea or set of ideas that will not only cover the complex manifestations of American life, but resolve its paradoxes.

A mere enumeration of characteristics does not suffice. Thus Henry Pratt Fairchild, pleading for restricted immigration, in order to preserve that "spiritual reality," that "complex of cultural and moral values" which constitutes Americanism, has listed certain traits on which there would be general agreement: "such things as business honesty, respect for womanhood, inventiveness, political independence, physical cleanliness, good sportsmanship, and others less creditable, such as worship of success, material-mindedness, boastfulness."[1] But how do these and other characteristics *go together*? What is the underlying idea which expresses itself in this aggregate of items and in their paradoxical balance of opposites?

It might be supposed that the continental vastness of America, and its unparalleled variety of climate, natural resources, race and creed, would make such an inquiry both impossible and unprofitable. But the fact is that identity is more easily traced when it dwells amidst variety. It is because there is something common to life in New England and California, Montana and Florida, in the arid deserts of Arizona and the lush Mississippi and Ohio lowlands, in great cities and small towns, that it is possible to find a meaning for Americanism. It

[1] *The Melting-Pot Mistake,* 1926, pp. 201–2.

is because this thing which is common within our boundaries stops so abruptly at the Mexican border, and so unmistakably though less abruptly at the Canadian border, and begins when one disembarks either at New York or at San Francisco, that it can be detected and set apart from the rest of human life, however similar this life outside may be, taken item by item. It is because Americans are English, Scotch, Irish, German, French, Spanish, Jewish, Italian, East-European, Asiatic and African that their common Americanism is something else again, something discernible and recognizable, however indescribable. The melting pot has not merely melted: it has cooked a broth with an unmistakable flavor of its own.

In conveying this pervasive and identical character of the American mind it is impossible to make any statement to which exception may not be taken. There is no indivisible Platonic essence of which America is the unique embodiment. There is no American characteristic which is not exemplified elsewhere, or which some Americans do not lack. All that one can possibly claim is that there is among the people of this half-continent taken as a whole, a characteristic blend of characteristics. The cast of the American mind is not a simple quality—but a physiognomy, a syndrome, a form of complexity, a contour, a total effect of the distribution and comparative densities of elements. Nor should one be expected to say on this subject anything that has not been known before. Any claim of original discovery should be distrusted. For America has not hidden its face; its character is not mysterious, but palpable—there are those who would say, flagrant.

Of what elements does a national character, mind, or soul, consist? Not of ideas in the strict sense of the term. The acceptance of attested facts, or of some portion of the body of scientific truth, does not go to the heart of the matter. No doubt most Americans believe that $2 + 2 = 4$, and that the Pacific Ocean is larger than the Atlantic, and that matter is composed of atoms. But Americanism consists not of what Americans believe to be true, but rather of what they believe *in*— their attitudes, their sentiments, their hopes and resolves, their scruples and maxims, or what are sometimes called their "valuations." It is here that Gunnar Myrdal, for example, looks for "the cultural unity" of America—"the floor space upon which the democratic process goes on." He finds such a common ground and sanction in "the fact that *most Americans have most valuations in common* though they are arranged differently in the sphere of valuations of different individuals and groups and bear different intensity coefficients." [2]

2

How America came to be American is a story that has been often told, and a story that can properly be told only by the historian. The present study is an interpretation of America, and not a history. Nevertheless, it is well that it should include a brief summary of the major influences which have formed the American mind and given it its peculiar cast or bias.

In the first place, America developed from a group of colonies. It began as the child of Europe, and while it has achieved maturity and independence it has never lost its parentage and ancestry. Its culture was transplanted after having flowered on other soil. Its thought, therefore, is rarely indigenous, and has always retained something of provincialism even in the manner and tone of its self-sufficiency. It diverged from the main stream of European culture in comparatively modern times, and in the realm of fundamental ideas it still imports more than it exports, thus reversing the balance of trade in the realm of commerce.

Therefore great importance attaches, in the second place, to the ideas which the colonists brought with them, or which were imported during the early formative period of the nation's history. These consisted of mediaeval European thought; of the literature and science of the Renaissance, and especially of Elizabethan England; and of the "new philosophy" of the Seventeenth and early Eighteenth Centuries, comprising Newton, Locke, Hutcheson, Berkeley, Adam Smith, Descartes,

---

[2] *An American Dilemma*, 1944, Vol. I, p. xliv. Myrdal's own idea of Americanism is not essentially different from that which is proposed here, though he uses a variety of different expressions such as "practical idealism," "bright fatalism," "rationalism" (in the sense of organized efficiency), "humanistic liberalism," "moral optimism." *Op. cit.*, Introduction.

Malebranche, and the broad currents of thought, and especially of political thought, known as the Enlightenment.

In the third place, the colonial mind of America was moulded by Protestant Christianity and in the main by Puritan and Evangelical Protestantism. Except for Maryland, the Catholicism of colonial days was peripheral; and the Catholicism of the later migrations not only came after the main characteristics of the American mind were already crystallized, but did not as a rule reach the upper economic, political and cultural levels of American society.

Fourthly, since the colonies which combined to form the United States were British colonies the institutions of the new nation were fundamentally British. The American Revolution was not a social revolution, or even a political revolution, but a war of liberation, in which the new entity retained the structural characteristics of the parent organism. The very principles invoked to justify the overthrow of British authority were themselves British—Magna Carta and the "higher law," the Common Law, representative parliamentary government, the rights of the individual, the pursuit of happiness. While these original social and institutional forms, together with their associated habits and sentiments, were modified in the course of time, they were never repudiated, but became the heroic memory and sacred legend, the ceremonial symbols, the norm of self-criticism, the core of conservatism, the dream of the future.

Fifthly, the original settlers of America, and many later immigrants, were products of the advancing capitalistic economy. They were yeomen, tradesmen, artisans, professional men, or small landowners, already emancipated from a feudal past—"rising men," jealous of authority, and seeking an opportunity under more favorable conditions to prove the capacity which they felt within themselves. Such men were neither hopeless nor self-satisfied, but ambitious to improve their condition and build for themselves a new society corresponding to their ideas and hopes.

Finally, the philosophical, religious, cultural, and social ideas brought or imported from Europe were modified by the experience of settlement. A sparsely inhabited area of wide expanse, rich in natural resources, presenting formidable but not insuperable obstacles, both stimulated and rewarded effort, and generated a sense of man's power to master nature. The temperate but variable climate, the freedom from economic pressure and congestion, the rugged and primitive life of the frontier, and the mixture of ethnic types produced men of physical robustness and energy who felt a contempt for the effeminacy and softening luxury imputed to older civilization.

Through the operation of these and other influences the American mind came to possess a specific character which, despite an immense variety of local, ethnic, and economic differences, pervades the whole from coast to coast and from border to border, is recognizable to visitors from abroad, and is sufficiently strong to stamp its imprint on successive generations and waves of immigration.

3

If one were limited to a single word with which to characterize America, one would choose the word "individualism"— used, however, with reservations. If individualism is taken to mean the cult of solitude, or the prizing of those personal traits which set one man apart from his fellows, or are the effect of retreat from the world, then no word could be less appropriate. American individuality is the very opposite of singularity. The people of the United States are highly gregarious and sociable. The individual who holds himself apart, who will not "join," who does not "belong," who will not "get together" and "play the game," who does not "row his weight in the boat," is viewed with suspicion. Americans find silence hard to endure, and if they develop an oddity they make a fad of it so that they may dwell among similar oddities. Their individualism is a *collective* individualism—not the isolation of one human being, but the intercourse and coöperation of many.

At the same time, there is a tonic quality of American life that imbues men with a feeling of buoyancy and resourcefulness. They believe that they can improve their condition, and make their fortunes; and that if they fail they have only themselves to blame. There is a promise of reward, not too remote, which excites ambition and stimulates effort. It is this prospect of abounding opportunity which constitutes that appeal of America abroad which attracted immigrants in colonial days, and still in 1949 causes multitudes in all parts of the world to look wistfully toward our half-closed doors. However harshly America is criticized, foreigners, including the critics themselves, come to America of their own free will. Seen from afar America is a land of promise; and that vision is never wholly obliterated by closer acquaintance, but remains in the form of gratitude and love of country. It is to be assumed that those who come find confirmation of this hopefulness in the reports received from those who have preceded them, and from their own experiences.

It follows that the people of the United States judge, and expect to be judged, by the standard of success, meaning something made of opportunity. There is the opportunity, in the sense of favorable conditions—the "opening," as it is sometimes called—and there is the seizing of the opportunity, the taking advantage of the opening. Success is thought of as the fruit of a marriage between circumstance and action.

American success must be recognized success—not by the God of Things as They Are, but by one's neighbors. Success must be not only measurable, but observed, recorded, applauded, and envied. Hence the close relation of success and publicity, attested by Mark Twain's famous description of the rival boy who went as an apprentice engineer on a Mississippi steamboat:

> That boy had been notoriously worldly, and I just the reverse; yet he was exalted to this eminence, and I left in obscurity and misery. . . . He would always manage to have a rusty bolt to scrub while his boat tarried at our town, and he would sit . . . and scrub it, where we could all see him and envy him and loathe him. . . . When his boat blew up at last, it diffused a tranquil contentment among us such as we had not known for months. But when he came home the next week, alive, renowned, and appeared in church all battered up and bandaged, a shining hero, stared at and wondered over by everybody, it

seemed to us that the partiality of Providence for an undeserving reptile had reached a point where it was open to criticism.[3]

This was a local and juvenile social experience, but modern facilities of communication—moving pictures, illustrated magazines, radio, national newspapers, and political conventions—have only enlarged the scale. Applause must follow hard upon achievement; and the volume of applause tends to become the measure of achievement.

The American belief in success is not based on blind faith, or on trust, or on a mere elasticity of spirit, but on experience. Nature makes things big in America—mountains, rivers, deserts, plants and animals. It is no secret, least of all from the American people, that the little enterprise launched on the banks of the Delaware in 1776 turned out to be a big success. As these people look back over their history, or out upon the life of their times, they see (easily, with the naked eye) American success achieved and in the making; and their confidence seems to them to be justified. They feel themselves to be on the march; toward precisely what is not always clear, but anyway toward something bigger and better.

In America the moving of mountains is not a symbol of the impossible, but a familiar experience. Major Hutton, the assistant engineer of the Grand Coulee Dam, is reported to have said: "If a hard mountain gets in the way, move it. If it's just a soft mountain, freeze the darn thing, forget it, and keep on going." [4] *Keep on going!*

American pride of achievement is local as well as national. Each state and city and region is out to make records —in population, in volume of business, or in the height of its skyscrapers. If the press report is to be trusted, patriots of the State of Washington now propose to alter the geologic map in order to outstrip their rivals. To quote a certain Dr. C. A. Mittun of that State:

> Man will re-do Mother Nature's work and give Mount Rainier back its prominence in the world of mountains. . . . These two almost unknown sand dunes in Colorado, and that reverse go-

[3] *Life on the Mississippi,* 1901, pp. 32–4.
[4] John Gunther, *Inside U.S.A.,* 1947, p. 124.

pher hole in California . . . are in for a bad time. . . . We're going to realize the dream of every Washington mountaineer who scraped the snow from the record-cairn at the top to pile something, anything—snow, rocks, ice—on the crater's rim so our mountain can regain the dignity it deserves.[5]

Here is movement, confidence, verified confidence, visible success, success on a large scale, efficiency, and, let it be confessed, a touch of boastfulness. For there is a belief in America, founded half on fiction and half on fact, that Americans owe their major blessings to themselves, rather than to history or inherited institutions—as though they had started from scratch with their bare hands.

It is largely because of a widespread belief in success that competition, while keen and intense, is, as a rule, not deadly or vindictive. No fight is taken to be the last fight. Defeat may not be accepted gracefully, but it is accepted cheerfully, because he who is defeated expects to fight again, with another opponent or on another field of battle. Sometime, somehow, somewhere, he expects to win.

Whether Americans are successful in their pursuit of happiness is another question; the contrary is often asserted. Nor is it clear that they pursue happiness methodically, or have, save for certain sects, such as Christian Science, developed any positive art of happiness. It would perhaps be more correct to say that they believe in the possibility of removing the causes of *un*happiness—pain, poverty, frustration, sickness, old age, and even death. They do not regard unhappiness as the necessary lot of man, to be accepted as a fatality and sublimated in tragic nobility. Even sin is regarded as curable; if not by divine grace, then by psychoanalysis.

American resourcefulness consists to no small extent in the fertility of its intellectual soil. America has become a universal seed bed and nursery for ideas from all the past and from all the world. The American public has become a sort of public at large—the great world-market for ideas. Its immense and voracious literacy creates the greatest aggregate demand for reading matter, for the visual arts, for music, for thoughts

[5] Quoted by the *N.Y. Times,* Aug. 13, 1948, p. 17.

and fancies, for anything communicable, in human history. Now while this does convey, and rightly conveys, a suggestion of shallowness and lack of discrimination, it also gives the Americans the sense that they have everything. If they do not make it they can buy it. This does not offend their pride for they feel that they buy it with that which they *have* made.

American self-reliance is a plural, collective, self-reliance —not "*I* can," but "*we* can." But it is still individualistic—a togetherness of several and not the isolation of one, or the absorption of all into a higher unity. The appropriate term is not "organism" but "organization"; *ad hoc* organization, extemporized to meet emergencies, and multiple organization in which the same individuals join many and surrender themselves to none. Americans do not take naturally to mechanized discipline. They remain an aggregate of spontaneities. Such organization develops and uses temporary leaders—"natural" leaders, and leaders for the business in hand, rather than established authorities.

This confidence in achievement through voluntary association and combined effort breeds among Americans a sense of invincible power, a tendency to centrifugal expansion, and a readiness to assume the rôle of a people chosen to head the march of human progress.

The idea of racial superiority did not begin with the political agitators of the South in the Reconstruction Era, nor has it been limited to the context of Negro slavery. It has been applied with equal arrogance to American Indians, to Mexicans, and to the "Mongolians" of the Orient. It was Thomas Hart Benton, voicing the spirit of the advancing westward frontier, and addressing the United States Senate in 1846, who said:

> For my part, I cannot murmur at what seems to be the effect of divine law. I cannot repine that this Capitol has replaced the wigwam—this Christian people, replaced the savages—white matrons, the red squaws—and that such men as Washington, Franklin, and Jefferson, have taken the place of Powhattan, Opechonecanough, and other red men, howsoever respectable they may have been as savages. Civilization, or extinction, has been the fate of all people who have found themselves in the track of the advancing Whites, and civilization, always the pref-

erence of the Whites, has been pressed as an object, while extinction has followed as a consequence of its resistance. The Black and the Red races have often felt their ameliorating influence.[6]

The sense of collective power, demonstrated in the rapidity and extent of westward expansion, has led Americans to confuse bigger and better, and to identify value with velocity, area, altitude, and number. Jefferson was concerned to refute the thesis of Buffon that animal and plant life is smaller on the Western continent than in Europe; and he has been proved right. Even human stature has increased in America. The same cult of magnitude has led to that strain of half-believing, half-joking exaggeration which is a feature of American legend and folk-lore. Stories, like everything else, must be "big stories." The hyperbole of the imagination reflects the sense of vital exuberance. When all things are deemed possible, the line between the actual and the preposterous is hard to draw.

This same collective self-reliance, this urge to do something together, gives to the American mind a peculiar aptitude for industrialization and for the development of the technological arts. The American does not readily become a tool, but he is a born user of tools—especially of tools which are a symbol of organized rather than of single-handed action. The American's love of achievement, his impulse to make and to build, to make faster, to build bigger, to rebuild, to exceed others in making and building, leads to the multiplication and quick obsolescence of gadgets, and the deflection of thought from the wisdom of ends to the efficiency of means.

Publicity in America is valued above privacy. This is only one of the phenomena which attest the fact that American individualism is collective and not singular. Regimentation did not begin with the New Deal, and government regulation is one of the least of its causes. Americans are made alike by imitation, and by the overpowering pressures of mass opinion and sentiment. Agencies of publicity create and inculcate clichés; national advertising and mass production create uni-

[6] "Superiority of the White Race," *Speech of Mr. Benton of Missouri on the Oregon Question,* Washington, Blair and Rives, 1846, p. 30.

formity of manners, clothing, and all the articles of daily life. Competition itself tends to uniformity among competitors, since they are matched against one another in like activities, calling for like talents. In order that a competitor may be exceeded he must be exceeded "at the same game."

This tendency to uniformity has been accentuated by modern developments of mass communication, but it is an old and persistent American trait. It was in 1837 that James Fenimore Cooper recorded the following impression of the difference between the English and the Americans:

> The English are to be distinguished from the Americans by greater independence of personal habits. Not only the institutions, but the physical condition of our own country has a tendency to reduce us all to the same level of usages. The steamboats, the overgrown taverns, the speculative character of the enterprises, and the consequent disposition to do all things in common aid the tendency of the system in bringing about such a result. In England a man dines by himself in a room filled with other hermits, he eats at his leisure, drinks his wine in silence, reads the paper by the hour; and, in all things, encourages his individuality and insists on his particular humours. The American is compelled to submit to a common rule; he eats when others eat, sleeps when others sleep, and he is lucky, indeed, if he can read a paper in a tavern without having a stranger looking over each shoulder.

At the same time Cooper reported the observation that "the American ever seems ready to resign his own opinion to that which is *made to seem* to be the opinion of the public." [7] In other words, the sanction of public opinion is invoked as an authority so coercive upon the individual that its name carries weight even in the absence of the fact.

4

The characteristic American blend of buoyancy, collective self-confidence, measuring of attainment by competitive success, hope of perpetual and limitless improvement, improvising of method and organization to meet exigencies as they

[7] James Fenimore Cooper, *Gleanings in Europe,* 1837, Vol. II, pp. 248–9.

arise, can be illustrated from various aspects of American life, some fundamental and some superficial: though which is fundamental and which superficial it would be difficult to say. This same blend of traits will at the same time serve to account for certain American ways which seem to non-Americans paradoxical, if not objectionable.

Thus Americans are at one and the same time law-abiding and lawless. They live within a frame of law, and seem often to make a fetish of their written constitution. The law is the usual road to public office, and the lawyers are perhaps the most influential members of the community, with the businessmen running them a close second. The business lawyer is the higher synthesis of the two. At the same time Americans have a certain contempt for the law, as something which they have made, and which they sometimes take into their own hands. As in the case of the Prohibition Law, one of the accepted methods of changing the law is to break it. Americans employ lawyers to enable them to evade the law, or at any rate to mitigate its inconveniences.

Americans are highly litigious. Opposing lawyers engage in lively combat; prosecuting attorneys score their convictions and acquire thereby a prestige that may start them on the road to the Presidency; criminal lawyers score their acquittals. Appeal follows appeal from court to court; but while a negative verdict is not lightly accepted, it usually *is* accepted after every legal resort has been exhausted. Americans are more insistent in claiming legal rights than scrupulous in respecting them: in other words, they tend to assume that each will look after his own—which he usually does.

5

American politics are harshly competitive but rarely bloody or fatal. Candidates do not, as in England, "stand" for office—they "run" for office. Major campaigns are conducted as though the survival of the country were at stake; but nobody really means it. On the morrow the defeated candidate "concedes" his defeat and congratulates the victor whom the day before he has slain with invectives. As in sport, the punch is followed by the handshake. A government based on division of powers has become a struggle between powers—between the legislative and executive branches, or between the upper and lower houses of Congress. Even party solidarities tend to dissolve amidst the rivalries of persons, lobbies and pressure groups. And yet there is a saving grace, which somehow triumphs over dissension—a saving grace which is in part an incurable sense of humor, in part a common underlying faith, but in the main the belief that there is enough for everybody, and that what is lost today can be regained tomorrow. Disputes among optimists rarely become irreconcilable conflicts.

The world would be glad to discover the key to the foreign policy of the United States, which it views with mingled hope and distrust. There is no key; but the American mentality here described may throw some dim light on a question which is of no little importance for the future of mankind.

The traditional isolationism, which is still to be reckoned with, was originally based on fear of becoming embroiled in the affairs of a Europe whose yoke had been cast off; and this cautious isolationism was confirmed by the fact that later waves of immigration were composed of persons who, having for one reason or another turned their backs on Europe, desired to keep them turned. But these motives of distrust have gradually been superseded by a sense of self-sufficiency. While the surpluses of production have led to a growing recognition of the need of world markets, the average American businessman is still interested primarily in the domestic market; and while the experience of the present century has brought home the menace of world-war, the fact remains that American territory has not been invaded or seriously threatened with invasion for 130 years, so that those who reside in the interior of a wide continent bounded by two wide oceans still feel secure at home. The airplane and the atomic bomb have modified this attitude; but whereas Europeans know from *experience* that for better or worse they are dependent on the rest of the world, Americans still have to be *persuaded* that this is the case, and they do not always stay persuaded.

Opposed to this sense of continental self-sufficiency and disposition to isolationism there is a missionary spirit which inclines to adventure abroad: a belief, more or less justified, that what is good for the United States is good for everybody, and should be extended to other peoples, whether they like it or not and whether or not they are ready to receive it. Americans are disposed to "sell" their goods abroad, whether automobiles, typewriters, moving pictures, democracy, or various brands of Christianity. There is a readiness to embark on far-flung enterprises without a full recognition of their costs; or to talk about them without being prepared to follow through. Bold utterances are discounted at home, but when taken at their face value abroad they have often led to disappointment and resentment, by friends as well as enemies. It is not that Americans do not mean what they say, but that they do not always weigh their words and the implications of their words. Americans speak freely and lightly. Add to this the fact that our foreign policy reflects all the uncertainties arising from differences between Congress and the Executive, and from changing party majorities, and it is small wonder that other nations have learned to keep their fingers crossed.

The foreign policy of the United States must always be close to the electorate, and there is never a time when a nation-wide election is more than two years away. A large section of the press is commercially motivated, and caters to emotion and prejudice in order to compete for circulation. All publicity agencies—radio, cinema, and forum—tend similarly to quantity production and to mass appeal.

That, nevertheless, public policy should on the whole and in the long run have been judged sound by the verdict of history evidently requires explanation; whether it be by a Providence that watches over drunkards and democracies, or by a basic intelligence and good sense which makes the American people as a whole receptive to the enlightenment which spreads from their thoughtful minority by a sort of osmosis. Somehow, in the end, the sober second thought tends to prevail.

Once the people of the United States feel themselves fully committed to an enterprise their virtues come into play, and their very weaknesses become sources of strength. They discover natural leaders, invent techniques, improvise organizations, and are imbued with a confident determination to win. And in so far as they are impregnated with a sense of human solidarity, they can contribute to international organization their peculiar faculty for combining effort with the cheerful acceptance of temporary defeat, and their inexhaustible confidence that what needs to be done *can* be done, even on a world-wide scale, and whatever the odds against it.

THE PARADOX OF SUCCESS AND FAILURE

William A. Clebsch

Since early colonial times, religion has been engaging American history in a special way. Instead of commanding that society conform to a preplanned City of God, the American way has been to marshal campaigns to inaugurate in this or that dimension of the common life a yearning to turn holy hopes into earthly fruition. This religion has been predominantly Christian and mainly Protestant during the three formative centuries of the Anglo-American experience, and to the extent that it saw obedience to God as attuning the common life to the divine will expressed to believers in Scripture, it has been Calvinistic as well. Yet only in those few utopian communities that arose far from the highways of historical flux has America seemed the place to build a permanent Eden under God's legislation.

What is remarkable is not the failure but the success of

Source: William A. Clebsch, *From Sacred to Profane America* (New York: Harper & Row, Publ., Inc., 1968), pp. 1–2, 7–14. Copyright © 1968 by William A. Clebsch. Reprinted by permission of Harper & Row, Publ., Inc.

William A. Clebsch (1923–   ), is professor of religion and humanities at Stanford University. He was educated at the University of Tennessee, the Virginia Theological Seminary, and the Union Theological Seminary, in New York; he has taught at Michigan State, the Virginia Theological Seminary, and the Seminary of the Southwest. In addition to *From Sacred to Profane America: The Role of Religion in American History* (1968), he has written *England's Earliest Protestants, 1520–1535* (1964), *Pastoral Care in Historical Perspective* (1966), "A New Historiography of American Religion" (1967), and *Christian Interpretations of the Civil War* (1969).

religious efforts to inspire hopes and summon energies for sanctifying the arenas of common life in America. Once won, however, the spoils of each such campaign belonged not to religious institutions but to society at large. In that sense the unintended but nevertheless salutary effect of religion on American history has been to make a nation profaned—a society standing *pro-fanum,* outside of religion's temple. Being without land of its own, as it were, organized religion realized in frustration that the improvements it made belonged to all America. To cite but the case that comes readiest to mind, churches have built hundreds of schools and seminaries to train saints and ministers, only to find that those institutions which flourished became the society's colleges and universities for making good citizens and public servants. Nor is the turnabout a strictly Protestant phenomenon; if the pattern was established by Calvinistic religion, by it was cut the cloth of American Catholicism. "Education in Roman Catholic schools has been 'virtually wasted' on three-quarters of the students so far as influencing their religious behavior is concerned, a study financed by the Carnegie Corporation and the Federal Office of Education has found." [1] Instruction under religious auspices flourished when and where it served the common welfare.

.   .   .   .   .

From the beginning, American Christianity has been ambidextrous. The story of its right hand's labors is well known as "American church history." The right hand summoned people to church, inculcated spirituality, taught doctrine, praised God, bought property, erected edifices, accumulated money, trained and hired and used personnel, and served the religious needs of members. But with its left hand religion strove to build certain qualities of life in America. Not that it has ever had a blueprint for the ideal America, nor even that it has ever been the real glue of American society; rather, it has built within American society several cultural cities by stimulating urgent desires for education, for participation of diverse peoples in a common life, for a sense of American novelty and na-

[1] *New York Times* story in *San Francisco Chronicle,* July 25. 1966, p. 2.

tionality, for good and acceptable morals and manners and the general welfare, and for variety in American institutions— including religious institutions.

By devoting itself to the American dream, religion has been not only ambidextrous but ambivalent as well. While the left hand's work has been owned by society at large and not by the churches, the right hand has usually known what the left hand was doing. Just when common claim has been laid to achievements inspired by religion, the denominations have usually sought title or possession—at least long enough to take credit for the work. This ambivalence has never been clearer than it is today.

American religion at the middle third of the twentieth century presented a peculiar paradox of success and failure. By any measurable standard it had climbed very near its perennial goal of subscribing the nominal allegiance of a majority of Americans. Nearly two-thirds of the people in the nation had their names on the rosters of one (or more) formal religious organizations, and all but a tiny fraction professed their belief in God of some kind or another. By contrast, at the genesis of the nation's independent career, less than one-tenth of the people were enrolled in religious denominations, and opinions diverging sharply from all traditional varieties of Christian theism were not only respectable but seemed to be the wave of the future.

These figures, to be sure, give a distorted picture of the facts. For it seems likely that, between the Declaration of Independence and the Treaty of Paris, the professed members of the congregations comprised a third of the persons commonly attending their worship services, while after World War II that was indeed a thriving congregation which drew a third to a half of its enrollment to an average Sunday's services, excepting perhaps the vernal feasts of Easter and Mother's Day. Early Americans who doubted traditional Christianity's God nevertheless acted in general as though He existed, while modern Americans who so fervently profess belief in Him are hard pressed to know how or whether that belief makes any difference in the ordinary affairs of life. Most believe in no literal hell but are convinced that after death their own immortal souls will live in some vague heaven. It would be difficult to find a decade in all American history when religion wore a face more appealing to American culture than it did during the 1950's; it is impossible to find a decade when its leading interpreters so nearly approached unanimity of concern for religion's failure.

It is, of course, not unknown for critics to cry "failure" at moments of success. American religion has raised up a long line of sometimes lonely prophets to denounce the accommodations by which religion made its impact upon American life. Solomon Stoddard protested Massachusetts Puritanism's making the Lord's Supper an instrument for excluding seekers from the fellowship of full saints. His grandson Jonathan Edwards decried men's claims to their own agency in achieving the salvation that he preached to them and, ironically, urged them to accept. Horace Bushnell (1802–1876) rejected revivalism, that hallmark of early national religion in America, as an "artificial firework." Washington Gladden (1836–1918) substituted social salvation for individual piety. William Jennings Bryan (1860–1925) spent the last years of his bombastic life campaigning to reenthrone God in a public education which in its infancy had nursed at the paps of religion. Reinhold Niebuhr denounced the Christian pacifism of the late 1930's for what he called theologically naïve optimism of the belief that the Prince of Peace was the real source of international peace. The list is long, and these are mere samples. These prophets cried that success of the church signaled failure of the gospel.

By turning the proposition around, a strong case can be made that when religion's spokesmen perceived a flowing gospel in America, church life and activity ebbed. Not that prophets usually rejoice in a faltering church, nor that they often acknowledge a flourishing gospel. Yet the same Reinhold Niebuhr once wrote, "It is no easy task to build up the faith of one generation and not destroy the supports of the religion of the other." His contrast between faith and religion correlates with that between gospel and church. Citing Niebuhr's incisive insight one writer concluded, "In a real sense the chief victims of fundamentalism were the fundamentalists themselves. Their insistence upon the literal truth of the Bible denied them not only the benefits of modern science but much of the beauty and spirit of the very religion they were attempting to preserve." [2] It seems hardly necessary here to enumerate examples which abound in the pages to follow. A vast literature, both scholarly and popular, predicting the effects of the Second Vatican Council on American Catholicism is almost gleeful over the prospect that reinvigorated faith will tumble or transform ecclesiastical institutions whose solidity made them seem grandly immune to historical change.[3] But this successful-gospel/failing-church attitude is not new, for it is not far distant in spirit from the attacks by Awakening preachers—in no case more vociferous than in that of the Reverend James Davenport (1716–1757)—on the ministers and congregations of mid-eighteenth-century Boston. Thus critics who noted that ecclesiastical flood tide coincides with low-water piety have been complemented by spokesmen who wanted rising piety to damage churchly shoreworks.

In the middle decades of the twentieth century this paradox of failure and success came to be polarized. Sweepingly put, the clientele of American religion, the laymen—the men, women, and children "in the pew"—gloried in a succeeding church while the religious professionals they acknowledged as their leaders adumbrated a gospel to check that success. Theologians pleaded the ministry of the laity while laymen urged the sanctity of the clergy. The churches waxed strong after World War II on traditionally sound American principles by accommodating themselves to a major new trend in society, specifically the trend of suburban living.

Meanwhile, the professional ideologies of the gospel had been learning their theology from German-speaking dogmaticians who, by working on traditionally sound European princi-

[2] Lawrence W. Levine, *Defender of the Faith* (New York: Oxford University Press, 1965), p. 292; Reinhold Niebuhr, *Leaves from the Notebook of a Tamed Cynic* (New York: Willett, Clark & Colby, 1929; Hamden, Conn.: Shoe String Press, 1956), p. 36.

[3] An interesting example is monasticism for women, the demolition of whose traditions was surveyed with unconcealed delight by Michael Novak in "The New Nuns," *The Saturday Evening Post,* July 30, 1966.

ples, were recovering the symbols of those ages in which continental Christianity was most self-confident. The European theologians were led by Karl Barth, but most of them either veered from his path or else ran out ahead of him; they adumbrated a new terminology for an old gospel to reawaken a church that had failed to protest nazism but not communism, alas, to the same extent—worse than that, a church that had failed to serve people. But when that renewed gospel for a failing European church found expression in American idioms, there was no failing church for it to challenge, because the church was succeeding without really trying—succeeding in protesting nazism and even more so communism, as well as in serving people.

The devotees of the so-called theological renaissance in America fell into a trap of their own manufacture, the trap of thinking that the best way to proclaim Christianity was to claim for it everything. Rather than saying which, if any, of modern man's questions Christianity answered, they insisted that moderns must learn from Christianity to ask antique questions, e.g., about the inner nature of God, in order to receive Christianity's answers to all human yearnings. What has been hailed as a renaissance of theology was more essentially a subtle return to dogmatism. Following its advice led many Americans to discover that the old questions are not our questions, that the ancient language is no longer our language, and that ex-Christians understand modernity better than Christians.[4] The so-called theological renaissance has largely bypassed the lay Christian of twentieth-century America, not because he failed to hear its message but because its message failed to encounter his life. In a sense, the man in the pew had to learn to sing his cherished "Nearer, My God, To

[4] An eloquent statement of disillusionment with Christian apologetics was made by William H. Poteat, "Christianity and the Intellectual," in *Viewpoints,* ed. John C. Coburn and W. Norman Pittenger (Greenwich, Conn.: Seabury Press, 1959), reprinted under the same title but with telling revisions in *The Church Review, 24* (April–May 1966), 3–5. Turmoil over the inapplicability of continental neo-orthodoxy to American secularity underlies and motivates Paul M. van Buren, *The Secular Meaning of the Gospel* (New York: Macmillan, 1963). The voluminous writings which make the point in very brash ways need not concern us here.

Thee" as descant to the preacher's "neo-orthodoxology." The clientele of American religion believed in the church while the professional class of American religion concentrated on a particular statement of gospel. This statement emphasized that, experience to the contrary notwithstanding, man stood under adverse judgment of God in solving his social problems to his own liking, and that man individually was too spiritually paralyzed to hear (much less comprehend) the word God spoke to him, that only when God provided the hearing—or at least the hearing aid—could His own word be understood, that only when the word was understood might true obedience to God arise. The radical message became more plausible to middle-class Americans when they read the clauses backward: since, as they thought, they lived in true obedience to God, what better evidence could there be that they understood God's word? If they understood it, they must have heard it; the doctrine of sin seemed aimed at somebody else.

To be sure, certain intellectuals, who had absorbed the literature and philosophy of pessimism which has fascinated Western thinkers since Kierkegaard and Nietzsche, comprehended the first word of the neo-orthodox gospel, but these rarely felt a need for what followed. T. S. Eliot's *Wasteland* was their home, and they drank Niebuhr's anthropology, intended as apéritif for the gospel, without becoming hungry for the main course of his theology. If, as this gospel asserted, Christianity provided the answers to the human predicament, the ordinary man in the pew seems to have heard that, since he subscribed to Christianity, his personal predicaments were being solved.

In the middle of the twentieth century these conflicting features of religion became polarized in America: sophisticated preachers adopted the new version of old dogmatism while their parishioners clung to the more available tradition in which Christianity improved the lives of those who subscribed it. That polarization of the success/failure paradox both culminated and transformed the dominant tradition of American religion. Since colonial times religion has encountered our society in a series of campaigns which ran through similar (but not identical) patterns. Here the similarities are chiefly interesting, but variants must be remarked where appropriate. Religion commanded attention by revealing a certain flaw or lack in the society, for which religion held the remedy. But when victory was in sight the society claimed the endeavor as its own and in doing so "profaned" it. At that point religion judged its success to be somehow a failure and it turned against the very feature of life it had fervently advocated. Then religion sought another point of contact at which to confront a problem with proffered cure, waged another campaign that led to success, condemned society's claim over the success, and so through the cycle again.

There have been, in the history of American religion prior to the middle years of the twentieth century, six such religious campaigns waged, won, embraced and condemned. This historical pattern in the social utility of American religion of course gives no warrant of future recurrence. The consensus of astute observers of religion and culture in America today indicates that the pattern has run a certain logical course to its own exhaustion, evidenced by the polarization we have been discussing. Professional religionists tend to insist that profane achievements pervert religious aspirations, while the public apparently rejoices in the achievements unperturbed by alterations of original hopes. But all this is not to say that profane America has become separated from or has lost interest in the sacral stimuli that helped elicit the dream. Perhaps the apparent stilling of interaction between the two promotes historical understanding of their patterned relation.

As Henry F. May noted in 1964, "For the study and understanding of American culture, the recovery of American religious history may well be the most important achievement of the last thirty years." He suggested that enough monographic studies of episodes in American religious history now exist from which "to build a convincing synthesis, a synthesis independent of political history, though never unrelated to it." May thought American history had been "brought . . . back into the great dialogue between secular and religious thought. It is to this dialogue, after all," he asserted, "that American culture itself owes much of its vigor and complexity." [5] During the

[5] Henry F. May, "The Recovery of American Religious History," *American Historical Review*, 70 (Oct. 1964), 79, 92. That such a synthesis had been

1950's American church historians outgrew the style of denominational chronicles, either taken one by one or else woven into "general" church histories of America, and began to view American religion in a genuinely synoptic way. Yet these explanations of the churches in their own language as belonging to a common religious movement fall short of "a convincing synthesis." American religious history as embodied in churches—or "the church," if the singular has a palpable referent—is, then, a far advanced field of study in our time. American religion is distinctive, however, precisely for the fact that the aspirations it nurtured have found profane embodiments.

If the "great dialogue between secular and religious thought" is really to be resumed, the stand-off of polarization which switches these patterns into one another's terms must be undercut by understanding historically the function of religion in America. In such an understanding the churches will be seen not as institutions owning distinct or composite histories. Rather it must be relearned that the American churches in most important ways undertook sacred programs which helped to make American history as they were profanely embodied by the society. For viewed as one of many strands (but a vigorous one) in the experience of the American people, religion repeatedly enriched, fashioned, and transformed—and having transformed also repeatedly blocked, truncated, and diverted—that people's aspirations and achievements. To identify the aspirations which religion in good measure elicited and to describe those achievements which at once fulfilled and terminated such aspirations would indeed be to enter a persistent dialogue between the religious and the worldly dimensions of the American experience. It would also be to discover that many proud accomplishments now encased and cherished in mundane form were once infused with religious zeal and, paradoxically, became true achievements only by shucking their religious husks, thereby inviting the enmity of the very religious forces by which they were earlier cultivated.

gained by church historians was noted by William A. Clebsch, "A New Historiography of American Religion," *Historical Magazine of the Protestant Episcopal Church,* 32 (Sept. 1963), 224–257.

III
BINARY PATTERNS IN AMERICAN CULTURAL HISTORY

PALEFACE AND REDSKIN

Philip Rahv

Viewed historically, American writers appear to group themselves around two polar types. Paleface and redskin I should like to call the two, and despite occasional efforts at reconciliation no love is lost between them.

Consider the immense contrast between the drawing-room fictions of Henry James and the open air poems of Walt Whitman. Compare Melville's decades of loneliness, his tragic failure, with Mark Twain's boisterous career and dubious success. At one pole there is the literature of the lowlife world of the frontier and of the big cities; at the other the thin, solemn, semi-clerical culture of Boston and Concord. The fact is that the creative mind in America is fragmented and one-sided. For the process of polarization has produced a dichotomy be-

Source: Philip Rahv, *Literature and the Sixth Sense* (Boston: Houghton Mifflin Company, 1969), pp. 1–5. Copyright © 1969 by Philip Rahv. Reprinted by permission of the publisher.

Philip Rahv (1908–   ), literary critic and editor, is professor of English at Brandeis University. He was born in Russia, came to the United States as a boy, and was educated in Providence, Rhode Island. In 1933 he and others founded the *Partisan Review,* regarded subsequently by T. S. Eliot as "America's leading literary magazine." In addition to *Image and Idea* (1949), he has written *The Myth and the Powerhouse* (1965), *Literature and the Sixth Sense* (1969), and edited *The Great Short Novels of Henry James* (1944), *The Short Novels of Tolstoy* (1946), *Discovery of Europe: The Story of American Experience in the Old World* (1947), *Great Russian Short Novels* (1951), *Literature in America* (1957), *Modern Occasions* (1966), *The Partisan Reader* (1946), *The New Partisan Reader* (1953), and *The Partisan Review Anthology* (1962).

tween experience and consciousness—a dissociation between energy and sensibility, between conduct and theories of conduct, between life conceived as an opportunity and life conceived as a discipline.

The differences between the two types define themselves in every sphere. Thus while the redskin glories in his Americanism, to the paleface it is a source of endless ambiguities. Sociologically they can be distinguished as patrician vs. plebeian, and in their aesthetic ideals one is drawn to allegory and the distillations of symbolism, whereas the other inclines to a gross, riotous naturalism. The paleface is a "highbrow," though his mentality—as in the case of Hawthorne and James —is often of the kind that excludes and repels general ideas; he is at the same time both something more and something less than an intellectual in the European sense. And the redskin deserves the epithet "lowbrow" not because he is badly educated—which he might or might not be—but because his reactions are primarily emotional, spontaneous, and lacking in personal culture. The paleface continually hankers after religious norms, tending toward a refined estrangement from reality. The redskin, on the other hand, accepts his environment, at times to the degree of fusion with it, even when rebelling against one or another of its manifestations. At his highest level the paleface moves in an exquisite moral atmosphere; at his lowest he is genteel, snobbish, and pedantic. In giving expression to the vitality and to the aspirations of the people, the redskin is at his best; but at his worst he is a vulgar anti-intellectual, combining aggression with conformity and reverting to the crudest forms of frontier psychology.

James and Whitman, who as contemporaries felt little more than contempt for each other, are the purest examples of this discussion.* In reviewing *Drum Taps* in 1865 the young James told off the grand plebeian innovator, advising him to stop declaiming and go sit in the corner of a rhyme and meter school, while the innovator, snorting at the novelist of scruples and moral delicacy, said "Feathers!" Now this mutual repul-

* According to Edith Wharton, James changed his mind about Whitman late in life. But this can be regarded as a private fact of the Jamesian sensibility, for in public he said not a word in favor of Whitman.

sion between the two major figures in American literature would be less important if it were mainly personal or aesthetic in reference. But the point is that it has a profoundly national and social-historical character.

James and Whitman form a kind of fatal antipodes. To this, in part, can be traced the curious fact about them that, though each has become the object of a special cult, neither is quite secure in his reputation. For most of the critics and historians who make much of Whitman disparage James or ignore him altogether, and vice versa. Evidently the high valuation of the one is so incongruous with the high valuation of the other that criticism is chronically forced to choose between them—which makes for a breach in the literary tradition without parallel in any European country. The aristocrat Tolstoy and the tramp Gorky found that they held certain values and ideas in common, whereas James and Whitman, who between them dominate American writing of the nineteenth century, cannot abide with one another. And theirs is no unique or isolated instance.

The national literature suffers from the ills of a split personality. The typical American writer has so far shown himself incapable of escaping the blight of one-sidedness: of achieving that mature control which permits the balance of impulse with sensitiveness, of natural power with philosophical depth. For the dissociation of mind from experience has resulted in truncated works of art, works that tend to be either naive and ungraded, often flat reproductions of life, or else products of cultivation that remain abstract because they fall short on evidence drawn from the sensuous and material world. Hence it is only through intensively exploiting their very limitations, through submitting themselves to a process of creative yet cruel self-exaggeration, that a few artists have succeeded in warding off the failure that threatened them. And the later novels of Henry James are a case in point.

The palefaces dominated literature throughout the nineteenth century, but in the twentieth they were overthrown by the redskins. Once the continent had been mastered, with the plebeian bourgeoisie coming into complete possession of the national wealth, and puritanism had worn itself out, degenerating into mere respectability, it became objectively possible and socially permissible to satisfy that desire for experience and personal emancipation which heretofore had been systematically frustrated. The era of economic accumulation had ended and the era of consummation had arrived. To enjoy life now became one of the functions of progress—a function for which the palefaces were temperamentally disqualified. This gave Mencken his opportunity to emerge as the ideologue of enjoyment. Novelists like Dreiser, Anderson, and Lewis—and, in fact, most of the writers of the period of "experiment and liberation"—rose against conventions that society itself was beginning to abandon. They helped to "liquidate" the lag between the enormous riches of the nation and its morality of abstention. The neo-humanists were among the last of the breed of palefaces, and they perished in the quixotic attempt to reestablish the old values. Eliot forsook his native land, while the few palefaces who managed to survive at home took to the academic or else to the "higher" and relatively unpopular forms of writing. But the novelists, who control the main highway of literature, were, and still are, nearly all redskins to the wigwam born.

At present the redskins are in command of the situation, and the literary life in America has seldom been so deficient in intellectual power. The political interests introduced in the nineteen-thirties have not only strengthened their hold but have also brought out their worst tendencies; for the effect of the popular political creeds of our time has been to increase their habitual hostility to ideas, sanctioning the relaxation of standards and justifying the urge to come to terms with semi-literate audiences.

The redskin writer in America is a purely indigenous phenomenon, the true-blue offspring of the western hemisphere, the juvenile in principle and for the good of the soul. He is a self-made writer in the same way that Henry Ford was a self-made millionaire. On the one hand he is a crass materialist, a greedy consumer of experience, and on the other a sentimentalist, a half-baked mystic listening to inward voices and watching for signs and portents. Think of Dreiser, Lewis, Anderson, Wolfe, Sandburg, Caldwell, Steinbeck, Farrell, Saroyan: all writers of genuine and some even of admirable accomplishments, whose faults, however, are not so much literary as faults of raw life itself. Unable to relate himself in any significant manner to the cultural heritage, the redskin writer is always on his own; and since his personality resists growth and change, he must continually repeat himself. His work is ridden by compulsions that depress the literary tradition, because they are compulsions of a kind that put a strain on literature, that literature more often than not can neither assimilate nor sublimate. He is the passive instead of the active agent of the *Zeitgeist,* he lives off it rather than through it, so that when his particular gifts happen to coincide with the mood of the times he seems modern and contemporary, but once the mood has passed he is in danger of being quickly discarded. Lacking the qualities of surprise and renewal, already Dreiser and Anderson, for example, have a "period" air about them that makes a re-reading of their work something of a critical chore; and one suspects that Hemingway, that perennial boy-man, is more accurately understood as a descendant of Natty Bumppo, the hero of Fenimore Cooper's Leatherstocking tales, than as the portentously disillusioned character his legend makes him out to be.

As for the paleface, in compensation for backward cultural conditions and a lost religious ethic, he has developed a supreme talent for refinement, just as the Jew, in compensation for adverse social conditions and a lost national independence, has developed a supreme talent for cleverness. (In this connection it is pertinent to recall T. S. Eliot's remark about Boston society, which he described as "quite refined, but refined beyond the point of civilization.") Now this peculiar excess of refinement is to be deplored in an imaginative writer, for it weakens his capacity to cope with experience and induces in him a fetishistic attitude toward tradition; nor is this species of refinement to be equated with the refinement of artists like Proust or Mann, as in them it is not an element contradicting an open and bold confrontation of reality. Yet the paleface, being above all a conscious individual, was frequently able to transcend or to deviate sharply from the norms of his group, and he is to be credited with most of the rigors and charms of the classic American books. While it is true, as John Jay Chapman put it, that his culture is "secondary and tertiary" and that between him and the sky "floats the Constitution of the United States and the traditions and forms of English literature"—nevertheless, there exists the poetry of Emily Dickinson, there is *The Scarlet Letter,* there is *Moby Dick,* and there are not a few incomparable narratives by Henry James.

At this point there is no necessity to enter into a discussion of the historical and social causes that account for the disunity of the American creative mind. In various contexts a number of critics have disclosed and evaluated the forces that have worked on this mind and shaped it to their uses. The sole question that seems relevant is whether history will make whole again what it has rent asunder. Will James and Whitman ever be reconciled, will they finally discover and act upon each other? Only history can give a definite reply to this question. In the meantime, however, there are available the resources of effort and understanding, resources which even those who believe in the strict determination of the cultural object need not spurn.

A CULTURE OF CONTRADICTIONS

Richard Chase

The imagination that has produced much of the best and
most characteristic American fiction has been shaped by the
contradictions and not by the unities and harmonies of our culture. In a sense this may be true of all literatures of whatever
time and place. Nevertheless there are some literatures which
take their form and tone from polarities, opposites, and irreconcilables, but are content to rest in and sustain them, or to
resolve them into unities, if at all, only by special and limited
means. The American novel tends to rest in contradictions and
among extreme ranges of experience. When it attempts to resolve contradictions, it does so in oblique, morally equivocal
ways. As a general rule it does so either in melodramatic actions or in pastoral idyls, although intermixed with both one
may find the stirring instabilities of "American humor." These
qualities constitute the uniqueness of that branch of the novel-
istic tradition which has flourished in this country. They help to

Source: Richard Chase, The American Novel and its Tradition (New York:
Doubleday & Company, Inc., 1957), pp. 1–11. Copyright © 1957 by Richard
Chase. Reprinted by permission of the publisher.

Richard V. Chase, Jr. (1914–1962) was professor of literature at Columbia
University. He was educated at Dartmouth and Columbia, and taught at Connecticut College and Indiana University. In addition to The American Novel
and Its Tradition (1957), he wrote Herman Melville, A Critical Study (1949),
Quest for Myth (1949), Emily Dickinson (1951), Walt Whitman Reconsidered
(1955), The Democratic Vista: A Dialogue on Life and Letters in Contemporary America (1958), and edited Melville: A Collection of Critical Essays
(1962).

account for the strong element of "romance" in the American "novel."

By contrast, the English novel has followed a middle way. It is notable for its great practical sanity, its powerful, engrossing composition of wide ranges of experience into a moral centrality and equability of judgment. Oddity, distortion of personality, dislocations of normal life, recklessness of behavior, malignancy of motive—these the English novel has included. Yet the profound poetry of disorder we find in the American novel is missing, with rare exceptions, from the English. Radical maladjustments and contradictions are reported but are seldom of the essence of form in the English novel, and although it is no stranger to suffering and defeat or to triumphant joy either, it gives the impression of absorbing all extremes, all maladjustments and contradictions into a normative view of life. In doing so, it shows itself to derive from the two great influences that stand behind it—classic tragedy and Christianity. The English novel has not, of course, always been strictly speaking tragic or Christian. Often it has been comic, but often, too, in that superior form of comedy which approaches tragedy. Usually it has been realistic or, in the philosophical sense of the word, "naturalistic." Yet even its peculiar kind of gross poetic naturalism has preserved something of the two great traditions that formed English literature. The English novel, that is, follows the tendency of tragic art and Christian art, which characteristically move through contradictions to forms of harmony, reconciliation, catharsis, and transfiguration.

Judging by our greatest novels, the American imagination, even when it wishes to assuage and reconcile the contradictions of life, has not been stirred by the possibility of catharsis or incarnation, by the tragic or Christian possibility. It has been stirred, rather, by the aesthetic possibilities of radical forms of alienation, contradiction, and disorder.

The essential difference between the American novel and the English will be strongly pointed up to any reader of F. R. Leavis's *The Great Tradition.* Mr. Leavis's "great tradition" of the novel is really Anglo-American, and it includes not only Jane Austen, George Eliot, Conrad, and Henry James but, apparently, in one of its branches Hawthorne and Melville. My assumption in this book is that the American novel is obviously a development from the English tradition. At least it was, down to 1880 or 1890. For at that time our novelists began to turn to French and Russian models and the English influence has decreased steadily ever since. The more extreme imagination of the French and Russian novelists has clearly been more in accord with the purposes of modern American writers than has the English imagination. True, an American reader of Mr. Leavis's book will have little trouble in giving a very general assent to his very general proposition about the Anglo-American tradition. Nevertheless, he will also be forced constantly to protest that there is another tradition of which Mr. Leavis does not seem to be aware, a tradition which includes most of the best American novels.

Ultimately, it does not matter much whether one insists that there are really *two* traditions, the English and the American (leaving aside the question of what writers each might be said to comprise) or whether one insists merely that there is a radical divergence within one tradition. All I hold out for is a provisional recognition of the divergence as a necessary step towards understanding and appreciation of both English and the American novel. The divergence is brought home to an American reader of Leavis's book when, for example he comes across the brief note allotted to the Brontës. Here is Leavis's comment on Emily Brontë:

> I have said nothing about *Wuthering Heights* because that astonishing work seems to me a kind of sport . . . she broke completely, and in the most astonishing way, both with the Scott tradition that imposed on the novelist a romantic resolution of his themes, and with the tradition coming down from the eighteenth century that demanded a plane-mirror reflection of the surface of "real" life. Out of her a minor tradition comes, to which belongs, most notably, *The House with the Green Shutters*.

Of course Mr. Leavis is right; in relation to the great tradition of the English novel *Wuthering Heights* is indeed a sport. But suppose it were discovered that *Wuthering Heights* was written by an American of New England Calvinist or Southern Presbyterian background. The novel would be astonishing and unique no matter who wrote it or where. But if it were an American novel it would not be a sport; it has too close an affinity with too many American novels and among them some of the best. Like many of the fictions discussed in this book *Wuthering Heights* proceeds from an imagination that is essentially melodramatic, that operates among radical contradictions and renders reality indirectly or poetically, thus breaking, as Mr. Leavis observes, with the traditions that require a surface rendering of real life and resolution of themes, "romantic" or otherwise.

Those readers who make a dogma out of Leavis's views are thus proprietors of an Anglo-American tradition in which many of the most interesting and original and several of the greatest American novels are sports. *Wieland* is a sport, and so are *The Scarlet Letter* and *The Blithedale Romance, Moby-Dick, Pierre,* and *The Confidence Man, Huckleberry Finn, The Red Badges of Courage, McTeague, As I Lay Dying, The Sun Also Rises*—all are eccentric, in their differing ways, to a tradition of which, let us say, *Middlemarch* is a standard representative. Not one of them has any close kinship with the massive, temperate, moralistic rendering of life and thought we associate with Mr. Leavis's "great tradition."

The English novel, one might say, has been a kind of imperial enterprise, an appropriation of reality with the high purpose of bringing order to disorder. By contrast, as Lawrence observed in his *Studies in Classic American Literature,* the American novel has usually seemed content to explore, rather than to appropriate and civilize, the remarkable and in some ways unexampled territories of life in the New World and to reflect its anomalies and dilemmas. It has not wanted to build an imperium but merely to discover a new place and a new state of mind. Explorers see more deeply, darkly, privately and disinterestedly than imperialists, who must perforce be circumspect and prudential. The American novel is more profound and clairvoyant than the English novel, but by the same token it is narrower and more arbitrary, and it tends to carve out of experience brilliant, highly wrought fragments rather than massive unities.

For whatever reason—perhaps the nagging scrupulosity of the Puritan mind has something to do with it—the American novel has sometimes approached a perfection or art unknown to the English tradition, in which we discover no such highly skilled practitioners as Hawthorne, Stephen Crane, Henry James, or Hemingway. These writers, often overestimated as moralists, seem content to oppose the disorder and rawness of their culture with a scrupulous art-consciousness, with aesthetic forms—which do, of course, often broaden out into moral significance.

In a well known passage Allen Tate refers to the "complexity of feeling" that everyone senses in the American novel and that, as Mr. Tate says, "from Hawthorne down to our own time has baffled our best understanding." The complexity of the American novel has been much exaggerated. With the exception of one or two of James's novels no American fiction has anything like the complexity of character and event of *Our Mutual Friend,* for example. In *The Scarlet Letter* or *Moby-Dick* the characters and events have actually a kind of abstracted simplicity about them. In these books character may be deep but it is narrow and predictable. Events take place with a formalized clarity. And certainly it cannot be argued that society and the social life of man are shown to be complex in these fictions.

But of course Tate says "complexity of feeling," and he is right about that. The states of feelings, and the language in which they are caught, are sometimes very intricate in American novels. Yet these musing tides of feeling and language that make such a rich poetry in our fiction often seem to be at variance with the simplified actions and conceptions of life our novels present. The origins of this apparent anomaly must be sought in the contradictions of our culture.

Marius Bewley takes up Tate's remark in an essay called "Fenimore Cooper and the Economic Age" and traces this "complexity of feeling" to a "tension" which he finds not only in Cooper but in Hawthorne and James. It is, he thinks, a political tension in its origins although as embodied in the works of these authors it assumes many forms. This tension, he says, "was the result of a struggle to close the split in American experience, to discover a unity that—for the artist especially—almost sensibly *was not there*. What was the nature of the division that supported this conflict? It took on many forms concurrently; it was an opposition between tradition and progress or between the past and the future; between Europe and America, liberalism and reaction, aggressive acquisitive economics and benevolent wealth. These same divisions existed in Europe also, but there they were more ballasted by a denser social medium, a richer sense of the past, a more inhibited sense of material possibilities."

Mr. Bewley's apt discussion of the matter needs to be amended in one fundamental way. The kind of art that stems from a mind primarily moved by the impulse toward aesthetic and cultural unities and thus "struggles to close the split in American experience" as an artist might wish to close it—this kind of art is practiced often, though not always, by Henry James, but less often by Hawthorne and Cooper, and much less often by Faulkner, Melville, and Mark Twain. The fact is that many of the best American novels achieve their very being, their energy and their form, from the perception and acceptance not of unities but of radical disunities.

Like many readers of American literature, Bewley makes the mistake of assuming both that our writers have wanted to reconcile disunities by their art and their intelligence and that this is what they *should* have wanted to do. Behind this assumption is a faulty historical view, as well as a certain overplus of moralism, which neglects to observe that there have been notable bodies of literature, as well as of painting and sculpture, that have proposed and accepted an imaginative world of radical, even irreconcilable contradictions, and that with some important exceptions, the American novel (by which I mean its most original and characteristic examples) has been one of these bodies of literature.

Surely Cooper (as will be noted later) is not at his best in a novel like *Satanstoe,* which is a "culture-making" novel and in which his mind is moved by an image of aesthetic and political harmony. On the contrary he is at his best in a book like *The Prairie,* where the search for unity is not at the center of the stage and he can accept without anxiety or thought the vivid contradictions of Natty Bumppo and his way of life— those contradictions which, as Balzac saw, made him so original a conception. In this book Cooper is not inspired by an impulse to resolve cultural contradictions half so much as by the sheer romantic exhilaration of escape from culture itself, into a world where nature is dire, terrible, and beautiful, where human virtues are personal, alien, and renunciatory, and where contradictions are to be resolved only by death, the ceaseless brooding presence of which endows with an unspeakable beauty every irreconcilable of experience and all the irrationalities of life.

Mr. Bewley is not alone in assuming it to be the destiny of American literature to reconcile disunities rather than to pursue the possibility it has actually pursued—that is, to discover a putative unity *in* disunity or to rest at last among irreconcilables. In *Democracy in America* Tocqueville tried to account for a number of related contradictions in American life. He noted a disparity between ideals and practice, a lack of connection between thought and experience, a tendency of the American mind to oscillate rather wildly between ideas that "are all either extremely minute and clear or extremely general and vague."

Tocqueville sought a genetic explanation for these disparities. He pointed out that in aristocratic societies there was a shared body of inherited habits, attitudes and institutions that stood in a mediating position between the individual and the state. This, he observed, was not true in a democracy, where "each citizen is habitually engaged in the contemplation of a very puny object: namely, himself. If he ever looks higher, he perceives only the immense form of society at large or the still more imposing aspect of mankind. . . . What lies between is a void." Tocqueville believed that this either/or habit of mind also owed much to the sharp distinctions made by Calvinism and its habit of opposing the individual to his God, with a minimum of mythic or ecclesiastical mediation. He found certain advantages in this "democratic" quality of mind, but he warned

Americans that it might produce great confusion in philosophy, morals, and politics and a basic instability in literary and cultural values, and that consequently Americans should try to discover democratic equivalents for those traditional habits of mind which in aristocracies had moderated and reconciled extremes in thought and experience.

Tocqueville knew that the dualistic kind of thought of which he spoke was specifically American only in the peculiar quality of its origin and expression. He saw that with the probable exception of England, Europe would characteristically concern itself during the nineteenth century with grand intellectual oppositions, usually more or less of a Hegelian order. But even though the tendency of thought Tocqueville predicted belonged to Western culture generally one is nevertheless struck by how often American writers conceive of human dilemmas according to his scheme, and how many make aesthetic capital out of what seemed to him a moral and intellectual shortcoming.

In his studies of the classic American writers, D. H. Lawrence presented his version of the contrariety, or, as he said, "duplicity" of the American literary mind by saying that he found in writers like Cooper, Melville, and Hawthorne "a tight mental allegiance to a morality which all their passion goes to destroy," a formulation which describes perfectly the inner contradiction of such products of the American imagination as the story of Natty Bumppo. In general Lawrence was thinking of an inherent conflict between "genteel" spirituality and a pragmatic experientialism which in its lower depths was sheer Dionysian or "Indian" energy and violence. Acute enough to see that the best American artistic achievements had depended in one way or another on this dualism, he seemed ready nevertheless to advocate, on moral grounds, a reconciliation of opposites, such as he thought he discerned in the poems of Whitman.

In short, like all the observers of American literature we are citing in these pages, Lawrence was trying to find out what was wrong with it. He is a sympathetic and resourceful reader —one of the best, surely, ever to turn his attention to the American novel. But he thinks that the American novel is sick, and he wants to cure it. Perhaps there is something wrong with it, perhaps it is sick—but a too exclusive preoccupation with the wrongness of the American novel has in some ways disqualified him for seeing what, right or wrong, it *is*.

Finally, there is the division of American culture into "highbrow" and "lowbrow" made by Van Wyck Brooks in 1915 in his *America's Coming-of-Age*. Brooks's essay is a great piece of writing; it is eloquent, incisive, and witty. But we have lived through enough history now to see its fundamental error —namely, the idea that it is the duty of our writers to heal the split and reconcile the contradictions in our culture by pursuing a middlebrow course. All the evidence shows that wherever American literature has pursued the middle way it has tended by a kind of native fatality not to reconcile but merely to deny or ignore the polarities of our culture. Our middlebrow literature—for example, the novels of Howells—has generally been dull and mediocre. In the face of Brooks's desire to unite the highbrow and the lowbrow on a middle ground, there remains the fact that our best novelists have been, not middlebrows, but either highbrows like James, lowbrows like Mark Twain, Frank Norris, Dreiser, and Sherwood Anderson, or combination highbrow-lowbrows like Melville, Faulkner, and Hemingway. Here again American fiction contrasts strongly with English. The English novel at its best is staunchly middlebrow. The cultural conditions within which English literature has evolved have allowed it to become a great middlebrow literature—the only one, it may be, in history.

Let us in all candor admit the limited, the merely instrumental value of the terms used in the last paragraph. They work very well, and are in fact indispensable, in making large cultural formulations. But in applying them to individual authors the terms must be constantly reexamined. We might ask, for example, whether from one point of view both Hawthorne and James performed the unlikely feat of becoming great middlebrow writers. Both of them, at any rate, achieve a kind of contemplative centrality of vision within the confines of which their minds work with great delicacy and equanimity. In so far as they do this, one certainly cannot chide them for shying away from some of the more extreme contradictions, the more drastic forms of alienation, the more violent, earthy, or sordid ranges of experience which engage the minds of Melville and

Faulkner, and the fact most of our best writers. Yet to achieve a "contemplative centrality of vision" certainly requires an action of the mind; whereas the word "middlebrow," although suggesting centrality of vision, inevitably suggests, judging by our American literature, a view gained by no other means than passivity and the refusal of experience.

To conclude this brief account of the contradictions which have vivified and excited the American imagination, these contradictions seem traceable to certain historical facts. First, there is the solitary position man has been placed in in this country, a position very early enforced by the doctrines of Puritanism and later by frontier conditions and, as Tocqueville skillfully pointed out, by the very institutions of democracy as these evolved in the eighteenth and nineteenth centuries.

Second, the Manichaean quality of New England Puritanism, which, as Yvor Winters and others have shown, had so strong an effect on writers like Hawthorne and Melville and entered deeply into the national consciousness. From the historical point of view, this Puritanism was a backsliding in religion as momentous in shaping the imagination as the cultural reversion Cooper studied on the frontier. For, at least as apprehended by the literary imagination, New England Puritanism—with its grand metaphors of election and damnation, its opposition of the kingdom of light and the kingdom of darkness, its eternal and autonomous contraries of good and evil—seems to have recaptured the Manichaean sensibility. The American imagination, like the New England Puritan mind itself, seems less interested in redemption than in the melodrama of the eternal struggle of good and evil, less interested in incarnation and reconciliation than in alienation and disorder. If we may suppose ourselves correct in tracing to this origin the prevalence in American literature of the symbols of light and dark, we may doubtless suppose also that this sensibility has been enhanced by the racial composition of our people and by the Civil War that was fought, if more in legend than in fact, over the Negro.

More obviously, a third source of contradiction lies in the dual allegiance of the American, who in his intellectual culture belongs both to the Old World and the New.

FENIMORE COOPER
AND THE ECONOMIC AGE

Marius Bewley

Cooper has been consistently underestimated as an artist. He ranks with Hawthorne, James, and Melville as one of the four greatest novelists America produced in the nineteenth century. Conrad called him a rare artist and one of his own masters, and his words deserve more attention than they have ever received. But the novels that must be considered in this chapter are by no means his masterpieces interesting as they are in many respects. The European political novels with which I shall be concerned first, greatly enlarged, or would have done had their example been heeded, the scope of the political novel as it then existed. In them Cooper presents a strikingly original analysis of history and of his own times, the brilliance of which has never received any recognition. In a day such as our own when the political novel largely concerns itself with the threat to democracies from the outside, it is salutary to consider Cooper's political novels, which are concerned with threats to democracy that arise from abuse of its own nature. The European political novels are, in effect, a

Source: Marius Bewley, *The Eccentric Design: Form in the Classic American Novel* (New York: Columbia University Press, 1959), pp. 47−48, 65−72. Reprinted by permission of the Columbia University Press.

Marius Bewley (1918−   ), is professor of English at Rutgers University. He was educated at St. Louis and Cambridge universities. He has taught at the Catholic University of America, Wellesley, Connecticut College, and Fordham University. In addition to *The Eccentric Design; Form in the Classic American Novel* (1959), he has written *The Complex Fate: Hawthorne, Henry James, and Some Other American Writers* (1952) *Masks and Mirrors: Essays in Criticism* (1970), and edited *Selected Poems of John Donne* (1966).

manifesto of Cooper's ardent democratic principles. . . . Ten years later, in the Littlepage trilogy, Cooper wrote three novels whose political philosophy seems diametrically opposed to that he had previously expressed. And yet Cooper had not really changed his views. The aristocratic Cooper of *The Chainbearer* and *The Redskins* is the democratic Cooper who had written *The Heidenmauer* and *The Bravo.* These two sets of novels exemplify the polarity in American experience. Cooper never really succeeded in resolving this polarity or conflict artistically in any one novel. The best he could do was to shift his attention back and forth from one aspect to the other, and in doing so he often gives what appears to be a contradictory performance. Out of this tension or spiritual conflict, Henry James was to evolve at last the structural dialectic of the international novel in which opposites are brought together, skilfully juggled or held in suspension, and at last resolved by mutually qualifying each other, as in *The Europeans.*[1] No one before James was equipped, either with the worldly knowledge or creative tact, to achieve so much, but many American writers had been brought face to face with the devastating problem. Two of them had been among America's greatest writers, and if Cooper and Hawthorne partially failed where James was later to succeed, it is possible that James himself would not have succeeded if Cooper and Hawthorne had not struggled with the tension before him. . . . Cooper and Hawthorne helped James to that preliminary knowledge of America—not indeed a knowledge of the mere surfaces of American life, but of her profoundest spiritual trials which was the necessary prelude of the full maturity of Jamesian art. In the following pages I wish to explore this basic tension as it occurs in Cooper's novels. If we can understand it fully in Cooper, we shall have a touchstone that may well prove helpful in guiding our critical explorations through the American novel as it developed after him.

· · · · ·

The Littlepage trilogy was written in the 'forties. The first novel in the series *Satanstoe* (1845), is perhaps Cooper's best

[1] See F. R. Leavis, 'The Europeans', *Scrutiny,* Vol. XV, No. 3, pp. 209–21.

novel after the Leatherstocking tales. The pastoral picture it gives of colonial life particularly among the Dutch settlers at Albany, reminds one of *The Pioneers. The Chainbearer,* also published in 1845, is almost as good; but *The Redskins* of the following year is a declamatory failure. The Littlepage trilogy traces the history of a single family through some three or four generations as they live their lives on their New York estates. The Littlepage family are landed proprietors, and the basis of interest in these novels is the way we see them acquiring their lands, surveying them, and building substantial houses on them, settling their thousands of acres with tenants, passing them on from father to son, and watching them rise in value as New York becomes more prosperous. Not least among the successes of these novels is the way in which one feels the lands acquire, not only greater money value, but an endowment of richer values through human association as they pass successively from heir to heir. Cooper's aim, of course, was to praise landed wealth, transmitted through families, at the expense of wealth gained by speculation or industrial enterprise. Landed wealth had a dignity, and carried certain values and responsibilities with it that no other kind of wealth could claim. 'The vulgar, almost invariably in this country, reduce the standard of distinction to mere money,' Cooper had written in *The Chainbearer*. His trilogy is intended as an illustration of everything, in addition to money, that land means when it becomes the focal point for the activities and interests of a family. His ideas on land and inheritance are adequately suggested in the following paragraph from *Satanstoe.*

'You see,' continued Herman Mordaunt, as we walked together conversing on this subject, 'that my twenty thousand acres are not likely to be of much use to myself, even should they prove to be of any to my daughter. A century hence, indeed, my descendants may benefit from all this outlay of money and trouble; but it is not probable that either I or Anneke will ever see the principal and interest of the sums that will be expended in the way of roads, bridges, mills, and other things of that sort. Years may go by before the light rents which will only begin to be paid a year or two hence, and then only by a few tenants, can amount to a sufficient sum to meet the expense of keeping up the settlement to say nothing of the quit-rents that must be paid to the Crown. . . .

'Every man who is at his ease in his moneyed affairs, Corny, feels a disposition to make some provision for his posterity. This estate, if kept together, and in single hands, may make some descendant of mine a man of fortune. Half a century will produce a great change in this colony; and at the end of that period, a child of Anneke's may be thankful that his mother had a father who was willing to throw away a few thousands of his own, the surplus of a fortune that was sufficient for his wants without them, in order that his grandson might see them converted into tens, or possibly into hundreds of thousands.'

We are confronted here with something that looks like a contradiction. If Cooper was embattled against the men of property, it was only when they were financiers or tycoons of the new class, men whose sources of wealth he distrusted, and whose desire to influence government for the welfare of vested interests he considered subversive of democratic principles. But the democratic principles Cooper championed were not broad enough to include a levelling interpretation of democracy. 'The tendency of democracies is, in all things, to mediocrity,' he had written in *The American Democrat*.[2] Like John Adams, Cooper was intensely conscious of the inequality of natural endowments, and he was never guilty of perverting the doctrine of equality of rights into equality of opportunity. He realized that such a formulation can only mean the suppression of opportunity for the specially talented. In words that sound remarkably like John Adams, he wrote:

> The rights of property being an indispensable condition of civilization, and its quiet possession everywhere guaranteed, equality of condition is rendered impossible. One man must labour, while another may live luxuriously on his means; one has leisure and opportunity to cultivate his tastes, to increase his information, and to reform his habits, while another is compelled to toil that he may live. One is reduced to serve, while another commands, and, of course, there can be no equality in their social conditions.[3]

[2] Op. cit., p. 64.
[3] Ibid., p. 32.

That was part of Cooper's explanation of what it meant to be a democrat in America—or, perhaps, what it ought to have meant. It is not surprising, then, that he once told the editor of the Albany *Argus* that he was a good Democrat because he was a good aristocrat.[4] When Cooper used the word 'aristocratic' in a benign sense, as when he applied it to himself, he interpreted it in its imaginative and chivalric mode, a sense which the romanticism of the day made popular, but which the economic trends of the past hundred years had drained of much practical meaning. Cooper believed that there must be a cultural élite at the top of society who functioned as custodians and dispensers of civilized values. It was his distinction that he recognized that such an élite was as becoming to a democracy as it was to a monarchy. He saw it as the guardian of democracy, not as a threat to it. Part of his indignation against the Whigs sprang from his perception of how they failed as guardians of any values beyond the most selfish economic ones. This role of the civilizing function of a cultivated upper class comes out very clearly in the Littlepage trilogy. In *The Chainbearer,* for example, we have this speech, perfectly representative of the values that are recommended throughout these three books, in which Mordaunt Littlepage's father is speaking to him:

> 'You will naturally think of marrying ere long, and your mother and I were just saying that you ought to build a good,

[4] Cited in Waples, op. cit., p. 206.

The recognition of this tension in Cooper is general among all biographers and critics who have written on him. Thomas R. Lounsbury, whose biography (*James Fenimore Cooper,* New York, 1900, p. 82) was first published in 1882, more or less sets a pattern:

> He was an aristocrat in feeling, and a democrat by conviction. To some this seems a combination so unnatural that they find it hard to comprehend it. That a man whose tastes and sympathies and station connect him with the highest class, and to whom contact with the uneducated and unrefined brings with it a sense of personal discomfort and often of disgust, should avow his belief in the political rights of those socially inferior, should be unwilling to deny them privileges which he claims for himself, is something so appalling to many that their minds strive vainly to grasp it. But this feeling was so thoroughly wrought into Cooper's nature that he almost disliked those of his countrymen whom he found not to share it.

substantial dwelling on this very spot, and settle down on your own property. Nothing contributes so much to the civilization of a country as to dot it with a gentry, and you will both give and receive advantages by adopting such a course. It is impossible for those who have never been witnesses of the result, to appreciate the effect produced by one gentleman's family in a neighbourhood, in the way of manners, tastes, general intelligence, and civilization at large.'

Or again, in *The Redskins,* which brings the trilogy down to Cooper's own day, we have this passage on New York City:

Will New York ever be a capital? Yes—out of all question yes. But the day will not come until after the sudden changes of condition which immediately and so naturally succeeded the revolution, have ceased to influence ordinary society, and those above again impart to those below more than they receive. This restoration to the natural state of things must take place as soon as society gets settled; and there will be nothing to prevent a town living under our own institutions—spirit, *tendencies* and all—from obtaining the highest tone that ever yet prevailed in a capital. The folly is in anticipating the natural course of events. Nothing will more hasten these events, however, than a literature that is controlled, not by the lower, but by the higher opinion of the country; which literature is yet, in a great degree, to be created.

Nothing could be more charming or superficially more plausible than this combination of democratic and aristocratic tendencies in their purity as they coalesced in Cooper's imagination. But the type of American democrat he looked forward to has failed to develop, at least in any numbers, while levellers and Babbitts have multiplied. The fact is that Cooper's American democrat was not a creature of the economic age in which he was compelled to take his place. Set down in the middle of nineteenth-century America there was something contradictory in his nature. His great virtues were to find an adequate stage only in literature—but here he was to be a complete success. The tensions that he could not resolve in politics were finally to make him into an artist. In the last analysis, it is not only Cooper, but Hawthorne and James who may be taken as the finest examples of what Cooper meant by being an American democrat.

There is a passage in Cooper's *Gleanings in Europe* which it will be well to bear in mind at this point. He and his family had just arrived in England, through which they were passing on their way to France, when they made a visit to the ruins of Netley Abbey:

> The Abbey was fine, without being a very imposing ruin, standing in the midst of a field of English neatness, prettily relieved by the woods. . . . The effect of these ruins on us proved the wonderful power of association. The greater force of the past than of the future on the mind can only be the result of questionable causes. Our real concern with the future is incalculably greater, and yet we were dreaming over our own graves, and the events and scenes which throw a charm around the graves of those who have gone before us.[5]

Cooper was one of the most astute politico-social critics America has ever had. But if he understood the new economic man so well, his clarity of vision was partly induced by hate. Of the elder Mr. Goldencalf in *The Monikins,* Cooper said, 'With him, to be born was but the commencement of a speculation, and to die was to determine the general balance of profit and loss.' It was a despicable way of life for a man as civilized as Cooper. The violence of his reaction was so great that in searching for an alternative he failed at times to preserve intact the precision of his critical judgment. To escape the financial aristocracy and its degraded image of the economic man, he embraced the remnants of feudal tenure in the New York land laws which were presently to be repealed under the new state constitution. In doing so he was dreaming over his own grave and the graves of those who had gone before him in a more literal sense than he had ever done while viewing the ruins of Netley Abbey.

It will not be necessary to discuss the nature of these feudal land laws except to say that they guaranteed the vast manorial system that New York had inherited from colonial days, and which was dominated by the great estate of Rensselaerwyck on the Hudson, covering an area of nearly eleven hundred square miles, and containing a number of villages and thousands of small farms which were rented on a basis of

[5] *Gleanings in Europe,* edited by Robert E. Spiller, New York, 1928–30, Vol. 1, p. 36.

feudal tenure.[6] The evolving pattern of American society fore-doomed the whole system to extinction, and Cooper, if anyone, should have known it. But at this point we encounter that cru-

[6] The most recent and exhaustive study of these land laws and the agitation that led to their repeal is to be found in Henry Christman, op. cit. The laws are discussed in relation to the Littlepage novels in 'Landlord Cooper and the Anti-Renters', by Granville Hicks, *Antioch Review*, Vol. V, pp. 95–109. An account narrowly sympathetic to the land-owners is given by Edward P. Cheyney, *The Anti-Rent Agitation in the State of New York, 1839–46*, Philadelphia, 1887. The style and tone of life on these old estates are described by Cooper in *The Pioneers*. A visually suggestive account is given in an article by General Egbert L. Viele, 'The Knickerbockers of New York Two Centuries Ago', *Harper's New Monthly Magazine*, December, 1876:

> The early Dutch residents of Albany and its vicinity constituted a kind of landed aristocracy, and, with their numerous retainers and slaves, held a sort of feudal court in the grand mansions which may still be found dotted here and there in the interior of the State. The family seat of the Knickerbockers at Schagticoke is one of these ancestral homes. . . . The spacious edifice is built in the Flemish style of architecture, with its steep pyramidally shaped roof. . . .
> The principal entrance is reached through an avenue of ancient trees, time-worn and scarred, that climb high above the roof. . . . The main hall is in itself a room. Quaint settees and an antique bookcase, with rare old engravings on the walls, constitute the furniture, while over all an air of quiet comfort and repose prevails. The principal stairway is in the second hall, separated from the first by folding doors. On either side of the main hall are the reception and drawing-rooms, while the diningroom and library open into the rear hall. In the olden time the diningroom contained the historic fireplace, with its tiled front and sides representing the scenes and events in Bible History. . . . Beyond the diningroom, in the large wing, are the kitchen and servants' apartments. The great cellar, which extends under the entire building, was the slaves' quarters in winter.

This description of the Knickerbocker ancestral estate reminds one of the description given by Henry Walcott Boynton (*James Fenimore Cooper*, New York, 1931, p. 8) of Otsego Hall, in which much of Cooper's boyhood was spent: a stately mansion made of brick, two stories high, above an enormous cellar, the entrance opening into a great central hall flanked by large rooms. The lands attached to the estate numbered 40,000 acres in 1786.

The aristocratic tone which pervaded wealthy New York society, which still thought in terms of land, is described by D. R. Fox (op. cit., pp. 130–3):

> The gentry who centred in the drawing-rooms of those fashionable streets running eastward from Broadway, all had their coats of arms, and

cial strain or tension which, if we probe deeply enough into their works, characterizes so many of the great American writers. Although he was always a devout Democrat, Cooper was also a man of an older and more imaginative order of things. In fact, this apparent paradox often exists in Americans—that men of High Tory mentality become Democrats, espousing the

> history of knights and squires and manor houses with wide stretching acres in the counties of old England. To lord it over docile tenantry, and ride at hunt through one's own forest, made up a part of what was most attractive in the family legends of a storied past. . . .
>
> So these families came, bringing in a spirit of aristocracy which left its mark, as we have seen, upon the county politics. That now they have for the most part disappeared adds a touch of pathos to the story. Theirs was a spirit foreign to the custom of the country; while others made their way into the wilderness to be rid of every vestige of the feudal system, these came to perpetuate so much of that tradition as could be saved. But the aloofness of this gentry, so proper to their social theory, could not be comfortably preserved, and, bound by an inflexible endogamous rule, these branches of the families slowly withered and passed into memory, though leaving after them an influence that increased respect for 'the few, the rich, and the well-born'.

This was essentially the class that Cooper admired, and with which he identified himself; and as I have remarked elsewhere in Chapter III, the intensity of his loyalty to it blinded him to the fact that the men of wealth in New York were no longer the old aristocrats, but men whose wealth came from speculation and business, and who, for that very reason, were pleased to identify themselves with the more honoured tradition of land, which not only shed a lustre of dignity over them, but proved profitable as well. Thus, the character of the old landowning class was gradually sapped by its fusion with those very elements Cooper distrusted. As Fox describes it (ibid., pp. 122–4):

> The men of wealth in New York City had no settled prejudice against holding real estate; not only were there close connections with the Schylers and the Van Rensselaers, but in most families of the gentry there were large-acred cousins, of whose prosperity there could be no doubt. . . . The attention of large investors was already fixed on these lands while they were still dispensed by the colony land office, and the bidding grew far brisker in the early days of statehood. As one glances down the pages of the *Calendar of Land Papers* one sees many familiar Federalist names, William Bayard, the Bleeckers, C. D. Colden, Duane, James Emott, Nicholas Fish, and many others. Alexander Hamilton invested all his surplus earnings in the lands about Oswego which would pay a rich dividend only after years of waiting, so that his tragic death left his widow 'land-poor'.

popular party, which they understand as the party of chivalry and the opponent of those vested interests that represent the triumph of a financial pseudo-aristocracy. Therefore, when Cooper turned from his criticism of Whig oligarchy, the position that attracted him most strongly was the feudalism of the landowners. The fervour of his attraction, based partly on his memory of his childhood on his father's great estate, prevented him from examining it with the same keen eye he had turned on the moneyed class who looked to speculation and commerce rather than to land for wealth. As for the feudal aspects of the landowners, by that date Cooper didn't care (if he ever had—which is doubtful). In the Preface to *The Redskins* he wrote: 'It is pretended the durable leases are feudal in their nature. We do not conceive this to be true; but, admitting it to be so, it would only prove that feudality, to this extent, is a part of the institution of the state.'

Cooper saw in the great landowning interests the last bulwark against the new financial mentality. It had been suggested that the Van Rensselaers sell the farms they rented to their tenants outright. In *The Redskins,* two of the characters, speaking for Cooper, comment on this:

> 'Do you suppose the Rensselaers would take their money, the principal of the rent at 7 per cent, and buy land with it, after the experience of their uncertainty of such possessions among us?'
>
> 'Not they,' said my uncle Ro laughing. 'No, no! They would sell the Manor House at Beverwyck, for taverns; and then one might live in them who would pay the principal sum of the cost of a dinner; bag their dollars, and proceed forthwith to Wall Street, and commence shaving the notes—that occupation having been decided to be highly honoured and esteemed accordingly.'

As I said, Cooper was dreaming 'on the events and scenes which throw a charm around the graves of those who have gone before us' when he wrote the Littlepage novels, and a man of his incisive intelligence ought to have known it: ought to have known that in so far as the old estates had a chance of surviving it was in that degree to which their interests had become allied with the new financial class. Nevertheless, if Cooper's grasp of reality seems momentarily relaxed in these novels, the idyllic scenes of American aristocratic life, the benevolent High Toryism that Cooper depicts in his land-lords, is as agreeable as anything he ever wrote, saving only the Natty Bumppo series. But it is astonishing that Cooper, who had described Signor Gradenigo so brilliantly, should suppose that in an age dominated by such men the relation-ship represented in the following passage from *The Chainbearer* could long endure:

> A rumour had gone forth among the people that their land-lord had arrived, and some of the older tenants, those who had known 'Herman Mordaunt' as they called my grandfather, crowded around me in a frank hearty manner, in which good feeling was blended with respect. They desired to take my hand. I shook hands with all who came, and can truly say that I took no man's palm into my own that day, without a sentiment that the relation of landlord and tenant was one that should in-duce kind and confidential feelings.

Cooper failed to examine New York feudal society criti-cally because he was enamoured of a way of life that, in imag-ination at least, it seemed to foster and protect. He could never have been convinced that the impoverished outlying farms of Rensselaerwyck were really open-air sweat shops. He remembered his own childhood in Otsego County too vividly to believe any such thing.

When we contrast the democratic European political nov-els with the aristocratic Littlepage novels, we see that Cooper was faced with a difficult dilemma. It was one he could not solve, at least by any of the courses that suggested them-selves as possible. Wedded to an older imaginative order, and cherishing the values that flourished under such an order no less than the democratic principles in which he believed, he looked in vain for a practical position in which to ground his values in his own time. And it is doubtful if he would have fared any better in ours. This dilemma which I have tried to isolate from two sets of his novels is important because it rep-resents a recurrent tension that we meet in later writers, and on many levels of American thought. At the somewhat elementary level at which it occurs in Cooper we are able to understand it in relation to the surrounding intellectual context in which it occurs more easily than we can with Hawthorne and James. Considered merely as a political statement, Cooper's Littlepage novels represent the desperation of his plight, and of those who came later. How were a cultured élite who were the dispensers of civilized and moral values to reconcile themselves to the economic framework which alone provided the leisure and opportunities for the discharge of their elegant responsibilities? And was not the purity of the democratic dogma, for example, its insurance against demagoguery, guaranteed alone by disciplines that were most readily fostered in aristocratic societies? And although America looked to the future for the fulfilment of her destiny, wasn't it the future, as things were going in the economic age, that gave the lie to the hopes the past had cherished? And finally, wasn't it old, guilt-ridden Europe that, over and over again, whispered insidious intimations to the startled imaginations of these democratic New World writers, that some—perhaps an important part—of the answers they were looking for were to be found in her ancient institutions and seasoned manners?

THE MYTH AND THE DIALOGUE

R. W. B. Lewis

   This book has to do with the beginnings and the first tentative outlines of a native American mythology. The period I cover runs from about 1820 to 1860; the scene, for the most part, is New England and the Atlantic seaboard. The cast of characters is large, and would be a great deal larger if every person were included who, by act or utterance, contributed to the formation of the American myth. But I am not concerned with matters of anthropology and sociology, or with folklore and legend; nor am I primarily concerned with the psychology of myth, any more than with the facts of economic geography and political history. I am interested rather in the history of ideas and, especially, in the representative imagery and anecdote that crystallized whole clusters of ideas; my interest is

   Source: R. W. B. Lewis, *The American Adam: Innocence, Tragedy and Tradition in the Nineteenth Century* (Chicago: University of Chicago Press, 1955), pp. 1–10. Copyright © 1955 by the University of Chicago Press. Reprinted by permission of the author and the publisher.
   R. W. B. Lewis (1917–   ), is professor of English and American Studies at Yale University. He was educated at Harvard and the University of Chicago, and has taught at Bennington College, the Salzburg Seminar in American Studies, Smith College, Rutgers and the University of Munich. In addition to *The American Adam: Innocence, Tragedy, and Tradition in the Nineteenth Century* (1955), he has written *The Picaresque Saint: Representative Figures in Contemporary Fiction* (1959), *The Presence of Walt Whitman* (1962), *Trials of the Word: Essays in American Literature and the Humanistic Tradition* (1965), *The Poetry of Hart Crane: A Critical Study* (1967), and edited *Herman Melville, A Reader* (1962), *Malraux: A Collection of Critical Essays* (1964), and *The Collected Short Stories of Edith Wharton* (1968).

therefore limited to articulate thinkers and conscious artists. A century ago, the image contrived to embody the most fruitful contemporary ideas was that of the authentic American as a figure of heroic innocence and vast potentialities, poised at the start of a new history. This image is the title of the book.

It was an image crowded with illusion, and the moral posture it seemed to indorse was vulnerable in the extreme. But however vulnerable or illusory, this image had about it always an air of adventurousness, a sense of promise and possibility —of a sort no longer very evident in our national expression. Its very openness to challenge, its susceptibility to controversy, made possible a series of original inquiries and discoveries about human nature, art, and history. I shall have many an occasion to comment on the present relevance of the Adamic myth. But here I should introduce the terminology and method I shall employ.

I want, first, to suggest an analogy between the history of a culture—or of its thought and literature—and the unfolding course of a dialogue: a dialogue more or less philosophic in nature and, like Plato's, containing a number of voices. Every culture seems, as it advances toward maturity, to produce its own determining debate over the ideas that preoccupy it: salvation, the order of nature, money, power, sex, the machine, and the like. The debate, indeed, may be said to be the culture, at least on its loftiest levels; for a culture achieves identity not so much through the ascendancy of one particular set of convictions as through the emergence of its peculiar and distinctive dialogue. (Similarly, a culture is on the decline when it submits to intellectual martial law, and fresh understanding is denied in a denial of further controversy.) Intellectual history, properly conducted, exposes not only the dominant ideas of a period, or of a nation, but more important, the dominant clashes over ideas. Or to put it more austerely: the historian looks not only for the major terms of discourse, but also for major pairs of opposed terms which, by their very opposition, carry discourse forward. The historian looks, too, for the coloration or discoloration of ideas received from the sometimes bruising contact of opposites.

As he does so and as he examines the personalities and biases of the men engaged in debate at any given historical moment, the historian is likely to discover that the development of the culture in question resembles a protracted and broadly ranging conversation: at best a dialogue—a dialogue which at times moves very close to drama.[1]

In America, during the second quarter of the nineteenth century, the chief intellectual spokesmen—novelists and poets, as well as essayists, critics, historians, and preachers —appear to have entered into just such a lively and creative dialogue. The subject, stimulated by the invigorating feeling that a new culture was in the making, touched on the moral, intellectual, and artistic resources of man in the new society. Whatever else they may have been talking about, all interested persons seem invariably to have been talking about that. And in the perspective of history, they give the impression of talking to and about one another—within separate fields of activity and across them. Historians, telling of the past, at the same time illuminated or contradicted the imagery of contemporary novelists; novelists enacted or challenged, in their stories, the patterns of experience proposed by theologians, the focus in all these cases being the peculiar capacities of the inhabitant of the new world. Among the terms and ideas that turned up most frequently in the debate were: innocence, novelty, experience, sin, time, evil, hope, the present, memory, the past, tradition. Almost any one of them can be found, in the documents of the day, paired off with or against almost any other; and there were consequently many changes of coloration and many unexpected conclusions. The shifting weight of emphasis and import is too rapid for accurate analysis; but these are some of the main ideas with which this book is concerned. It is one of my aims to account for the dialogue that emerged as those ideas were invoked by American writers and speakers, from 1820 onward, in their contentious effort to define the American character and the life worth living.

[1] An excellent example of intellectual history seizing upon the dialectical and dramatic qualities of its subject has been the volumes on the New England mind by Perry Miller.

But the purpose of a cultural conversation, to judge from our American example, is not, after all, simply to settle the terms of discussion. It goes beyond that to provide materials for the creative imagination. The intellectual historian should accordingly look beyond the terms of discussion for something else. He should, in fact, look for the images and the "story" that animate the ideas and are their imaginative and usually more compelling equivalent. For what is articulated during the years of debate is a comprehensive view of life, in an ideal extension of its present possibilities. And while the vision may be formulated in the orderly language of rational thought, it also finds its form in a recurring pattern of images—ways of seeing and sensing experience—and in a certain habitual story, an assumed dramatic design for the representative life. (The Passion of Christ, for example, is the story behind most Christian argumentation.) The imagery and the story give direction and impetus to the intellectual debate itself; and they may sometimes be detected, hidden within the argument, charging the rational terms with unaccustomed energy. But the debate in turn can contribute to the shaping of the story; and when the results of rational inquiry are transformed into conscious and coherent narrative by the best-attuned artists of the time, the culture has finally yielded up its own special and identifying "myth."

The relation between idea and story is considered further, in the practical illustrations offered in this book. This much can be said in advance: the narrative art inevitably and by nature invests its inherited intellectual content with a quickening duplicity; it stains ideas with restless ambiguity. For the *experience* of the aims and values of an epoch is apt to be more complex and more painful than the simple statement of them; and narrative deals with experiences, not with propositions. The narrative art, moreover, dramatizes as human conflict what is elsewhere a thoughtful exchange of ideas; and art projects —in a single packed dramatic image—conflicting principles which the discursive mind must contemplate separately and consecutively.

Perhaps the rather narrow context in which I am using words like "myth" and "mythology" can be explained by citing an instance from classical culture. The Roman myth received its final magnificent and persuasive form in the *Aeneid* of Virgil. The *Aeneid*, however, was unmistakably a dramatization on a vast scale of the humanistic ideas set forth and debated in the philosophical dialogues of Cicero, two or three decades earlier. Cicero, in his turn, had only brought together the conflicting opinions of the contemporary schools of thought; and these opinions reflected an earlier imaginative feeling about the limits and aims of human experience. Cicero discovered *the* dialogue of his generation. It became the matter for the myth consciously created by Virgil: an essentially political myth, the myth of "the city" or "the republic"; a vision of life as shaped and bounded by the *polis,* with all other human concerns (love, for example, or scientific investigation) subordinated to the political and moral. And what Virgil was able to do in his mythical narrative of the origins of the city was, as one historian has observed, to provide the "dynamic [which] was needed in order to impart to Ciceronianism the vitality which it lacked." [2] But "the tears of things" so prevalent in the *Aeneid* reflect Virgil's poetic ambivalence toward the Roman ideals that his poem nonetheless affirmed.

My intention, then, is to disentangle from the writings and pronouncements of the day the emergent American myth and the dialogue in which it was formed. The American myth, unlike the Roman, was not fashioned ultimately by a single man of genius. It was and it has remained a collective affair; it must be pieced together out of an assortment of essays, orations, poems, stories, histories, and sermons. We have not yet produced a Virgil, not even Walt Whitman being adequate to that function.[3] *Leaves of Grass* (1855) did indeed set to a music of remarkable and original quality many attitudes that had been current for several decades. . . . But *Leaves of*

[2] Charles N. Cochrane, *Christianity and Classical Culture* (Oxford, 1946).

[3] It is worth noting that the one poem which set out quite deliberately to provide America with its definitive myth—Hart Crane's *The Bridge* (1930)—was inspired at once by Whitman and Virgil. The Whitman strain is, of course, very evident throughout *The Bridge;* but Crane remarked in letters and conversations that his ambition was to do for his own age what Virgil had done for his, and that the *Aeneid* was the exemplary poem.

Grass is scarcely more than a bundle of lyrics which gives us only one phase of the story imbedded in the American response to life; to round it out, other writings had to follow.[4]

Unlike the Roman myth, too—which envisaged life within a long, dense corridor of meaningful history—the American myth saw life and history as just beginning. It described the world as starting up again under fresh initiative, in a divinely granted second chance for the human race, after the first chance had been so disastrously fumbled in the darkening Old World. It introduced a new kind of hero, the heroic embodiment of a new set of ideal human attributes. America, it was said insistently from the 1820's onward, was not the end-product of a long historical process (like the Augustan Rome celebrated in the *Aeneid*); it was something entirely new. "Our national birth," declaimed the *Democratic Review* in 1839, "was the beginning of a new history . . . which separates us from the past and connects us with the future only." "American glory begins at the dawn," announced Noah Webster in 1825. Edward Everett found an acceptable prescription for national health in the simple italicized phrase, *separation from Europe* —separation from its history and its habits.

The new habits to be engendered on the new American scene were suggested by the image of a radically new personality, the hero of the new adventure: an individual emancipated from history, happily bereft of ancestry, untouched and undefiled by the usual inheritances of family and race; an individual standing alone, self-reliant and self-propelling, ready to confront whatever awaited him with the aid of his own unique and inherent resources. It was not surprising, in a Bible-reading generation, that the new hero (in praise or disapproval) was most easily identified with Adam before the Fall. Adam was the first, the archetypal, man. His moral position was prior to experience, and in his very newness he was fundamentally innocent. The world and history lay all before him.

---

[4] More than one critic of Henry James has suggested that James's last three novels—*The Ambassadors, The Wings of the Dove,* and *The Golden Bowl,* all published in the very early 1900's—may be taken as a trilogy comprehending the totality of the distinctively American vision of experience.

And he was the type of creator, the poet par excellence, creating language itself by naming the elements of the scene about him. All this and more were contained in the image of the American as Adam.[5]

Such were the first impulses which begot the myth. Such were the first fertile illusions. The changes they suffered and the further insights they elicited, as they were challenged, transcended, and dramatized over the years, are precisely the burden of this study. But it is worth remarking that while the Adamic image was invoked often and explicitly in the later stages of our history, during earlier stages it remained somewhat submerged, making itself felt as an atmospheric presence, a motivating idea. It was the concealed cause of an ethical polemic, and it lurked behind the formal structure of works of fiction. The image was slow to work its way to the surface of American expression; and the reader will notice that it tends to appear toward the end of sections or discussions in this book. The significant fact is that the literal use of the story of Adam and the Fall of Man—as a model for narrative— occurred in the final works of American novelists, the works in which they sought to summarize the whole of their experience of America. *The Marble Faun* and *Billy Budd,* where the Adamic imagery is altogether central and controlling, were the last finished writings of Hawthorne and Melville. And it was in *The Golden Bowl* of Henry James that the protagonist's name was Adam. Those novels were perhaps as close as American culture ever came to the full and conscious realization of the myth it had so long secreted.

It is also worth remarking that the ideal of newborn innocence was both rejoiced in and deplored. The opposed reactions set the dialogue in motion that later constituted the energizing conflict in narrative fiction. Emerson, recoiling from the sense of antique pressures in Europe, might voice the epochal

[5] Here, and occasionally later, I must distinguish between the notion of progress toward perfection and the notion of primitive Adamic perfection. Both ideas were current, and they overlapped and intertwined. On the whole, however, we may settle for the paradox that the more intense the belief in progress toward perfection, the more it stimulated a belief in a present primal perfection.

remark: "Here's for the plain old Adam, the simple genuine self against the whole world." But Henry James the elder, that formidable and explosive man, came back (in 1857) with the contention that "nothing could be more remote . . . from distinctively *human* attributes . . . than this sleek and comely Adamic condition." This was not, in fact, an effort simply to repudiate the current mythology. James wanted rather to enrich it, by educating his listeners in the fact and the value of tragedy, for, as he said, "Life flowers and fructifies out of the profoundest tragic depths." And just as the more optimistic moral principles were challenged and converted in the course of the dialogue, so the narrative figure of Adam—introduced as the hero of a new semidivine comedy—was converted into the hero of a new kind of tragedy, and grew thereby to a larger stature. It was the tragedy inherent in his innocence and newness, and it established the pattern for American fiction.

This brings me to a final word about the several "voices" in our dialogue and the names I will give them. We might begin by noticing that Emerson saw no dialogue at all, but only a "schism," a split in culture between two polarized parties: "the party of the Past and the party of the Future," as he sometimes called them, or the parties "of Memory and Hope, of the Understanding and the Reason." The schism began, according to Emerson's retrospective mediation of 1867, in about 1820. But Emerson subscribed too readily perhaps to a two-party system in intellectual affairs; and he was always puzzled by the attitude of a man like Hawthorne, who seemed skeptically sympathetic toward both parties and managed to be confined by neither.

Historians after Emerson have either gone along with his dichotomies and have talked about the "dualism" of American culture; or they have selected one of Emerson's two parties as constituting *the* American tradition, rejecting the other as a bleak foreign hangover or as immature native foolishness. But if we attend to the realities of American intellectual history, we must distinguish in it at least *three* voices (sometimes more). American culture has traditionally consisted of the productive and lively interplay of all three.

In the chapters which follow, I adopt one of Emerson's

pairs of terms to identify the two parties he himself recognized: the party of Hope and the party of Memory. For the third party, there is no proper name: unless we call it the party of Irony.

As an index to the "hopeful" stand on national morality, I cite the editorial (of 1839) which hailed the birth in America of "a clear conscience unsullied by the past." The national and hence the individual conscience was clear just because it was unsullied by the past—America, in the hopeful creed, had no past, but only a present and a future. The key term in the moral vocabulary of Emerson, Thoreau, Whitman, and their followers and imitators consequently was "innocence." To the "nostalgic"—that is, to the party devoted to Memory—the sinfulness of man seemed never so patent as currently in America. As the hopeful expressed their mounting contempt for the doctrine of inherited sin, the nostalgic intoned on Sundays the fixed legacy of corruption in ever more emphatic accents; and centers of orthodox Calvinism, like Andover and Princeton, became citadels of the old and increasingly cheerless theology. But the ironic temperament—as represented, say, by the elder Henry James—was characterized by a tragic optimism: by a sense of the tragic collisions to which innocence was liable (something unthinkable among the hopeful), and equally by an awareness of the heightened perception and humanity which suffering made possible (something unthinkable among the nostalgic).

The debate over morality echoed the general debate over time: the connecting links, or the lack of them, between the present and the past. And in this respect the parties of Hope and of Memory virtually created each other. The human mind seems by nature to be "contrary," as by nurture it becomes dialectical. This was demonstrated afresh in early nineteenth-century America, when a denial of the past generated, by compensation, a new nostalgia, a new veneration for the past in its pastness. As the present and the future became objects of worship and inquiry, historical research began greatly to increase and the past to be discovered; there had been no need to discover it previously, for it had never been lost. But now statistical guesses about the material growth of the new society were countered by the efforts of a Prescott to re-create the historical reality of the old societies. The prescription of Edward Everett (*separation from Europe*) cut both ways. It was steadily more difficult to decide which of the two continents had been isolated; separation from Europe resulted in the first American expatriates.

Although Emerson listened with pleasure to "the clangor and jangle of contrary tendencies," there were those—and I collect them under my third heading—who found that constant discord unsatisfying. This group inspected the opposed tendencies and then arrived at a fresh understanding of the nature of tradition and America's practical involvement with the past. Their conclusion was a curious, ambivalent, off-beat kind of traditionalism. It expressed itself in many forms, but it was particularly striking in the field of fiction. For here it affected both form and content: an organic relation between past experience and the living moment became a factor in narrative—a recurring theme *of* narrative; and at the same time—most notably in the novels of Hawthorne and Melville—the narrative revealed its design through an original use of discredited traditional materials. And beyond fiction the resources of tradition, dispensed with by one sort of theologian in the name of religious freedom, were re-established by another as the essential means of human redemption.

There may be no such thing as "American experience"; it is probably better not to insist that there is. But there has been experience in America, and the account of it has had its own specific form. That form has been clearest and most rewarding when it has been most dialectical. Only recently has the dialogue tended to die away. For only recently has the old conviction of the new historical beginning seemed to vanish altogether, and with it the enlivening sense of possibility, of intellectual and artistic elbow-room, of new creations and fresh initiatives. Our culture will at the very least be a great deal drearier without it.

The dangers, both to life and to letters, of the Adamic ideal were acknowledged at once and have been repeated endlessly. The helplessness of mere innocence has been a primary theme of novelists in almost every decade, and a source of bewilderment to our political and diplomatic historians. The dismissal of the past has been only too effective: America, since the age of Emerson, has been persistently a one-generation culture. Successive generations have given rise to a series of staccato intellectual and literary movements with ever slighter trajectories. The temper which despised memory not unnaturally fostered a habit of forgetfulness, and writers who even forgot that there was anything to remember have found themselves remote alike from their predecessors and their contemporaries. The unluckiest consequence, however, has not been incoherence, but the sheer dullness of unconscious repetition. We regularly return, decade after decade and with the same pain and amazement, to all the old conflicts, programs, and discoveries. We consume our powers in hoisting ourselves back to the plane of understanding reached a century ago and at intervals since.

The vision of innocence and the claim of newness were almost perilously misleading. But they managed nonetheless to provide occasions for reflection and invention, for a testing of moral and artistic possibilities. The illusion of freedom from the past led to a more real relation to the continuing tradition. The vision of innocence stimulated a positive and original sense of tragedy. Without the illusion, we are conscious, no longer of tradition, but simply and coldly of the burden of history. And without the vision, we are left, not with a mature tragic spirit, but merely with a sterile awareness of evil uninvigorated by a sense of loss. For the notion of original sin draws its compelling strength from the prior notion of original innocence. Recent literature has applauded itself for passing beyond the childlike cheerfulness of Emerson and Whitman; but, in doing so, it has lost the profound tragic understanding—paradoxically bred out of cheerfulness—of a Hawthorne or a Melville.

A century ago, the challenge to debate was an expressed belief in achieved human perfection, a return to the primal perfection. Today the challenge comes rather from the expressed belief in achieved hopelessness. We stand in need of more stirring impulsions, of greater perspectives and more penetrating controversies. Perhaps a review of that earlier debate can help us on our way. We can hardly expect to be persuaded any longer by the historic dream of the new Adam. But it can pose anew, in the classic. way of illumination as it did in the American nineteenth century, the picture of what might be against the knowledge of what is, and become once more a stimulus to enterprise and a resource for literature.

VENTUROUS CONSERVATIVE:
ON TOCQUEVILLE'S
IMAGE OF THE DEMOCRAT

Marvin Meyers

Alexis de Tocqueville's classic commentary on American democracy [1] has been consulted by historians for every purpose but the simplest: as a key to the immediate subject of the work, Jacksonian America. In the sober view of history Tocqueville has figured as a philosopher, a prophet, a personage, and a source of brilliant phrases. Why not restore to him the office of observer, interpreting the scene he visited between the spring of 1831 and the late winter of 1832? Plainly, it

Source: Marvin Meyers, The Jacksonian Persuasion: Politics and Belief (Stanford: Stanford University Press, 1957), pp. 24–41. Copyright © 1957 by the Board of Trustees of the Leland Stanford Junior University. Reprinted by permission of the publisher.

Marvin Meyers (1921–   ) is Harry S Truman Professor of American Civilization at Brandeis University. He was educated at Rutgers and Columbia universities, and taught at the University of Chicago and the University of Puerto Rico before coming to Brandeis in 1963. In addition to The Jacksonian Persuasion: Politics and Belief (1957), he is co-editor of Sources of the American Republic: A Documentary History of Politics, Society, and Thought (1960–61).

[1] Democracy in America, originally published in French in two volumes, 1835 and 1840. I am much indebted to Professor George Pierson for his full, meticulous account of Tocqueville and Beaumont in America (1938), although I have not always followed his interpretations; so rich is the book in documentary quotation that it becomes as much a source book as a history. It should be clear that I am proposing an additional use of Tocqueville, one especially suited to the purpose of this study and consistent with Tocqueville's intention. Certainly his importance as a political and social analyst is not restricted to the particular subject of Jacksonian Democracy.

would be absurd to treat Tocqueville as one more garrulous nineteenth-century tourist; but that is not the only way open. His work offers just what is most needed by the student of Jacksonian times: an integrative view of society and culture, grounded in experience.

The venturous conservative is my construction of the man beneath the skin of Americans met everywhere in Tocqueville's pages. This image—compounded of consistent human qualities perceived by Tocqueville in the institutions, laws, ideas, customs, manners, and feelings of the American democracy—reflects Jacksonian experience within the basic form of the democratic social situation. The central character of the *Democracy* is, at once and congruously, a recognizable Jacksonian contemporary; a representative American; inherently, the universal democratic man.

Among these interpenetrating aspects of social character, and their corresponding environments, Tocqueville plainly gives least weight to the immediate and particular. The Jacksonian era, in his perspective, has no unique structure. Observed traits of society and character and culture simply illustrate the consequences of a great seven-century democratic revolution in its American—penultimate—expression. This stress on continuity makes for sound general history: in the long view, comprehending Europe and America, there is compelling force in Tocqueville's bold comment that he saw "the destiny of America embodied in the first Puritan who landed on those shores." And so he can interpret the Jacksonian world as a democratic microcosm, refer the actions of its citizens to the generic social responses of the democrat as American.[2]

I would propose further that the particular experiences of the Jacksonian generation formed a pattern of their own, which reinforced the general effects ascribed by Tocqueville to a persistent social situation; and that the venturous conservative was, in a brief incarnation, exactly the Jacksonian who helped to work a social transformation as he invoked the virtues of the Old Republic. The value of this notion for the un-

[2] *Democracy in America*, I, 290.

derstanding of Jacksonian Democracy and its persuasion cannot be established in a short argument. Its merits can be judged only in the whole design of my study, which attempts an extended development of Tocqueville's lead.

The following discussion offers an interpretation of *Democracy in America,* intended first to recover a searching portrait of the new-world democrat as a historical social type. Implicitly, I shall be sketching out an analytic scheme to guide further inquiry into the contemporary meaning of the Jacksonian appeal. Tocqueville's sometimes doubtful incidental judgments on Jacksonian public affairs have been rebuked more than enough. One does not ask a visitor to grasp esoteric family references; and especially not when one can get instead the testimony of a mind with a rare gift for using the contrast between object and observer to reveal essential and determinative qualities. If Tocqueville missed political details, he found a most rewarding general approach to democratic politics. With the appraisal of social character and its conditions—of the venturous conservative in his American democratic situation—Tocqueville starts us toward a fresh understanding of the Jacksonians. In their community, as the *Democracy* suggests persuasively, politics becomes a medium for the expression of influences compounded at the heart of democratic society, a mirror more than a creator of the common life. "What is understood by a republican government in the United States," Tocqueville comments, "is the slow and quiet action of society upon itself." [3]

The Democratic Situation

America is an illuminating case and not a realized blueprint of democratic development: a case uniquely valuable as the fully recorded experience of a people born to equality and tranquilly unfolding their endowment almost to its natural limits. The great democratic revolution in the Western world, extending over seven centuries, has thrown America into its vanguard to explore, within a special history and place, varieties

[3] *Ibid.,* I, 416.

upon a providential theme: equality. Tocqueville's general analysis of democracy represents an effort to define the common social situation created by equality, through which accident and choice must operate.

Every page of Tocqueville, beginning with the first sentence of the introduction, is an argument that equality of condition "is the fundamental fact from which all others seem to be derived"—at once the principle and the substance of the great social revolution.[4] Condition is, in this usage, the total social situation:

> Gradually the distinctions of rank are done away with; the barriers that once severed mankind are falling; property is divided, power is shared by many, the light of intelligence spreads, and the capacities of all classes tend towards equality. Society becomes democratic, and the empire of democracy is slowly and peaceably introduced to institutions and customs.[5]

The primary theoretical task for Tocqueville is to discover how equality, the primal active element, can constitute a social system, democracy.

In searching out the social design of democracy, Tocqueville confronts the possibility that equality does not create a community at all, but the negation of community. Radical equality is a solvent of bonds; of tradition, hierarchy, authority, and every joint articulating contemporaries and generations. Viewed strictly, from the elevation of an ideal aristocracy, democracy would seem a state of bedlam, a vast aberration, with system only in the mode of its departure from the norms of human association. Approaching democracy from above and behind, Tocqueville in America, one feels, could never quite subdue a sense of shock at what he saw: not a black void but a viable human condition with remarkable powers of expansion and persistence. It is as if a man removed the main supports of a massive structure and felt its terrible weight in his own hands; then withdrew and saw it still standing. Here I think Tocqueville's aristocratic values served him wonderfully, at first to find the essential contrast of the old and new condi-

---

[4] *Ibid.*, I, 3.
[5] *Ibid.*, I, 9.

tion; and then to force him to construct in theory a coherent order out of chaos.

In a dazzling passage Tocqueville sketches the primary response to leveled condition:

> Among democratic nations new families are constantly spring- ing up, others are constantly falling away, and all that remain change their condition; the woof of time is every instant broken and the track of generations effaced. Those who went before are soon forgotten; of those who will come after, no one has any idea: the interest of man is confined to those in close pro- pinquity to himself. As each class gradually approaches others and mingles with them, its members become undifferentiated and lose their class identity for each other. Aristocracy had made a chain of all the members of the community, from the peasant to the king; democracy breaks that chain and severs every link of it. . . .
>
> Thus not only does democracy make every man forget his ancestors, but it hides his descendants and separates his con- temporaries from him; it throws him back forever upon himself alone and threatens in the end to confine him entirely within the solitude of his own heart.[6]

This is the original democratic chaos—"individualism"— from which Tocqueville derives the essential pattern of the new order. Men set apart upon a social plain confront their strength and then their weakness. To think and act alone breeds boundless independence. To doubt or fail in indepen- dence out of common human insufficiency compels submis- sion to the only eminence equality permits, the equal brother- hood. The masterless of democratic times invent the only authority tolerable, even conceivable, in their condition: them- selves *en masse*.[7] In the absence of countervailing influence extraneous to the social structure, Tocqueville expects always to find democracy somewhere in the passage from an insup- portable liberty-in-isolation toward an abject dependence on the majority. This logic of development cannot be reversed; at most its consequences can be modified, and then only by un- derstanding the process, accepting its limits, and employing

[6] *Ibid.,* II, 99.
[7] *Ibid.,* I, 254–70; II, 8–12, 258–63, 316–21.

the peculiar means which it presents.[8] Thus the urgent call: "A new science of politics is needed for a new world."[9]

I do not wish to impose more rigor and completeness upon Tocqueville's ideal conception of the democratic situation than the author himself intended. The *Democracy* never pulls together a formal structure with all elements nicely integrated and all tendencies precisely specified. Perhaps it is misleading to apply the term "ideal type" to a broad characterization of a historical trend, used as a kind of wire master key for opening strange new things to view. At any rate my purpose here has been not to systematize Tocqueville's system, a major theoretical task in its own right, but to locate its central theme, as an aid to recognition of the democrat as American.

American Variations

The *Democracy* is so full of paradox that the casual reader is moved to suspect the author either of a muddled head or of a willful eccentricity. Man in his pride, portrayed in bold primaries, gives way to man reduced to a gray mass; then reappears; then disappears again. There is no simple formula in Tocqueville for composing the antagonistic figures; yet there are guides which bring the difference within the range of comprehension. The fundamental source of paradox lies in the double potentiality of the democratic situation: toward radical independence; toward submergence in the brotherhood. The most powerful and enduring tendency in "pure" democracy is the passage from the former toward the latter: toward a soft totalitarianism peopled by shapeless men. If all the counter-forces of accident and statecraft should converge, there could not be a second coming of the aristocratic virtues. Uniformity, conformity, mediocrity, and the rule of the felicific calculus are fixed returns of the equalitarian society.[10]

And yet, within the democratic range, variety remains significant: the independence unloosed by killing off the gods of

[8] *Ibid.*, I, 418; II, 287–96, 316–21.
[9] *Ibid.*, I, 7.
[10] *Ibid.*, I, 252–53; II, 332–34.

traditional society persists in varying degrees, in different spheres of social action, according to the reinforcements brought by history, place and the creative use of political means available to democratic leaders. Thus the American of the *Democracy* is the compound product of the universal democratic situation and a unique national experience. If the fundamental fact of American history has been the quiet unfolding of an equalitarian society [11]—the basic democratic situation—yet there are lesser facts which, in aggregate, weigh heavily upon the outcome. A historical beginning in the modern era, under conditions of substantial equality and middle-class homogeneity, has meant in Tocqueville's view not only the quick and thorough elaboration of a democratic society, but a unique deliverance from social revolution and its special consequences—notably, class hatred and a strengthened state. The English-Puritan heritage transplanted to America carried the most advanced democratic elements of the Old World, to shape the New exclusively along democratic lines; but further, the heritage brought special gifts which significantly altered the course of democratic development: especially, the values of individual liberty, local freedom, and morality grounded in religious belief.[12]

Historical influences count in giving American democracy a distinctive turn only as they are grounded in customs and institutions. Tocqueville credits America with several political inventions of critical importance for preserving its historical gifts; the most brilliant innovation, perhaps, is the design of the dual federal system, with a wide distribution of administrative functions. The constitutional separation of church and state, the guarantee of private rights, the assignment of important functions to the judiciary are further instances of a prudent statecraft, effecting the translation from historical possibility, through legal and institutional forms, into "habits of the heart" and mind which alter the consequences of the basic democratic situation.[13] And yet the greatest achievement of the American democracy in recasting its fate Tocqueville sees

[11] *Ibid.,* I, 46–54.
[12] *Ibid.,* I, 26–29, 30–35, 43–44, 62–67, 290–91; II, 6–7, 101, 243–44, 256.
[13] *Ibid.,* I, 244–47, 271–72, 280, 299, 300–314, 324–25.

as an unintended process, a fortunate result of choices made with other ends in view. Returning to the fundamental analysis of the leveled society, contrasted with a model aristocracy, Tocqueville recalls the essential feature of nonarticulation, of shapelessness—"individualism" when expressed in terms of members' responses. As a result of local freedom, the broad extension of political rights, and a bold commitment to almost unlimited civil liberty, the Americans have stumbled upon the chief expedient in democratic times for avoiding the new despotism: voluntary association. The leading virtue of political democracy in America turns out to be the capacity to penetrate the citizen's isolation, join his self-interest to a wider group, and educate him in the wonderworking skills of organization; thus to fill the void between the weak individual and the overbearing mass with a buzzing congeries of voluntary ("civil") associations. Ironically, the achievement of American politics has been to convert political into private affairs, to train men for private action.[14]

So history and art intervene to give variety to providence, and the look of paradox to Tocqueville's pages. The accidents of geography have less autonomous influence: Tocqueville anticipates some recent critics of Turner by asking why comparable conditions in South America, Canada, and the United States have yielded such unlike national careers; and finds the answers in decisive differences of law and above all custom, introduced by varying historical beginnings.[15] The gift of space, rich resources, and unmenaced borders has meant a free field for the fulfillment of the democratic revolution: specifically, a full provision for material equality; a wide margin for error; elbowroom for liberty.[16] In Tocqueville's phrase, "Nature herself favors the cause of the people." [17] The sheer abundance of natural endowment—"a field for human effort far more extensive than any sum of labor that can be applied to work it" [18]—sustains the recessive tendency in democracy,

[14] *Ibid.*, I, 191–98, 241–44, 248–52; II, 102–20.
[15] *Ibid.*, I, 319–23; see also pp. 316–17.
[16] *Ibid.*, I 288–98.
[17] *Ibid.*, I, 291.
[18] *Ibid.*, I, 297.

the tendency toward independence. In a sense, the American environment perpetuates the democratic state of nature, the world of liberated equal isolates, by promising fabulous rewards to brave spirits. Brave *economic* spirits, one should add, excited by the material rewards which loom so large in the city of equality; not independent minds and characters.

Venturous Conservative

Unique American conditions work selectively upon the basic democratic situation to give a mixed, even a paradoxical, aspect to American society, in Tocqueville's wide perspective. One might conclude simply that the double potentiality in democracy—toward independence, toward dependence—made possible a certain interesting and in some respects hopeful variety in American life, which Tocqueville rendered in alternating images of equalitarian freedom and servitude. This easy resolution would, however, cost us some of the most powerful historical insights in the *Democracy*. Primarily, we would miss Tocqueville's most ambitious and, I think, most productive contribution toward a concrete synthesis of American character; i.e., his recurrent attempt to identify a patterned response to the American situation, in both its typical democratic and its unique American features. The phrase "venturous conservative" is mine, and the assembled argument for using it as a central expression for the antithetic elements in American character is mine again, derived from scattered interpretations in the text suggestive of a common theme.

"They love change," Tocqueville's provocative formula for American democrats goes, "but they dread revolutions." [19] Thus:

> Two things are surprising in the United States: the mutability of the greater part of human actions, and the singular stability of certain principles. Men are in constant motion; the mind of man appears almost unmoved. . . . In the United States general principles in religion, philosophy, morality, and even politics do not vary, or at least are only modified by a hidden and often an

[19] *Ibid.*, II, 255.

imperceptible process; even the grossest prejudices are obliterated with incredible slowness amid the continual friction of men and things.[20]

In elucidating the distinction between change and revolution, in exploring the interplay of mutable actions and frozen principles, Tocqueville provides a brilliant lead for the understanding of Jacksonian Americans.

Speaking from his full elevation—the French aristocrat looking down upon a dull provincial show—Tocqueville sometimes, rarely, dismisses his own problem with a noble yawn. What does all the shuffling of possessions, laws, and notions amount to in the scale of dramatic high policy, philosophic heresy, great revolution?

It is true that they [democracies] are subject to great and frequent vicissitudes, but as the same events of good or adverse fortune are continually recurring, only the name of the actors is changed, the piece is always the same. The aspect of American society is animated because men and things are always changing, but it is monotonous because all these changes are alike.[21]

But sympathy and curiosity force Tocqueville beyond mere boredom: the spectacle suggests man's fate, all of reality which can reasonably be expected to appear; and therefore a thing to be understood internally. Indeed, I would argue that Tocqueville often, in unguarded moments, forgot that he was conceding the world reluctantly to the providential dictum of the lesser good for the greatest number; and that he gaped and marveled at the American miracle—the continuous social explosion which contained itself, and prospered mightily.

The ultimate sources of American character are found in that radical equality of condition which makes men masterless and separate. Everything seems possible, nothing certain, and life short: the American "clutches everything, he holds nothing fast, but soon loosens his grasp to pursue fresh gratifications." [22] As traders the Americans overwhelm their rivals with the audacity of French Revolutionary generals,[23] as workers they are never "more attached to one line of opera-

[20] *Ibid.*, II, 257.
[21] *Ibid.*, II, 228–29.
[22] *Ibid.*, II, 236.
[23] *Ibid.*, I 422–25.

tion than to another" and have "no rooted habits."[24] Commerce is "like a vast lottery."[25] Turner's famous sketches of a westering people are almost watery beside the restless image in the *Democracy,* of a "continuous removal of the human race" without parallel since "those irruptions which caused the fall of the Roman Empire."[26] Thus,

> It would be difficult to describe the avidity with which the American rushes forward to secure this immense booty that fortune offers. . . . Before him lies a boundless continent, and he urges onward as if time pressed and he was afraid of finding no room for his exertions. . . . They early broke the ties that bound them to their natal earth, and they have contracted no fresh ones on their way. Emigration was at first necessary to them; and it soon becomes a sort of game of chance, which they pursue for the emotions it excites as much as for the gain it procures.[27]

All this rootless, anxious, driving quality Tocqueville invests in a panoramic view of American careers:

> In the United States a man builds a house in which to spend his old age, and he sells it before the roof is on; he plants a garden and lets it just as the trees are coming into bearing; he brings a field into tillage and leaves other men to gather the crops; he embraces a profession and gives it up; he settles in a place, which he soon afterwards leaves to carry his changeable longings elsewhere. If his private affairs leave him any leisure, he instantly plunges into the vortex of politics; and if at the end of a year of unremitting labor he finds he has a few days' vacation, his eager curiosity whirls him over the vast extent of the United States, and he will travel fifteen hundred miles in a few days to shake off his happiness. Death at length overtakes him, but it is before he is weary of his bootless chase of that complete felicity which forever escapes him.[28]

So far the social basis of American character, equality of condition, has been treated in a generalized way, as the unstructured social environment playing into a rich and spacious physical environment, giving to American life the qualities of

[24] *Ibid.,* I, 425.
[25] *Ibid.,* II, 236.
[26] *Ibid.,* I, 293.
[27] *Ibid.,* I, 294–95.
[28] *Ibid.,* II, 136–37.

"a game of chance, a revolutionary crisis, or a battle," and shaping the American as "a man of singular warmth in his desires, enterprising, fond of adventure and, above all, of novelty." [29] It is equally clear that restlessness, anxiety, insatiability are permanently embedded in an enterprising nature: Tocqueville's venturous American is no more the heroic Renaissance individual than he is a flexible Poor Richard, deriving his actions from his balance sheet.

A grinding tension is inherent in that bold pursuit of a success which

> perpetually retires from before them, yet without hiding itself from their sight, and in retiring draws them on. At every moment they think they are about to grasp it; it escapes at every moment from their hold. They are near enough to see its charms, but too far off to enjoy them; and before they have fully tasted its delights, they die. . . .
>
> In democratic times enjoyments are more intense than in the ages of aristocracy, and the number of those who partake in them is vastly larger; but, on the other hand, it must be admitted that man's hopes and desires are oftener blasted, the soul is more striken and perturbed, and care itself more keen.[30]

In America Tocqueville saw "the freest and most enlightened men placed in the happiest circumstances that the world affords; it seemed to me as if a cloud habitually hung upon their brow, and I thought them serious and almost sad, even in their pleasures." [31] Indeed, so central was this worried quality in American experience that Tocqueville suspected life "would have no relish for them if they were delivered from the anxieties which harass them." [32]

Perhaps it is already evident how Tocqueville will discover tameness in the marrow of the tiger's bones. But the case will be clearer if first we trace the argument from condition to character along a more concrete line. All the previous references involve the pursuit of material success, the handling of material things. This is not, of course, accidental to Tocqueville's thesis. Most democratic energies, heightened by the ex-

[29] *Ibid.,* I, 426.
[30] *Ibid.,* II, 138–39.
[31] *Ibid.,* II, 136.
[32] *Ibid.,* II, 222.

traordinary flux and freedom of American life, are channeled into one outlet. The direct pursuit of rank, privilege, honor, power, intellectual distinction has an aristocratic taint; money and goods alone are legitimate counters for the social competition of dissociated equals. The existence of competition is a given democratic fact: human energies must go somewhere in a society which does not prescribe fixed places and goals, which makes everything possible. But its intensity and direction are best understood from the conception of a social order in which men see first themselves and then a mass of almost-equals.[33]

In Tocqueville's penetrating analysis:

> Whatever efforts a people may make, they will never succeed in reducing all the conditions of society to a perfect level. . . . However democratic, then, the social state and the political constitution of a people may be, it is certain that every member of the community will always find out several points about him which overlook his own position; and we may foresee that his looks will be doggedly fixed in that direction. When inequality of conditions is the common law of society, the most marked inequalities do not strike the eye; when everything is nearly on the same level, the slightest are marked enough to hurt it. Hence the desire of equality always becomes more insatiable in proportion as equality is more complete.[34]

Thus the intensity of democratic American striving. The direction, already partially explained, can now be given fuller definition. A major component of social equality in America is the narrowed spread of property differences, with a heavy concentration in the middle range: the typical figures are "eager and apprehensive men of small property."

> As they are still almost within the reach of poverty, they see its privations near at hand and dread them; between poverty and themselves there is nothing but a scanty fortune, upon which they immediately fix their apprehensions and their hopes.[35]

The case is very similar for the democratic rich and poor: "When . . . the distinctions of ranks are obliterated and privi-

[33] *Ibid.*, II, 128–30, 136–39, 154–57, 228–29, 244–47.
[34] *Ibid.*, II, 138.
[35] *Ibid.*, II, 253.

leges are destroyed, when hereditary property is subdivided and education and freedom are widely diffused, the desire of acquiring the comforts of the world haunts the imagination of the poor, and the dread of losing them that of the rich." [36] In total effect, then: "The love of well-being has now become the predominant taste of the nation; the great current of human passions runs in that channel and sweeps everything along in its course." [37]

With the urgent, worried striving for indefinite material success Tocqueville finds a marked propensity toward industrial and commercial callings; i.e., toward the most flexible pursuits which afford the quickest openings to large returns.[38] The seeming contradiction, in the heavy predominance of agricultural employment among Americans, Tocqueville resolves first by pointing to the rapid rate of growth in nonagricultural lines and then, more effectively, by attaching a special meaning to American farming.

> Almost all the farmers of the United States combine some trade with agriculture; most of them make agriculture itself a trade. It seldom happens that an American farmer settles for good upon the land which he occupies; especially in the districts of the Far [i.e., Middle] West, he brings land into tillage in order to sell it again, and not to farm it: he builds a farmhouse on the speculation that, as the state of the country will soon be changed by the increase of population, a good price may be obtained for it. . . . Thus the Americans carry their businesslike qualities into agriculture, and their trading passions are displayed in that as in their other pursuits.[39]

Tocqueville does not hesitate to accept one of the sweeping consequences of his argument: that America is essentially a one-dimensional society, with a single basic life style, a single character type. Equality of condition, American-style, defines a common social situation and enforces a common pattern of response (along the lines sketched above). Examining the possibility of sectional variation, Tocqueville concludes

---

[36] *Ibid.,* II, 129.
[37] *Ibid.,* II, 130.
[38] *Ibid.,* II, 154–57.
[39] *Ibid.,* II, 157.

that the American South alone has preserved a unique social universe, founded upon the glaring anomaly, within a democratic order, of Negro slavery, and even this difference must collapse eventually. The West is partially distinct in nature and effects, yet basically within the unitary pattern.[40] In a fascinating set of wilderness notes [41] (which some future editor of the *Democracy* should append to the text), Tocqueville wrote that he had indeed expected geography to count for more in America, and abandoned this among other "traveller's illusions" only in the face of strong evidence.

> In America, even more than in Europe, there is only one society. It may be either rich or poor, humble or brilliant, trading or agricultural; but it is composed everywhere of the same elements. The plane of a uniform civilization has passed over it. The man you left in New York you find again in almost impenetrable solitudes: same clothes, same attitude, same language, same habits, same pleasures. Nothing rustic, nothing naive, nothing which smells of the wilderness, nothing even resembling our [French] villages. . . . Those who inhabit these isolated places have arrived there since yesterday; they have come with the customs, the ideas, the needs of civilization. They only yield to savagery that which the imperious necessity of things exacts from them. . . .[42]

The most remarkable quality of the West, in short, is not its somewhat looser, rougher ways, but its capacity to reproduce almost from the moment of settlement the typical society and character of American democracy.[43]

At the center of this turbulence Tocqueville exposes—what he scarcely expected his French readers to credit—the soul of an arch-conservative: the steady citizen, the meek thinker, the pillar of property and propriety. To deal convincingly with such a strange compound he calls upon all his resources in history, politics, sociology, and psychology. His point is not to distinguish differences and place them sepa-

---

[40] *Ibid.*, I, 356–81, 392–95, 405.
[41] "Quinze jours au Désert," quoted in Pierson, *Tocqueville and Beaumont*, pp. 231–84.
[42] *Ibid.*, pp. 236–37.
[43] Tocqueville, *Democracy*, I, 290–92, 297, 316–17.

rately upon plausible grounds, but to reconstruct a dynamic whole, a venturous conservative.

The men of the middle, preponderant in democratic times and overwhelmingly so in America, are unquiet souls, whipped into motion by acquisitive hunger and then arrested by possessive fears.[44] When Tocqueville portrays such men as the "natural enemies of violent commotions," [45] he has in mind no inert lump of a dozing bourgeois but a nervous striver whose apprehensions mount with his success. The democratic competitor, shifting his efforts fluidly toward the quick opening to relative economic success (as the key to all felicity), finds himself in the midst of a universal competition of equals. With all the parts of his universe, himself included, in erratic motion, with no fixed terminus and no secure resting place, the democrat develops an acute awareness of loss and failure. He is never the contented success; rarely the jealous miser; and typically the unrelenting acquisitor, casting a nervous backward glance at what he has already gained.[46] The economic radical, in style of work, becomes the property-minded conservative: "between poverty and themselves there is nothing but a scanty fortune upon which they immediately fix their apprehensions and their hopes." [47]

In the basic democratic situation, the strenuous pursuit of private welfare means the draining of vital concern from alternative commitments, notably to ideas and politics. There is simply very little attention available for revolutionary agitation.[48] This analysis has only a limited application to America, however, where free, democratic political institutions infuse the habits of freedom into almost the entire population: [49] "but

[44] *Ibid.*, II, 128–30, 252–53.

[45] *Ibid.*, II, 252.

[46] *Ibid.*, II, 136–39, 154–57, 228–29, 244–48.

[47] *Ibid.*, II, 253. Even failure is not a clean-cut, ultimate catastrophe leading to emotional rejection of the economic system. The bankrupt has fallen in an equal competition, has a standing offer of new chances in new places, and so responds normally by renewing the struggle, abnormally by escaping into insanity, almost never by overt rebelliousness. (Tocqueville reports, as a common opinion, that American insanity rates are unusually high.) *Ibid.*, II, 139, 236.

[48] *Ibid.*, II, 253–55, 260.

[49] *Ibid.*, I, 249–52.

if an American were condemned to confine his activity to his own affairs, he would be robbed of one-half of his existence; he would feel an immense void in the life which he is accustomed to lead, and his wretchedness would be unbearable." [50] It is not, then, political apathy which tames the American; instead he shapes the quality of his political participation to correspond to and conserve his private-welfare interests.

> An American attends to his private concerns as if he were alone in the world, and the next minute he gives himself up to the common welfare as if he had forgotten them. At one time he seems animated by the most selfish cupidity; at another, by the most lively patriotism. The human heart cannot be thus divided. The inhabitants of the United States alternately display so strong and so similar a passion for their own welfare and for their freedom that it may be supposed that these passions are united and mingled in some part of their character. And indeed the Americans believe their freedom to be the best instrument and surest safeguard of their welfare; they are attached to the one by the other. They by no means think that they are not called upon to take a part in public affairs; they believe, on the contrary, that their chief business is to secure for themselves a government which will allow them to acquire the things they covet and which will not debar them from the peaceful enjoyment of those possessions which they have already acquired. [51]

With such passionate devotion to the gains he has and seeks, the venturous American creates within himself a counterforce to his furious energies: "They love change but they dread revolutions." [52] Under a regime of almost unlimited political and civil liberty, the American democrat is perhaps the safest citizen in the world. Yet this is not the full measure of American conservatism: "amid the continual friction of men and things," Tocqueville observes, "the mind of man appears almost unmoved." [53] Here his classic analysis of equalitarian conformity, scarcely modified by anything unique to the American situation, records the suicide of individuality unbounded. If elsewhere Tocqueville emphasizes the "wide verge" of the

[50] *Ibid.*, I, 250.
[51] *Ibid.*, II, 142.
[52] *Ibid.*, II, 255.
[53] *Ibid.*, II, 257.

"fatal circle" defined by a democratic social condition, it now becomes clear that accident and choice are critically significant only in one direction: the avoidance of political despotism (the total domination of "an immense and tutelary power"), mainly be releasing and focusing vast stores of private energy for the nonpolitical accomplishment of social tasks. Against the natural tendency of democracy to press minds into a dead uniformity Tocqueville's "new science of politics" uncovers no deep-rooted, durable restraints.[54]

The leveling of society, especially when accomplished by violent revolutionary means, initially unhinges all authority relations. But the shock of leveled liberty puts an insupportable strain upon the democrat:[55] "A principle of authority must then always occur, under all circumstances, in some part or other of the moral and intellectual world."[56] The location is determined by the basic democratic situation:

> When the inhabitant of a democratic country compares himself individually with all those about him, he feels with pride that he is the equal of any one of them but when he comes to survey the totality of his fellows and to place himself in contrast with so huge a body, he is instantly overwhelmed by the sense of his own insignificance and weakness. The same equality that renders him independent of each of his fellow citizens, taken severally, exposes him alone and unprotected to the influence of the greater number. The public, therefore, among a democratic people, has a singular power, which aristocratic nations cannot conceive; for it does not persuade others to its beliefs, but it imposes them and makes them permeate the thinking of everyone by a sort of enormous pressure of the mind of all upon the individual intelligence.[57]

Thus democrats—and Americans—turn toward public opinion as their source of moral and intellectual authority.[58] That a pervasive public opinion should exist in democratic society to assume the functions of authority, is understood by Tocqueville as a simple consequence of equality:

[54] *Ibid.*, II, 318, 332–33.
[55] *Ibid.*, II, 3–12.
[56] *Ibid.*, II, 9.
[57] *Ibid.*, II, 10.
[58] *Ibid.*, I, 263–65.

Men who are equal in rights, in education, in fortune, or, to comprise all in one word, in their social condition, have necessarily wants, habits, and tastes that are hardly dissimilar. As they look at objects under the same aspect, their minds naturally tend to similar conclusions; and though each of them may deviate from his contemporaries and form opinions of his own, they will involuntarily and unconsciously concur in a certain number of received opinions. . . . The leading opinions of men become similar in proportion as their conditions assimilate: such appears to me to be the general and permanent law; the rest is casual and transient.[59]

The democratic heretic who seeks a public hearing must speak at once to all: he has a legal permit, but no social platform—no claim to the attention of a busily preoccupied crowd, no initial concession of confidence in private intellectual authority to build upon.[60] "He strains himself to rouse the indifferent and distracted multitude and finds at last that he is reduced to impotence, not because he is conquered, but because he is alone." [61]

Summary

The image of the democrat as American which I have assembled from Tocqueville's pages represents a most ambitious attempt to derive from the basic social situation of democracy (with local variations) a characteristic pattern of psychological response manifested broadly in the culture and life style of Jacksonian Americans. Certainly the boldest and possibly the most revealing feature of the portrait is the joining in dynamic tension, of two major tendencies—toward independence, toward dependence. Tocqueville discovers the antithetic trends in the basic democratic situation, finds them in varying relations through every aspect of American life, and sees them exposed again in that duality of character which I have summed up in the phrase "venturous conservative." Con-

[59] *Ibid.,* II, 258. See also *ibid.,* I 303–7; II, 6, 10–11, 26–28, on the conservative reinforcement provided by religion, adapted to democratic circumstance and accepted "as a commonly received opinion."
[60] *Ibid.,* II, 258–63.
[61] *Ibid.,* II, 255.

densing drastically, I would suggest that Tocqueville sees the process shaping the venturous conservative in two related ways. A comprehensive social equality is the common point of departure. Along one line: a world of almost-equals creates an anxious, urgent, flexible seeker of the next, most precious, most elusive increment of wealth and status; a seeker who, out of fear for his possessions and hope for his opportunities, becomes a firm conservative on property matters; and one who, from the depth of his material preoccupations, has little concern for radical revaluations of his moral universe. Along the second line: the masterless man, free to invent a fresh world, finds all the important value answers (and many petty ones) given in familiar, comfortable form by his own self-image magnified to authoritative dimensions—by the majority. In this direction little adventure survives; only a sort of surface confusion masking a congealed mass of values.

Tocqueville's venturous conservative is a historical type, perceived in wide focus. The portrait is built out of Jacksonian materials, but composed primarily to elucidate the enduring family traits of the democrat, with special reference to the American branch. As Tocqueville abstracted the democratic type from his Jacksonian observations, so I think one can profitably reverse the process, reviewing Jacksonian times in the light of Tocqueville's synthesis. His image of the venturous conservative pervades much of my discussion of the Jacksonian persuasion. Tocqueville does not himself make the connection between social situation, typical response, and the specific content of the Jacksonian political appeal; yet it seems to me a highly plausible association. The American who was involved in the continuous re-creation of his social world, the continuous relocation of his place within it, became the anxious witness of his own audacity. The consequence, Tocqueville suggests, was the renewal of frenetic activity and, at the same time, a powerful attachment to property and order. A further response is evidenced, I would propose, in the effectiveness of the Jacksonian political appeal: to hard money, personal enterprise and credit, rural simplicity, and, broadly, to the pristine values of the Old Republic.

IV
POLARITY
IN AMERICAN POLITICS
AND FOREIGN POLICY

THE FEDERALIST—
A SPLIT PERSONALITY

Alpheus Thomas Mason[*]

In his address of September 27, 1836, John Quincy Adams suggested that the line of demarcation separating the political thought of Madison from that of his collaborator, Hamilton, was easily discernible in the *Federalist* papers. "In examining closely the points selected by these great co-operators to a common cause and their course of argument for its support," Adams observed, "it is not difficult to perceive that diversity of genius and character which afterwards separated them so widely from each other on questions of public interest, affecting the construction of the Constitution which they so ably de-

[*] In preparing this article for publication, I have had the assistance of Gordon E. Baker and Joseph G. La Palombara.

Source: Alpheus Thomas Mason, "The Federalist—A Split Personality," *American Historical Review* 57 (April 1952): 625–43. Reprinted by permission of the author and publisher.

Alpheus Thomas Mason (1899–   ) is McCormick Professor of Jurisprudence, emeritus, at Princeton University. He was educated at Dickinson College and at Princeton where he taught from 1925 until his retirement. He is the author of *Organized Labor and the Law* (1925), *Brandeis: Lawyer and Judge in the Modern State* (1933), *The Brandeis Way: A Case Study in the Workings of Democracy* (1938), *Bureaucracy Convicts Itself: The Ballinger-Pinchot Controversy of 1910* (1941), *Brandeis: A Free Man's Life* (1946), *The Supreme Court: Vehicle of Revealed Truth or Power Group, 1930–1937* (1953), *Security Through Freedom: American Political Thought and Practice* (1955), *Harlan Fiske Stone: Pillar of the Law* (1956), *The Supreme Court from Taft to Warren* (1958), *The Supreme Court in a Free Society* (1959), *The Supreme Court: Palladium of Freedom* (1962), and *William Howard Taft: Chief Justice* (1965).

fended, and so strenuously urged their country to adopt."[1]

But was this "diversity" as distinct as Adams would lead one to believe? Six years earlier, John Mercer viewed the *Federalist* in a somewhat different light, insisting that

> He who studies it with attention, will perceive that it is not only argumentative, but that it addresses different arguments to different classes of the American public, in the spirit of an able and skillful disputant before a mixed assembly. Thus from different numbers of this work, and sometimes from the same numbers, may be derived authorities for opposite principles and opinions. For example, nothing is easier to demonstrate by the numbers of *Publius* than that the government . . . is, or is not a National Government; that the State Legislatures may arraign at their respective bars, the conduct of the Federal Government or that no state has any such power.[2]

Measured by the trouble editors and scholars have experienced in sorting out and identifying internal evidence of authorship of the eighty-five essays, Mercer's comment would appear to be more discerning than Adams'. Scholars are still not sure about the authorship of certain numbers.[3]

Apparently Madison's philosophy had not been precisely understood by Hamilton himself. In any event, the latter was taken aback in 1792 when Madison began "cooperating with Mr. Jefferson . . . at the head of a faction decidedly hostile to me [Hamilton] . . . and actuated by views . . . subversive to

---

[1] John Quincy Adams, *An Eulogy on the Life and Character of James Madison* (Boston, 1836), pp. 31–32. See also *The Writings of James Madison,* ed. Gaillard Hunt (New York, 1900–10), V, 55.

[2] *Proceedings and Debates of the Virginia State Convention of 1829–1830* (Richmond, 1830), p. 187.

[3] "There is still some doubt," Benjamin F. Wright observes in a recent article, "concerning the authorship of from six to twelve of the eighty-five essays." "The Federalist on the Nature of Man," *Ethics,* LIX (January, 1949), 3. See also Max Beloff, ed., *The Federalist, or the New Constitution . . .* (Oxford and New York, 1948), who, in this painstaking edition, continued the practice of labeling certain "disputed" numbers "Hamilton and/or Madison." Apparently the only recent edition of this classic which makes unqualified identification of authorship is that of Carl Van Doren, ed., *The Federalist* (New York, 1945). All quotations from the *Federalist* included herein are taken from this edition.

the principles of good government and dangerous to the Union, peace, and happiness of the country." [4] Hamilton insisted that he "knew of a certainty, it was a primary article in his [Madison's] creed, that the real danger in our system was the subversion of the national authority by the preponderancy of the State governments." [5] This not unwarranted assumption helps to explain why the arch Federalist was surprised and chagrined after 1790 to find Madison high "among those who are disposed to narrow the federal authority." [6] Besides Madison's invaluable assistance with the *Federalist,* Hamilton may have been thinking of an earlier collaboration in the Continental Congress where the two men provided the leadership for those legislators who were sensitive to basic defects in the Articles of Confederation and bent on achieving strong federal union.

[4] Alexander Hamilton to Edward Carrington, May 26, 1792, *The Works of Alexander Hamilton,* ed. Henry Cabot Lodge (New York, 1904), IX, 513.

[5] *Ibid.,* For evidence of Hamilton's confidence, see Madison's preconvention essay, "The Vices of the Political System of the United States," April, 1787, *The Writings of James Madison,* ed. Gaillard Hunt (New York, 1900–10), II, 361. In a letter to Jefferson prior to the Constitutional Convention, Madison contended that the weaknesses of the Articles of Confederation could best be rectified by providing "the federal head with a negative in all cases whatsoever on the local legislatures." *Letters and Other Writings of James Madison,* published by order of Congress (4 vols., Philadelphia, 1865), I, 285. In reply Jefferson said: *"Prima facie* I do not like it. It fails in an essential character that the hole and the patch should be commensurate." Jefferson to Madison, June 20, 1787, *The Writings of Thomas Jefferson,* ed. Paul Leicester Ford (New York, 1892–99), IV, 390–91. Later, in *Federalist* no. 45, Madison reaffirmed his fear of the centrifugal tendencies of state legislatures: "The more I resolve the subject, the more fully I am persuaded that the balance is much more likely to be disturbed by the preponderancy of the last [state governments] than of the first scale."

[6] Alexander Hamilton to Edward Carrington, *Works of Alexander Hamilton,* IX, 513. Henry Jones Ford, in his sympathetic biography of Hamilton, asserts that it was generally assumed at the time of the Constitutional Convention that Hamilton and Madison were philosophical bedmates: "Nobody," Ford observes, "then thought there was any important difference between Madison and Hamilton in their political principles. They were then working in close accord." *Alexander Hamilton* (New York, 1920), p. 198. The same view was held by another student of Madison, J. Mark Jacobson: "While he later became a follower of Jefferson, at this time he was an ardent nationalist and conservative." *The Development of American Political Thought* (New York, 1932), p. 171.

In 1783 Madison had even disregarded specific instructions from Virginia and presented a set of resolutions firmly endorsing the federal import duties, previously passed by Congress and opposed by the states.[7]

As late as October 12, 1789, Hamilton apparently felt that Madison was firmly on his side. In a letter to his former collaborator Hamilton asked the Virginian to forward in writing his suggestions for the best methods of increasing the federal revenue and of modifying the structure of the public debt in the interest of both public and creditors.[8] Further evidence of Hamilton's confident expectation of Madison's support is the pleasure he expressed on learning that Madison had been elected to the House of Representatives. Hamilton's faith that Madison would join him in pressing forward his nationalist program was not shaken, as his letter to Colonel Carrington shows, until some time after the Virginian had become an articulate member of the opposition in Congress.[9]

Hamilton's mistaken assumptions, as well as the uncertainty of scholars regarding the diverging political creeds of Hamilton and Madison, lay partly in the fact that, in the struggle over ratification, strategic considerations drove the contestants on both sides to minimize and to exaggerate. To quiet the fears of opponents, advocates of ratification said things which, in later years, proved embarrassing to themselves and misleading to scholars. On the other hand, certain of the Constitution's enemies turned alarmist, portraying the proposed national charter in the most extreme terms. This strategy obscured positions on all sides and made the Constitution's meaning less than crystal clear.

[7] See Adrienne Koch, *Jefferson and Madison: The Great Collaboration* (New York, 1950), pp. 8–9. At this time Madison felt extremely confident of Jefferson's support. He assumed that the latter would work diligently in the Virginia legislature to promote enlargement of national power.

[8] *Works of Alexander Hamilton*, IX, 462–63. It may be significant that this letter, one of several which Hamilton wrote to his former colleague during this period, was apparently never answered.

[9] Ford, *Hamilton*, pp. 211–212. From an analysis of the earlier co-operation between the two men, Ford draws the wholly unwarranted conclusion that Madison's antagonism toward Hamilton was not rooted in basic principles but stemmed primarily from regional political rivalry.

The Constitution itself was neither altogether satisfactory, nor free from ambiguity. To friends of "firm union" and energetic government, like Hamilton, it was bitterly disappointing; to defenders of the "sovereign" states, it made for a "consolidated" system, an "aristocratic" government calculated to be as obnoxious as that which the colonists had thrown off in 1776.[10] Jefferson's position is distinguishable from that of both Federalists and anti-Federalists. Particular provisions of the document impressed him less than the Constitution as a gratifying demonstration of the power of reason to bring varying interests and divergent views into constructive accord. Jefferson cited the new instrument as a glorious-example of "changing a constitution, by assembling the wise men of the State, instead of assemblying armies. . . ."[11] "I am captivated," he wrote James Madison, December 20, 1787, "by the compromise of the opposite claims of the great and little States, of the last to equal, and the former to proportional influence."[12]

[10] See my article, "The Nature of Our Federal Union Reconsidered," *Political Science Quarterly*, LXV (December, 1950), 503, 510.

[11] Jefferson to David Humphreys, Mar. 18, 1789, *Memoir, Correspondence, and Miscellanies from the Papers of Thomas Jefferson,* ed. Thomas Jefferson Randolph (Boston and New York, 1830), II, 449. Jefferson apparently never felt, as did Hamilton and other nationalists, that after 1783, the really crucial need was "firm Union." Far from considering Union, as did Hamilton, of "utmost moment to the peace and liberty of the States," he regarded "the State governments" as "the true barriers of liberty in this country." In explaining Jefferson's failure to appreciate the need for strong union growing out of the weaknesses of the Articles of Confederation, Hamilton observed that Jefferson "left the country before we had experienced the imbecilities of the former." Hamilton to Carrington, May 26, 1792, *Works of Alexander Hamilton,* IX, 513. And, in pointing out a fundamental difference between Madison and Jefferson on this point, Adrienne Koch, pp. 44–45, indicates that Madison had witnessed rash acts of state legislatures, driving him to support the move for a strengthened general government. At this same time, Jefferson was in France watching powerful "wolves" in Europe devour the "sheep"—the people. In justice to Jefferson it should be pointed out that he did give consideration to strong union; indeed, he was a staunch advocate of union, but the ingredients he envisaged as contributing to its achievement were far different from those of Hamilton. See in this connection, Julian P. Boyd, "Thomas Jefferson's 'Empire of Liberty,'" *Virginia Quarterly Review*, XXIV (Autumn, 1948), 538–54.

[12] *Writings of Jefferson,* ed. Ford, II, 274.

But was not the accommodation Jefferson saw, or thought he saw, reflected in the Constitution more apparent than real? Do not Hamilton and Madison display a sharp theoretical split while at the same time making concessions to views they could not honestly support, and in language so equivocal as to disguise the Constitution's true import? Obviously the Constitution did not draw the boundary lines between general government and the states, nor "define" the powers of Congress, nor indicate the source of such powers, with enough distinctness to escape bitter disagreement, protracted controversy, and finally civil war. But, did not the *Federalist,* instead of elucidating and clarifying the points of contention within the fundamental law, actually gloss these over and thereby add to the confusion? This paper may help to answer these questions.

Though first public reaction to the proposed Constitution was favorable in most states, strong and dangerous opposition soon asserted itself. In scores of pamphlets and speeches its critics—notably Elbridge Gerry in Massachusetts, Luther Martin in Maryland, George Mason and Richard Henry Lee in Virginia, Robert Yates and John Lansing in New York—began an unorganized but effective opposition.[13] This lack of organization, however, did not prevent them from agreeing that the Constitution established a most objectionable "system of consolidated government." In the vital state of New York, Governor Clinton's stubborn fight frightened friends and supporters of ratification, and with good reason. For even if enough states ratified (which seemed not unlikely), it was recognized on all hands that any system omitting New York State would be analagous to *Hamlet* without Hamlet.

It was this crucial situation in New York that prompted Hamilton to plan the now famous *Federalist* papers as ammu-

[13] See, for example, Luther Martin, "The Genuine Information," in Max Farrand, ed., *The Records of the Federal Convention of 1787* (New Haven, 1911), III, 172 ff.; Elbridge Gerry, "Observations on the New Constitution and on the Federal and State Conventions," in Paul L. Ford, ed., *Pamphlets on the Constitution of the United States* (Brooklyn, 1888), pp. 8–14; Richard Henry Lee, "Letters from the Federal Farmer to the Republican," *ibid.,* p. 282; Robert Yates and John Lansing, "To the Governor of New York Containing their Reasons for not Subscribing to the Federal Constitution," *Senate Documents,* 60 Congress, 2 Session, Dec. 7, 1908–Mar. 4, 1909, p. 191.

nition for use there and in other states. That the essays literally constituted a debaters' handbook for Federalist delegates in the ratifying conventions of several states is an indication of the persuasiveness in these papers, if not the clarity of the arguments they contain.

In this enterprise—propaganda we might call it today—Hamilton joined with him John Jay, seasoned diplomat and expert in foreign affairs, and James Madison, Father of the Constitution. Jay was a key participant because of his extensive experience in and knowledge of external relations. Madison was indispensable not only because he was "the best informed Man of any point in debate" [14] but also because, as the convention's semiofficial note-taker, he had gained unrivaled command of its proceedings.

These papers were published anonymously under the pseudonym "Publius," and for many years following 1787 neither Hamilton nor Madison, for political reasons, was disposed to take the public into his confidence. During the writing of the essays they took special pains to guard the secrecy of authorship. When the two men corresponded with each other on matters concerning the papers, they frequently spoke of "Publius" as a third person, at times going so far in this deception as to speculate about the possible authorship of the essays.[15]

An interesting aspect of this period of "silence" has to do with Madison's relationship to Jefferson. The two friends had carried on a regular correspondence while the papers were in preparation, yet Madison, apparently, never divulged his share in the Federalist until a two-volume edition of the work had been in circulation for over two months. Madison, it is true, referred to the progress being made in the struggle over ratification but never alluded to the essays of "Publius" that figured so significantly in that contest. When, finally, Madison did take

[14] "Notes of Major William Pierce on the Federal Convention of 1787," American Historical Review, III (January, 1898), 331.

[15] In a letter to Madison, written as the task was drawing to a close, Hamilton remarked: "I send you the Federalist from the beginning to the conclusion of the commentary on the Executive Branch. If our suspicions of the author be right, he must be too much engaged to make a rapid progress of what remains." Hamilton to Madison, Apr. 3, 1788, Works of Alexander Hamilton, IX, 427. See also ibid., p. 431.

his friend into his confidence, he did so almost as an after-thought in a letter primarily concerned with other matters.

> Col. Carrington tells me [he] has sent you the first volume of the *Federalist,* and adds the 2d by this conveyance. I believe I never have yet mentioned to you that publication. It was under-taken last fall by Jay, Hamilton, and myself. The proposal came from the two former. The execution was thrown, by the sick-ness of Jay, mostly on the two others. Though carried on in concert, the writers are not mutually answerable for all the sides of each other, there being seldom time for even a perusal of the pieces by any but the writer before they were wanted at the press, and sometimes hardly by the writer himself.[16]

Adrienne Koch suggests that Madison was probably un-easy about revealing to Jefferson the nature of this collabora-tion with Hamilton. The Republican struggle against the New Yorker had not yet flared openly, but "Madison knew the tenor of Hamilton's contempt for democracy and democratic republicanism." [17] And Madison went out of his way, as his let-ter to Jefferson makes clear, to point out that the authors were not "mutually answerable" for the other's arguments. Nor was Madison's silence due wholly to the desire to keep his author-ship absolutely unknown, since he had strongly intimated his part in the essays to General Washington shortly after the pro-ject was begun and nine months before the "confession" to Jefferson.[18]

If Jefferson was surprised or chagrined at Madison's co-operation with Hamilton, he did not clearly divulge his feelings in reply: "With respect to the *Federalist,* the three authors had been named to me. I read it with care, pleasure and improve-ment, and was satisfied that there was nothing in it by one of those hands, and not a great deal by a second. It does the highest honor to the third, as being, in my opinion, the best commentary on the principles of government which ever was written." In addition to perceiving this distinction of talent and

[16] Madison to Jefferson, Aug. 10, 1788, *Writings of James Madison,* ed. Hunt, V, 246.

[17] Koch, p. 52.

[18] Madison to Washington, Nov. 18, 1787, *Writings of James Madison,* ed. Hunt, V, 55.

genius, all in Madison's favor, Jefferson evidently saw clearly, as did John Mercer, the concessions which Madison made to opposite viewpoints: "In some parts it is discoverable that the author means only to say what may be best said in defense of opinions in which he did not concur." [19]

So successful were the major authors of the *Federalist* in keeping their secret that one careful student has concluded that throughout the period in which the papers were written there were not more than a dozen individuals who could identify the three authors.[20] But two days before his fatal duel with Aaron Burr, Hamilton went to the law office of a friend, Egbert Bensen, and "ostentatiously" concealed in the lawyer's bookcase a slip listing what was presumably an accurate accounting of the authorship of various numbers. As was not unusual under the circumstances, Hamilton claimed numbers he did not write. In 1818, Madison counterattacked, being prepared to state under oath that he had written twenty-nine of the essays instead of the fourteen accredited to him by Hamilton. Because of this conflict of claims, editors of the *Federalist* have been wont to elude the issue, using the "and/or" formula for the "disputed" numbers. This is no longer necessary. Professor Douglass Adair makes it clear that of the eighty-five essays, Jay wrote only five (numbers 2-5 inclusive and 64); Hamilton did numbers I, 6-9, 11-13, 15-17, 21-36, 59-61, and 65-85 inclusive. Numbers 18, 19, and 20 appear to have been the result of the combined effort of Hamilton and Madison.[21] The remaining numbers were written by Madison, making the authenticated tally Hamilton 51, Madison 26.

In a joint literary endeavor of such dimensions, done under great pressure, a distribution of labor was as necessary

[19] Jefferson to Madison, Nov. 18, 1788, *Writings of Thomas Jefferson,* ed. Ford, V, 433–34.

[20] Douglass Adair, "The Authorship of the Disputed Federalist Papers," *William and Mary Quarterly,* 3d Ser., I (April and July, 1944).

[21] However, Carl Van Doren, *The Federalist,* p. vi, asserts: "As to 18, 19, 20 . . . both Madison's manuscripts and his statement make it clear that, while Hamilton did turn over some notes on historic confederacies to Madison, it was Madison who wrote the three essays and sent them to the printer." On the basis of this editor's findings, Madison would be accredited with twenty-nine of the essays.

as it was natural. It was reasonable, too, that the division made should represent the special interests of the authors. Hamilton had diagnosed "the fundamental defect" in the Articles of Confederation as early as 1780: "want of power in Congress." "The first step must be," he said, "to give Congress powers competent to the public exigencies." [22] As to the state constitutions he was less categorical: "Perhaps the evil is not very great . . . for, not withstanding their imperfections . . . they seem to have, in themselves . . . the seeds of improvement." [23] But later, in Philadelphia, behind closed doors, he urged the necessity of "a general government completely sovereign," the annihilation of "State distinctions and State operations, . . . State governments reduced to corporations with very limited powers." [24]

Madison, on the other hand, though not ignoring the need for more power in Congress, had pointed especially to troubles growing out of flagrant abuses in state legislatures, especially the subversive effect of laws affecting vested rights of property and contract. He had dealt with these inadequacies at length in his preconvention essay, "The Vices of the Political System of the United States." [25] These evils were still in the forefront of his mind at Philadelphia when, on June 6, he queried Roger Sherman's statement of "the objects of Union" as primarily "defense against foreign danger," "treaties with foreign nations," "regulating foreign commerce and drawing revenue from it," etc. All these objects were important, Madison agreed, but he "combined with them the necessity of providing more effectually for the securing of private rights, and the steady dispensation of justice." "Interferences with these," he maintained, "were evils which had, more perhaps than anything else, produced this convention." [26] Madison reinforced his convictions on June 26; [27] he gave the same ideas full-dress treatment in the *Federalist,* numbers 10 and

[22] *Works of Alexander Hamilton,* I, 213, 223.

[23] *Ibid.,* I, 247.

[24] Farrand, ed., *Records of the Federal Convention of 1787,* 1, 287, 323.

[25] See n. 5 above.

[26] Farrand, I, 131, 134.

[27] *Ibid.,* I, 421–23, 430–32. Madison reiterated this basic argument in the Virginia Constitutional Convention of 1829–30. *Proc. and Debates . . . Virginia State Convention of 1829–30,* pp. 538, 574.

51. For him an important object of the Constitution was to limit state legislative power. Article I, Section 10, was therefore among its most important provisions. For Hamilton, on the other hand, the new Constitution was chiefly significant as a grant of power. The heart of it was the congressional authority enumerated in Article 1, Section 8, paragraphs 1 to 18 inclusive, and in the supremacy clause, Article VI, paragraph 2.

That Hamilton and Madison co-operated effectively in this joint enterprise is a matter of history. One reason is that there were between them certain important areas of agreement. Both men entertained an extremely pessimistic view of human nature.[28] Government is necessary, they agreed, because men are not angels. "What is government itself," Madison queried in essay 51, "but the greatest of all reflections on human nature?" "Why has government been instituted at all?" Hamilton asked in essay 15. "Because the passions of men will not conform to the dictates of reason and justice, without constraint." This distrustful refrain (with exceptions to be hereafter noted) runs indistinguishable throughout the various numbers of the *Federalist.*

Human beings are seen as "timid and cautious" (no. 49). The essays stress the "caprice and wickedness of man" (no. 57), the "depravity of human nature," "the folly and wickedness of Mankind" (no. 78). In Madison's essays, no less than in Hamilton's one notes the conviction that "men are ambitious, vindictive, and rapacious," that "momentary passions and immediate interests" (no. 6), "the infirmities and depravities of the human character" (no. 37), rather than "considerations of policy, utility, or justice" (no. 6), are dominant drives in politics. Here, at least, one supposes, is an element or factor that can be regarded as constant, giving politics whatever scientific criteria it may possess. The authors of the *Federalist,* like Montesquieu, the oracle to whom both Hamilton and Madison paid great deference, were convinced that "virtue itself has need of limits." [29]

Nor did the *Federalist* collaborators look forward, eventu-

[28] For a detailed discussion of this thesis, see B. F. Wright, "The Federalist on the Nature of Man" (see n. 3 above).

[29] Montesquieu, *The Spirit of the Laws,* trans. from the French by T. Nugent (4th ed., 1766), I, book II, p. 220.

ally, as did Karl Marx in 1848, to some earthly paradise, emerging either from changed economic and social environment or spiritual regeneration. "Have we not already seen enough," Hamilton observed with disdain, "of the fallacy and extravagance of those idle theories which have amused us with promises of an exemption from the imperfections, weaknesses, and evils incident to society in every shape? Is it not time to awake from the deceitful dream of a golden age, and to adopt as a practical maxim for the direction of our political conduct that we, as well as the other inhabitants of the globe, are yet remote from the happy empire of perfect wisdom and perfect virtue?" (no. 6). Human nature being what it is, man must employ his feeble contrivance of reason in building institutional fences around unconquerable human avarice and greed.

Hamilton and Madison also agreed that the Articles of Confederation were inadequate to cope with "the variety of controversies" which grow out of the "caprice and wickedness of man" (no. 57). Hamilton called the Articles of Confederation "an odious engine of government," so "radically vicious and unsound, as to admit not of amendment but by entire change in its leading feature" (no. 16). Madison's language was somewhat less drastic, and his stand less unequivocal, as we shall see, but he concurred in holding that the Articles were based on "principles which are fallacious; that we most consequently change this first foundation, and with it the superstructure resting on it" (no. 37).

Finally, Hamilton and Madison agreed that in a free society, "inequality of property" is inevitable. For them it was axiomatic that "inequality will exist as long as liberty existed," and the primary task of government is to protect "liberty," i.e., "the different and unequal faculties of acquiring property," from which the different degrees and kinds of property immediately result." [30] Growing out of these inevitable inequalities,

[30] Madison, in *Federalist* no. 10. "It was certainly true," Hamilton remarked on the floor of the Philadelphia Convention, June 26, 1787, "that nothing like an equality of property existed: that an inequality would exist as long as liberty existed, and that it would unavoidably result from that very liberty itself. This inequality of property constituted the great and fundamental distinction in Society." Farrand, I, 424.

both men envisaged society as torn by strife and struggle, the major manifestation of discord being identified as "factions."

These points of agreement should not, however, blind us to divergences so great as to prompt Professor Adair to speak of America's illustrious political classic as afflicted with a "split personality." At what points can this charge be documented?

Generally speaking, both men addressed themselves to the problem of finding a "republican" remedy for the evil to which popular government is peculiarly addicted. Madison described the disease as "faction." An ineradicable malady, the "factious spirit" will exist "as long as the reason of man continues fallible, and he is at liberty to exercise it." This phenomenon is present whenever "a number of citizens, whether amounting to a majority or a minority of the whole [is] united and actuated by some common impulse of passion, or of interest adverse to the rights of other citizens or to the permanent and aggregate interests of the community" (no. 10).

Madison is especially concerned with "factions" having "the superior force of an interested and overbearing majority," and therefore capable of sacrificing to "its ruling passion or interest both the public good and the rights of other citizens." A minority faction may, he admits, "clog the administration" or "convulse the society," but he concludes, too easily perhaps, that the Republican principle will enable "the majority to defeat its sinister views by regular vote" (no. 10). In the preconvention essay, mentioned above, Madison had gone so far as to say that a luxuriance of "vicious legislation" had brought "into question the fundamental principle of republican Government, that the majority who rule in such governments are the safest Guardians both of the public Good and private rights." [31]

The "latent causes of faction are thus sown in the nature of man," Madison observed in essay 10. They are "everywhere brought into different degrees of activity according to the different circumstances of civil society. A zeal for different opinions concerning religion, concerning government, and many other points, as well of speculation as of practice; an attachment to different leaders ambitiously contending for pre-emi-

[31] *Writings of James Madison,* ed. Hunt, II, 366.

nence and power; or to persons of other descriptions whose fortunes have been interesting to the human passions, have, in turn, divided mankind into parties, inflamed them with mutual animosity." Madison saw "the most frivolous and fanciful distinctions" exciting the "most violent conflicts." "Property" was "the most common and durable source of factions," not, as Harold Laski "quotes" him as saying, "the only" foundation.[32]

For this many-faceted evil there was no easy remedy. Pure democracy was no cure because it is "incompatible with personal security or the rights of property." Two other possible remedies suggested themselves, but these were also rejected. One would destroy liberty and create in the community a will "independent of the majority," as in monarchy; the other would give all citizens the same interests, the same passions, the same opinion, as in, say, communism (no. 51). Neither of these authoritarian correctives was acceptable: the first was unthinkable, the second impracticable.

"A Republic," "a well-constructed union," opened for Madison "a different prospect," for it comprehends society in many descriptions of parties, sects, interests, thus making an unjust combination of the whole very improbable, if not impossible. Madison's thesis is that the evil of factions and the social chaos which they breed could be ameliorated, consistently with republican principles, by establishing a limited federal government, by a system of indirect election "to refine and enlarge the public views, by passing them through the medium of a chosen body of citizens, whose wisdom may best discern the true interest of their country, and whose patriotism and love of justice will be least likely to sacrifice it to temporary or partial considerations." Far from destroying the states, he would utilize them in the "refining" process, and as vital units of government. Furthermore, the vast size of the country, with its multiplicity of economic, geographic, social, religious, and sectional interests, was a blessing. "Extend the sphere," Madison reasoned, "and you take in a greater variety of parties and interests; you make less probable that a majority of the

[32] Harold J. Laski, *A Grammar of Politics* (London, 1925), p. 162. See Wright, p. 22.

whole will have a common motive to invade the rights of other citizens." "The influence of factious leaders may kindle a flame within their particular states," but will be unable to encompass the entire nation (no. 10). Madison would carry over this self-correcting remedy into the organization of government itself, "by so contriving the interior structure of the government as that its several constituent parts may, by their mutual relations, be the means of keeping each other in their proper place" (no. 51).

Hamilton was as sensitive to the evil of "factions" as his collaborator, but whereas Madison saw them as multifarious, and "the various and unequal distribution of property" as only the "most common and durable source" thereof, Hamilton saw the social cleavage more exclusively grounded in economics. For him every community was divided "into a few and the many," rich and poor, debtors and creditors. Hamilton's cure in Philadelphia had been monarchical government similar to that of England. He queried whether a "good" executive "could be established on Republican principles." "The aristocracy," he had told the convention, "ought to be entirely separated; their power should be permanent. . . . They should be so circumstanced that they can have no interest in change. . . . 'Tis essential there should be a permanent will in the community." [33] "A firm union," a national government with "coercive" powers acting directly on individuals, were necessary "to repress domestic factions and insurrections," he concluded in essay 9. John Quincy Adams did not take the trouble to spell it out, but he had hit upon a most significant aspect of the "diversity" in this great collaboration when he described Hamilton's number 9 and Madison's number 10 as "rival dissertations upon Faction and its remedy." [34]

Adams might have made the contrast even sharper by adding Madison's number 51 and Hamilton's numbers 70, 71, 76, and 78 in which the New Yorker elaborated his remedy for factions, stressing "the advantage of permanency in a wise system of administration," of duration in office of "consider-

[33] Farrand, I, 288, 299, 304–10, *passim*. See also *Federalist* nos. 35 and 36.

[34] Adams, *Eulogy on . . . James Madison,* p. 32.

able extent," of "independence" in government. "The republican principle," he wrote in *Federalist* 71, "demands that the deliberate sense of the community should govern the conduct of those to whom they intrust the management of their affairs; but it does not require an unqualified complaisance to every sudden breeze of passion or to every transient impulse which the people may receive from the arts of men, who flatter their prejudices to betray their interests." "There is an idea, which is not without its advocates," he observed, "that a vigorous Executive is inconsistent with the genius of republican government." Hamilton rejected this categorically, saying that "energy in the Executive is a leading character in the definition of a good government. It is essential to the protection of the community against foreign attacks; it is not less essential to the steady administration of the laws; to the protection of property against those irregular and high-handed combinations which sometimes interrupt the ordinary course of justice; to the security of liberty against the enterprises and assaults of ambition, of faction, and of anarchy." The arch-Federalist went on to illustrate the point:

> Every man the least conversant in Roman story knows how often that republic was obliged to take refuge in the absolute power of a single man, under the formidable title of Dictator, as well against the intrigues of ambitious individuals who aspired to the tyranny, and the seditions of whole classes of the community whose conduct threatened the existence of all government, as against the invasions of external enemies who menaced the conquest and destruction of Rome [no. 70].[35]

Hamilton placed perhaps even greater reliance on the federal judiciary—especially because of the provision for indefinite tenure of judges—as a safeguard against factions. "In a monarchy," he explained, holding office during good behavior "is an excellent barrier to the despotism of the prince; in a republic it is a no less excellent barrier to the encroachments and oppressions of the representative body." Nor did judicial

[35] Hamilton cited this example with evident approval. Years later Jefferson recalled his own unfavorable reaction to Hamilton's remark that "the greatest man . . . that ever lived, was Julius Caesar." *Writings of Jefferson*, ed. Ford, XI, 168.

review involve any violation of republican principles. "It is far more rational to suppose, that the Courts were designed to be an intermediate body between the people and the legislature, in order . . . to keep the latter within the limits assigned to their authority. . . . It only supposes that the power of the people is superior to both; and that where the will of the legislature, declared in its statutes, stands in opposition to that of the people, declared in the Constitution, the judges ought to be governed by the latter rather than the former" (no. 78). In addition to serving as guardian of the people against Congress and against themselves, Hamilton emphasized as of equal, if not greater, importance, judicial review of state legislation and of state court decisions (nos. 16 and 22). The judiciary thus became the symbol of "firm union," of national prestige and power. "The majesty of the national authority," he wrote in *Federalist* 16, "must be manifested through the medium of the courts of justice."

The authoritarian note is evident throughout Hamilton's discussion of executive and judicial power. In essay 71 one encounters Rousseau's sentiments that though the "people commonly *intend* the PUBLIC GOOD," they do not "always *reason right* about the *means* of promoting it." [36] The exalted role carved out for the executive and judiciary, especially the latter, is faintly suggestive of Rousseau's "Legislator"—"a superior intelligence beholding all the passions of men without experiencing any of them." [37] Hamilton was naturally less outspoken in the *Federalist,* than he had been at the Philadelphia convention, but he made no less clear his conviction that an independent will in government, immune from fluctuating gusts of popular passion, is an essential safeguard against "domestic insurrection and factions." The effect, he tells us, is not to enthrone authoritarianism nor flout popular government, but rather to safeguard "the people" when their "interests are at variance with their inclinations," thus protecting them from the

[36] Rousseau put it this way: "Of itself, the people will always the good. The general will is always right, but the judgment which guides is not always enlightened." *The Social Contract,* Everyman's Library (New York, 1935), p. 34.

[37] *Ibid.,* p. 35.

"arts of men, who flatter their prejudices to betray their interests," giving them "time and opportunity for more cool and sedate reflection" (no. 71).

But does not such executive and judicial pre-eminence call for considerable qualification of those unseemly qualities Hamilton elsewhere attributed to the general run of mankind? It would seem so if he were to avoid the logical inconsistency we are accustomed to associate with Hobbes. Hamilton, considering himself in this connection "as a man disposed to view human nature as it is, without either flattering its virtues or exaggerating its vices," maintained: "The sole and undivided responsibility of one man will naturally beget a livelier sense of duty and a more exact regard to reputation. . . . This supposition of universal venality in human nature is little less an error in political reasoning, than the supposition of universal rectitude" (no. 76).[38]

One discovers in Madison's essays no such confidence in the purifying effect of power.[39] "The truth is," he said on the floor of the Philadelphia convention, "all men having power ought to be distrusted to a certain degree." [40] In *Federalist* 51

[38] Cf. Farrand, I, 82.

[39] In *Federalist* no. 55, Madison seems to qualify his earlier misgivings on human nature, but the context makes clear the contrast with Hamilton. "As there is a degree of depravity in mankind which requires a certain degree of circumspection and distrust, so there are other qualities in human nature which justify a certain portion of esteem and confidence. Republican government presupposes the existence of these qualities in a higher degree than any other form. . . . Were the pictures which have been drawn by the politically jealous of some among us faithful likeness of the human character, the inference would be, that there is not sufficient virtue among men for self-government; and that nothing less than the chains of despotism can restrain them from destroying and devouring one another." In the Virginia Constitutional Convention of 1829–1830, Madison again cautioned that government means power and that the necessity of placing power in human hands means that it is liable to abuse. The danger of abuse is greatest when men act in a body, and since conscience alone is not a sufficient check, safeguards for minority rights must be found in the structure of government. Thus Madison conceded that the slavery interest would have to be incorporated into the government in order to guard against oppressive taxation which might result from the government falling into the hands of non-slaveowners. *Proc. and Debates . . . Virginia State Convention of 1829–30*, p. 538.

[40] Farrand, I, 584.

he held that government must be obliged "to control itself" through a policy of supplying "by opposite and rival interests the defects of better motives." In number 48 he had observed: "It will not be denied that power is of an encroaching nature, and that it ought to be effectually restrained from passing the limits assigned to it." Even when Madison spoke of energy and stability as being essential to security and good government he was wont to temper his stand with caution. In the achievement of his principal objective—"energy in government" combined "with the inviolable attention due to liberty and the republican form"—there is no suggestion of Hamilton's faith that "responsibility" and office-holding "during good behavior" will develop "impartiality" and the "requisite integrity" in government (nos. 76 and 78). "On comparing . . . these valuable ingredients [energy and stability] with the vital principles of liberty," Madison commented in essay 37, "we must perceive at once the difficulty of mingling them together in their due proportions." No such "difficulty" troubled Hamilton.

Madison's approach was consistently pluralistic. For him the states need not be obliterated; they were adapted to a broad expanse of territory and helpful in serving the ends of a "well-constructed union," of liberty and justice. "If they were abolished, the general government," he wrote in number 14, "would be compelled by the principle of self-preservation, to reinstate them in their proper jurisdiction." Hamilton, on the other hand, saw the great size of the country, torn by warring factions, as necessitating a consolidated system with "unconfined," "coercive power," poised at one center. If the states continued, as under the Articles of Confederation, as members of a "partial" union, "frequent and violent contests with each other" would be inevitable (no. 6). In contrast, Madison envisaged a counterpoised, confederate system, a "compound republic" with the power of the people divided between the states and the nation and national power "sub-divided among distinct and separate departments" (no. 51). Just as in a society, composed of sects, interests, classes, and parties, ambition checks ambition, vice checks vice, and interest is set against interest, so the governmental structure itself provided an institutional expression of social diversity, of action and counteraction.

Hamilton's and Madison's divergence is further reflected in their views on the Constitution and the government it established. For Hamilton the crucial infirmity of the existing system was congenital—"it never had ratification by the people." To avoid the "gross heresy" that a *"party* to a *compact* has a right to revoke that *compact,"* "the fabric of American empire ought to rest on the solid basis of THE CONSENT OF THE PEOPLE" (no. 22). The Constitution corrected "the great radical vice . . . legislation for States . . . as contradistinguished from the individuals of which they consist." "If we are unwilling," Hamilton commented, going to the heart of his nationalist creed, "to be placed in this perilous situation; if we still adhere to the design of a national government, or, which is the same thing, of a superintending power, under the direction of a common council, we must resolve to incorporate in our plan those ingredients which may be considered as forming the characteristic difference between a league and a government; we must extend the authority of the union to the persons of the citizens,—the only proper objects of government" (no. 15).

Hamilton, like the opponents of ratification, saw the proposed Constitution as designed to establish a "consolidated system," "Union under one government," "perfect subordination [of the states] to the general authority of the union" (no. 9).[41] "If the federal system be not speedily renovated in a more substantial form," the "plain alternative" was "dissolution of the union" (no. 16). A critic of the proposed Constitution, Richard Henry Lee, had also identified "consolidation" as its objective, but had queried "whether such a change could ever be effected, in any manner; whether it can be effected without convulsions and civil wars."[42] Madison was not so unequivocal as either his collaborator or those fighting ratifi-

---

[41] However, Hamilton cautiously added: "It would still be, in fact and in theory, an association of states, or a confederacy. The proposed Constitution, far from implying an abolition of the State governments . . . leaves in their possession certain exclusive and very important portions of sovereign power."

[42] Lee, "Letters . . ." (see n. 13 above), p. 283.

cation. "This assent and ratification is to be given by the people," he wrote in essay 39, "not as individuals composing one entire nation, but as composing the distinct and independent States to which they respectively belong. It is to be the assent and ratification of the several States, derived from the supreme authority in each State,—the authority of the people themselves. The act, therefore, establishing the Constitution, will not be a *national,* but a *federal* act."[43]

The Madisonian distinction between *confederacy* and *consolidation,* so much labored in essay 39, Hamilton had brushed aside lightly in essay 9 as "a distinction more subtle than accurate," "in the main, arbitrary, . . . supported neither by principle nor precedent." In this he was in full accord with the Constitution's most rabid opponents, but not with his collaborator, Madison. In a word, Hamilton interpreted the Consti-

---

[43] It should be noted, however, that in the opening sentence of the paragraph in which this statement occurs, Madison says that "the Constitution is to be founded on the assent and ratification of the people of America. . . ." It is important also to recall Dr. Johnson's observation that in the Philadelphia Convention "states" were considered in two different senses: "as districts of people comprising one political society" and "as so many political societies." (Farrand, I, 461.) Madison endorsed Dr. Johnson's distinction, but "thought too much stress was laid on the rank of states as political societies." (*Ibid.,* 463–64.) The context in which this matter is discussed, both in essay 39 and in Madison's notes, makes it altogether clear that, in speaking of "assent and ratification" by the "several States," he is thinking of states as "districts of people comprising one political society"—that is, as "agents." On the floor of the Convention he had "considered the difference between a system founded on the Legislatures only, and one founded on the people, to be the true difference between a *league* or *treaty* and a *Constitution.*" (Farrand, II, 93.) He "thought it indispensable that the new Constitution should be ratified . . . by the supreme authority of the people themselves." (Farrand, I, 123.) Many years later, Chief Justice Marshall had likewise considered the states as "districts of people comprising one political society." "It is true," Marshall agreed, "that they [the people who ratified the Constitution] assembled in their several states—and where else could they have assembled? No political dreamer was ever wild enough to think of breaking down state lines and of compounding the American people in one common mass. Of consequence, when they act, they act in their States. But the measures they adopt do not, on that account, cease to be the measures of the people themselves, or become the measures of the State governments." (*McCulloch v. Maryland,* 4 Wheat. 316, 403; but compare *Writings of James Madison,* ed. Hunt, VI, 348–49.)

tution as designed to correct "fundamental errors in the structure of the building." It was intended to slay "the political monster of an *imperium in imperio*" (no. 15). It may be that Hamilton's caveat thrown down to enemies of the Constitution —"let us not attempt to reconcile contradictions, but firmly embrace a rational alternative" (no. 23)—might have been more appropriately addressed to his colleague, Madison.

Nor were Hamilton and Madison fully agreed as to the nature and scope of the power granted to the national government. For Madison the task of the convention was not to abolish the Articles of Confederation, but to "reduce" them: "The truth is, that the great principles of the Constitution proposed by the convention may be considered less as absolutely new than as an expansion of the principles which are found in the Articles of Confederation" (no. 40). "If the new Constitution be examined with accuracy and candor," he wrote in essay 45, "it will be found that the change which it proposes consists much less in the addition of NEW POWERS to the Union, than in the invigoration of its ORIGINAL POWERS." "The powers delegated by the proposed Constitution to the federal government," he explained in number 45, "are few and defined."

For Hamilton, on the other hand, the objects of the national government were general, and the powers granted for achieving them were undefined—indeed, undefinable. It would be, he declared, "both unwise and dangerous to deny the federal government an *unconfined authority* as to all those objects which are entrusted to its management. . . . Not to confer . . . a degree of power commensurate to the end, would be to violate the most obvious rules of prudence and propriety, and improvidently to trust the great interests of the nation to the hands which are disabled from managing them with vigor and success" (no. 23). Thus the powers granted the national government differed not merely in degree, as Madison insisted, but in kind. In Hamilton's mind Article I, Section 8, paragraphs 1 to 18 inclusive, combined with Article VI, paragraph 2, meant far more than "invigoration of original powers." Here was a grant of power broad enough to meet any and all unforeseeable exigencies. Nor was the force of the new government to be applied so exclusively as Madison suggested in

Federalist 45 to the field of foreign relations, or "in times of war and danger." Hamilton conceived of the national government as dominant in domestic affairs, especially as a positive coercive force to suppress "factions and insurrections."

How could men whose opinions took paths so widely separated co-operate effectually—indeed, work together at all? There are numerous possible answers. The particular division of labor served to preclude any head-on clash, or at least obscure a basic antagonism. For those unable to detect the seeds of future strife, the split rendered the Constitution more, rather than less, acceptable.

Nor can one always be certain in identifying the stand of either Hamilton or Madison. Their interpretations become less categorical when either author enters the province of the other. Thus Madison's nationalism in *Federalist* 14 is qualified in essays 39 and 40. The diminutive scope of the power he accorded Congress in essays 40 and 45 was lost sight of in essay 44: "No axiom is more clearly established in law, or in reason, than that whatever end is required, the means are authorized; whenever a general power to do a thing is given, every particular power necessary for doing it is included." In later years these words were easily fashioned into an effective instrument of national statesmanship.[44]

Similarly, Hamilton's bold nationalist stand in numbers 9, 15, and 22, his inference that the proposed Constitution, as a logical necessity, eliminated every essential vestige of the old relationship of states as members of a "League," is toned down, even neutralized, elsewhere. "An entire consolidation," he remarked in *Federalist* 32, "of the States into one complete national sovereignty would imply an entire subordination of the parts; and whatever powers might remain in them, would be altogether dependent on the general will. But as the plan of the convention aims only at a partial union or consolidation,

---

[44] Daniel Webster, in his brief submitted on behalf of the plaintiffs in the *Dartmouth College* case, cites number 44 in support of his contention that the Constitution was intended to impose severe curbs on the powers of the several states. *The Trustees of Dartmouth College v. Woodward*, 4 Wheaton, 589, 608. For other examples, see Adair, "Authorship of the Disputed Federalist Papers" (see n. 20 above), p. 103.

the State governments would clearly retain all the rights of sovereignty which they before had, and which were not by that act, *exclusively* delegated to the United States." In case of conflict even in the crucial matter of taxation Hamilton suggested the desirability of "reciprocal forbearance" (no. 32). Anticipating the provisions of Amendment X, he declared "that the States will retain all *pre-existing* authorities which may not be exclusively delegated to the federal head" (no. 82). And in essay 26, he cast the states in the role of "jealous guardians of the rights of the citizens against the encroachments from the federal government."

Madison's balanced purpose—to combine "energy in government, with the inviolable attention due to liberty and the republican form"—made a certain degree of equivocation quite natural. And when, during Washington's administration, Madison began his retreat from the nationalist stronghold, Hamilton discerned the underlying ambiguity in the Virginian's statesmanship. Madison's "attachment to the government of the United States," Hamilton told Colonel Carrington in 1792, was "more an affair of the head than of the heart; more the result of a conviction of the necessity of Union than of cordiality to the thing itself." [45] Madison's essays in the *Federalist* bear this out.

On the surface Hamilton's motives were elusive. In the opening number of the *Federalist* he confessed mixed feelings toward the project he had launched: "The consciousness of good intentions disdains ambiguity," he said. "My arguments will be open to all, and may be judged of by all. . . . My motives must remain in the depository of my own breast." No such obscurity cloaked his attitude on September 17 when he signed the Constitution. Then it was "impossible to deliberate between anarchy and Convulsion on one side, and the chance of good to be expected from the plan on the other." [46] He knew that even this chance would be lost unless a strong national authority could be immediately established. "A good administration will conciliate the confidence and affection of the people, and perhaps enable the government to acquire more

[45] *Works of Alexander Hamilton*, IX, 531.
[46] Farrand, II, 646.

consistency than the proposed constitution seems to promise for so great a country. It may triumph altogether over the State governments, and reduce them to an entire subordination, dividing the larger States into smaller districts." [47]

This Machiavellian twist in Hamilton's reasoning, foreshadowed in his letters to Duane and in the *Continentalist*, suggests what he had in mind—squeeze out by interpretation whatever power was necessary to achieve an adequately energetic government. "A statesman," he had remarked earlier, "ought to walk at the head of affairs and produce the event." This was a far easier job than even he dared hope, for the ambiguity lay far less in the language of the Constitution than in the "diversity of genius" John Quincy Adams noted in the *Federalist*.

[47] *Works of Alexander Hamilton*, I, 423. Compare these sentiments with those expressed in the *Federalist*, nos. 26, 28, 32, 81, and 82.

SOLDIERS AND POLITICIANS
IN THE AMERICAN CIVIL WAR

Marcus Cunliffe

We cannot do without generalizations. Our minds need something to hang on to; and categories are easiest to hang on to when they can be expressed as a dualism, a pair of opposed ideas, forces, tendencies.

In historical writing, indeed in history itself, these dualisms abound. No-one, for example, can gain much sense of American history unless he sees "American" and "Europe" as a dualism, and not merely a couple of geographical designations. "America" and "Europe" function as polarities: as opposite terms in a tension between democracy and aristocracy, innovation and conservatism, the future and the past. Within the United States, "North" and "South" are likewise much more than geographical labels. They are resonant with argument and antagonism. They symbolize antipathetic attitudes. "North" stands for a polyglot, mobile, urban, industrial society:

Source: Marcus Cunliffe, "Soldiers and Politicians in the American Civil War," *American Studies in Scandinavia,* 2 (Winter 1969): 6–23. Reprinted by permission of the author and publisher. A fuller treatment of this theme can be found in Marcus Cunliffe, *Soldiers and Civilians: The Martial Spirit in America, 1775–1865* (Boston: Little, Brown & Company, 1968).

Marcus F. Cunliffe (1922–   ), is professor of American Studies at the University of Sussex, England. He was educated at Oxford and Yale universities, and has taught at the University of Manchester and Harvard. His publications include *The Literature of the United States* (1954), *George Washington: Man and Monument* (1958), *The Nation Takes Shape, 1789–1837* (1959), *Soldiers and Civilians: The Martial Spirit in America, 1775–1865* (1968), and *The American Presidency* (1968).

a "Yankee" society. "South" stands for a more homogeneous, static, agrarian, planter-and-slave society: a "Cavalier" society.

On a smaller scale, we find that in the same way American *military* history seems to fall into a persistent dualism. On the one side there is the "professional" or "regular" principle, with the U. S. Military Academy at West Point as its particular symbol. On the other side there is the "amateur", or "volunteer" or "citizen" soldier, symbolized by the militia, and in particular by the "Minutemen" who rushed from their ploughs to confront the British redcoats at Lexington and Concord in 1775. These two opposing principles, the professional and the amateur, have a long tradition of mutual hostility—and of course not only in the United States. The professional soldier thinks of the amateur as—at best—amateurish; and, at worst, as a meddler, an intriguer, a person who owes his place in the army to political influence. In his own eyes the professional soldier is, by definition, a man above politics. Politics is an unscrupulous, civilian activity which he ignores and despises. In the words of a British general of seventy years ago (Lord Baden-Powell, the founder of the Boy Scout movement): "From what I know of them, I would not trust an ordinary politician with my grandmother's toothbrush." By contrast the citizen soldier, or the politician interested in military affairs, regards the regular soldier as—at best—conventional, slow-moving, clannish; and, at worst, as a person of inordinate vanity, tempted to use his momentary power or popularity to break in upon the civilian sphere of authority.

Two books sum up this long-standing American rivalry, both written in the aftermath of the American Civil War. One, entitled *The Military Policy of the United States,* is the work of a professional soldier, a graduate of West Point, named Emory Upton. Upton's thesis is that in all America's conflicts, including the Civil War, the professionals only just managed to avert the ruin threatened by civilian, and especially political folly. The other book, entitled *The Volunteer Soldier of America,* is by a politician-turned-amateur-soldier, John A. Logan. Logan's thesis is that in all America's conflicts, including the Civil War, the amateurs and politicians only just managed to avert the ruin threatened by the incompetence of the professional soldiers.

The interesting thing is that Upton's thesis has in the past half-century gained quite general acceptance among historians in the United States. Textbooks now commonly explain that in the Civil War, as in previous conflicts, the regular officers on the Northern (Union) side were bedevilled with "politics." It was because of political interference, we are told, that the much stronger Union armies took so long to defeat the South. Only when West Pointers were in control, and were trusted by Lincoln's administration, could the North sweep forward unhindered. The Union generals, it must be confessed, often said this at the time. One of them, David Hunter, declared in 1864 that "the United States government has nearly destroyed the vast resources of the people. Thousands and thousands of lives and millions of property have been sacrificed to the filthy demon of politics."

The filthy demon of politics!

One trouble with these dualisms—America *versus* Europe, North *versus* South, professional *versus* politician—is that they tend to be seen also as a moral dualism: good *versus* bad, or even good *versus* evil. America thus becomes the repository of virtue, and Europe of vice. Another trouble is that, for contemporaries and for subsequent historians, they exercise a polarizing or magnetizing effect. Loose evidence, like loose iron filings, is drawn into one corner or the other in obedience to this oversimplifying pull. So, in speaking of "America" and "Europe," we have tended to exaggerate the "American" and "European" qualities belonging respectively to the two continents, and to ignore what "European" elements actually pertain also to the United States, or what "American" elements in fact pertain also to Europe. Similarly, we have tended to exaggerate the differences between North and South in the United States—though of course in both cases the differences are real enough.

And, to come back to my subject, soldiers and politics in the American Civil War, we have tended to exaggerate the differences between the West Point professional and the ordinary American—as General David Hunter did. Categories are neat;

we could not get along without them. But history is an untidy affair, as I shall now illustrate in what I fear will be a most untidy discussion.

The Union army did have legitimate grievances against politics and politicians in the Civil War, at least according to its own lights. There were the initial and continuing senior appointments dished out to the Bankses, the Butlers, the Schenckses, the McClernands. There was the prodigious politicking, at all levels, of the (predominantly) volunteer army: the elections within units to choose company officers, the power left in the hands of state governors to nominate field officers, the maneuvers of Congressmen to promote their friends and demote their enemies. There was the constant interference with the formations fighting near to Washington. Given the muddled American military heritage, and his own consequent uncertainty, it is hard not to sympathize with the Union's general in chief McClellan in 1861–62. Whatever his failings he behaved no worse, to say the least, than his predecessor Winfield Scott might have done in similarly trying circumstances. He was not the first or the last soldier to complain that the damned civilians were trying to run him. Those who came after, when matters were somewhat better regulated, still detested their proximity to Washington. John Sedgwick, as a corps commander under General George G. Meade, received a letter in November 1863 from an old lady which concluded: "May God preserve you from all dangers in the battle field and in the camp, and especially from commanding the Army of the Potomac." Sedgwick commented that from this last danger he was safe: "I know my name has been mentioned, . . . but nothing could induce me to take it. Meade is twenty years older than when he took command."

Above all, regulars within reach of Washington—which in greater or lesser degrees meant most of them—had cause to fear and loathe the activities of the Committee on the Conduct of the War which Congress established in December 1861. Its terms of reference were sweeping. Its members were not only unversed in military affairs: they looked with suspicion on any soldier who had been at West Point. They were the spokesmen of the extreme, radical wing of the Republican party; the Committee's two Democratic members were largely ignored. The ferocity of the radicals is displayed in a typical subsequent utterance of one of the Committee, George W. Julian of Indiana:

> Democratic policy, in the year 1861, gave us as commanders of our three great military departments McClellan, Halleck, and Buell, whose military administrations have so terribly cursed the country; while it impressed upon our volunteer forces in the field such officers as Fitz-John Porter, General Nelson, General Stone, and very many more whose sympathies with the rebels were well known throughout the country . . .

Porter and Charles Stone were of course regulars. William ("Old Bull") Nelson was a former naval officer— obligingly removed from the Committee's list by an aggrieved comrade who shot him dead in September 1862. Julian went on:

> Of the major-and brigadier-generals in our armies Democratic policy has favored the Republican administration, if I am not mistaken, with over four-fifths,—certainly an overwhelming majority; while those great hives of military patronage the Adjutant-general's Department, the Quartermaster's Department, the Commissary Department, the Ordnance Department, and the Pay Department are all under Democratic control and have been during the war.

Senators Benjamin F. Wade, and Zachariah Chandler, Representative Julian and the other prime movers on the Committee, were supported by a good many members of Congress, by influential newspapers such as Greeley's New York *Tribune* and Raymond's New York *Times,* and by a large section of the public. They regarded Lincoln as weak, evasive, and lukewarm on the slavery issue. They convinced themselves that the army, thanks largely to West Point, was beset with apathy and defeatism, and that any officer known to be a Democrat was guilty of these sins until proved innocent.

Secretary of War Edwin Stanton shared their creed, and gave audience to Wade and Chandler every day that Congress was in session. It was Stanton who clapped General Charles P. Stone under arrest, and then denied him a fair hearing, after the fiasco at Ball's Bluff which led to the establishment of the

Committee. Its members, eager to believe the worst, decided that Stone was guilty of treasonable relations with the enemy, and harried an innocent man into ignominy and imprisonment. Stone was released after six months and served again, but never in positions of responsibility. After the war he was almost a man without a country. His wanderings took him to Egypt, where he became chief of staff of the Khedive's army. Pasha Stone eventually returned to the United States and in his closing days, with an irony that cannot have been lost on him, was entrusted with the construction of the pedestal for the Statue of Liberty in New York harbor.

The Committee treated other suspect generals with the same scant ceremony. Witnesses appeared alone, sometimes to find they were being interrogated by only one or two members of the Committee. Relevant testimony was withheld; they did not know whether they were merely witnesses, or whether like Stone they had been selected as victims. At least, soldiers who were under suspicion of "disloyalty" were handled in this fashion; the Committee maintained a dossier of the known or supposed political views of senior officers. It opposed the promotion or recommended the dismissal of men who did not meet its requirements. The Committee was by contrast heavily biased in favor of "reliable" citizen-soldiers such as Benjamin Butler, Lew Wallace and John C. Frémont. It encouraged officers thought to be radical in sentiment, planned military policy so as to push these officers forward, and thus helped to split the army into rival factions by setting one commander against another.

In vain might McClellan protest that his Democratic leanings held no military significance. As the spring of 1862 approached without apparent signs of haste on his part, the Committee grew almost morbidly suspicious. His plan to withdraw from the Washington front and advance on Richmond from the east, by way of the James Peninsula, struck them as not merely weak but possibly treacherous. At their insistence Lincoln ordered McClellan to regroup the twelve divisions of the Army of the Potomac into four corps under the senior division commanders, Irvin McDowell, S. P. Heintzelman, E. V. Sumner and Erasmus Keyes. The first three men had voted against McClellan's scheme at a previous conference, while

Keyes had supported it only with reservations. All four, more-over, were considered "radicals," whereas the other divisional commanders—now to be their juniors—were for the most part politically "conservative," and strong supporters of McClellan. The immediate defenses of Washington were placed under the command of a political appointee, Brigadier-General James S. Wadsworth of New York. Another political general, Nathaniel P. Banks of Massachusetts, was to be entrusted with a sepa-rate corps created from the forces in the Harper's Ferry-Shen-andoah Valley area. The radicals and Stanton also convinced Lincoln that McClellan had unduly weakened the defensive line covering Washington. On their urging he decided to with-hold McDowell's corps from McClellan's Peninsula expedition. It is conceivable that the Committee may have had ulterior, party motives, akin to those of President Polk in the Mexican War. According to this theory, the radicals did not believe that the capital was in serious danger: they hoped to give their man McDowell a chance to dash forward and capture Rich-mond while McClellan was embroiled elsewhere with the main Confederate army.

The Peninsula campaign proved inconclusive. The radi-cals then backed John Pope, and ensured his promotion over McClellan in the summer of 1862. The defeat at Second Bull Run destroyed most of Pope's glamor, but he was let off lightly. Popular hostility was directed instead at Fitz-John Por-ter, a warm admirer of McClellan. Porter, serving as a corps commander in the Bull Run battle, was denounced by Pope and by McDowell (another corps commander). Accused of de-liberately sabotaging Pope's maneuvers, Porter was found guilty at a court-martial arranged by Stanton, and cashiered. This miscarriage of justice, on a level with the deplorable treatment of General Stone, was not finally corrected until 1886.

The Committee's desire for vengeance was aroused by the further Union defeat at Fredericksburg in December 1862.[1]

[1] Politics of another sort may have been involved in the removal from their commands in November 1862 of McClellan, Porter and Buell, all Demo-crats. Their fall was not announced until after the mid-term Congressional elections. Warren G. Hassler, *McClellan: Shield of the Union* (Baton Rouge, 1967), 314–322.

Four Committee members descended on the camp of Pope's successor, Ambrose Burnside, to collect testimony. Burnside was a friend of McClellan. But he escaped their wrath by revising his opinions: he assured his inquisitors that far from condoning slavery he was working to end it. Reassured that Burnside's heart, and so presumably his head, was in the right place, the Committee sought another scapegoat for the Fredericksburg disaster. They found an acceptable victim in one of Burnside's generals, William B. Franklin. Though Franklin was more fortunate than Stone or Porter, he was never again given an important command. Once a highly regarded professional, he resigned from the army in despair in 1866.

Committee members were, following the familiar pattern, lenient with General Joe Hooker, a fellow-radical; they allowed him to escape censure after his inglorious performance at Chancellorsville in May 1863. They were less inclined to look kindly upon Hooker's successor George Meade (a conservative). Though they could not demand Meade's dismissal for his generalship at Gettysburg in July 1863, they criticized his subsequent slowness and gradually began to hound him: hence the force of Sedgwick's remark that "Meade is twenty years older than when he took command." They were not sure what to make of General Grant. Then he too incurred their displeasure for the inconclusive and bloody Wilderness campaign of 1864, and they urged the President to add Grant's name to the dismal roll of rejected generals.

There could well have been a committee to investigate the conduct of the Committee on the Conduct of the War. Or so some of the Union's luckless generals might have felt. There was some substance, along with exaggeration, in the comment of the London *Times* that America's Jacobins were repeating the extremist tendencies of the French Revolution: "The denunciation is precisely the same as those launched against the Girondins by the Mountain in the old French Convention. Disasters in the field have divided the Republican Party, and the zealots impute the reverses, not to the want of generals able to win victories, but to lack of faith in a principle." Vigilantism was rife. But then, the crisis was acute; and not all the faults were on one side.

This was, to reiterate, a civil war, with some of the elements of a revolution. In the confusion, opportunities for corruption abounded; it is hardly surprising that the venal side of politics—bribery, toadying, influence-peddling—flourished. Yet many Americans regarded politics in a higher spirit. It was one of the mechanisms which might enable the Union to wrest victory out of dire emergency. The New Yorker George Templeton Strong, an active member of the Sanitary Commission, recorded in his diary an argument at the Union League Club, shortly before the 1864 presidential election. The Club had drawn up a resolution that its duty was to use its influence to promote the re-election of Lincoln. A few members objected on the ground that this would convert the Club into a "mere political machine." Strong exploded:

> A "mere political machine," indeed! What subject of human thought and action is higher than politics, except only religion? What political issues have arisen for centuries more momentous than those dependent on this election? They are to determine the destinies . . . of the millions and millions who are to live on this continent for many generations to come.

Politics was in this sense far more than a cynical game. The crisis was deeper and deadlier in its divisiveness than that of the Mexican War. The response was inevitably more alarmist. If the Congressional radicals exceeded the proper limits of their authority, so by normal standards did the President—by expending money without previous sanction, by suppressing newspapers and arresting civilians. Accusation and counter-accusation were therefore virulent in the extreme. Stanton and the Committee on the Conduct of the War suspected McClellan of treasonable sloth: McClellan in his memoirs charged Stanton with "treasonable conspiracy."

Even for those who behaved more coolly, political could not be separated from military issues. Should the war be pressed hard against the South? Against all parts, or against certain regions? Should the border states be treated gently, in order not to drive them into the Confederacy? What should be done about slavery, not merely in the abstract but as a practical and urgent problem facing Union commanders? Should they respect Southern property, and return escaped slavers to their owners? Or should they treat the runaways as "contraband of war" (Butler's solution), or declare them liberated (Frémont's view)? Should the aim be to reach a settlement with the South and seek a swift end to the fighting, or to shatter the slavocracy as the only sure means of reconstituting its social base? Should Northern morale be sustained by the avoidance of heavy casualties, or by waging aggressive warfare? There was unanimity neither in the government nor in the army on such thorny and fundamental questions.

From the standpoint of energetic Union men, a number of propositions seemed incontrovertible. The training of regular soldiers, in this view, made them too deliberate, too fortification-minded. Second, regulars were by training and association committed to a warped idea of the Union. The annual Boards of Visitors had kept on assuring the American public that West Point imbued cadets with a love of the Union. But a large number of West Pointers had joined the rebellion. The affection they appeared to show was for one another: an affection that made Northern West Pointers reluctant to strike hard against their Confederate fraternity.[2] Hence the recurrent rumor that such-and-such a Union general, under criticism for sluggishness, had actually slipped across the lines to consort with the enemy commander. In the third place, it was assumed that most Democrats were untrustworthy, and could only exculpate themselves—like Benjamin F. Butler—by displaying the fanaticism of the newly converted. A Democrat was a potential Copperhead; some Democrats, such as Manton Marble, editor of the *New York World,* were regarded as vicious traitors. It followed, fourthly, that the most dangerous of Union commanders was a West Point graduate who admitted to being a Democrat and who had close social or family ties with the Confederacy. According to this rough yet not entirely absurd formula, several Union commanders were objects of legit-

[2] The Radicals would have been angered but not surprised if they could have read the diary-entry for 6 May 1861 of the retired soldier Ethan Allen Hitchcock: "Many friends urge my return to the army. But I have no heart for engaging in a civil war . . . If fighting could preserve the Union (or restore it) I might consider what I could do to take part—but when did fighting make friends?" *Fifty Years in Camp and Field,* 430.

imate suspicion. Don Carlos Buell, for example, was a cousin of old Daniel Twiggs, the general who surrendered the Department of Texas to the Confederacy in 1861 and then joined the rebellion. George Meade was the brother-in-law of the Confederate general Henry A. Wise, the former governor of Virginia.

Such prejudice was not confined to Northern radicals. Indeed the very term "radical" is misleading. The Committee on the Conduct of the War was not the only voice of vehement Republicanism. Secretary of War Stanton was at least as implacable as the Committee. Lincoln, though attacked by extreme antislavery men as weak and conservative, was himself impatient with McClellan and other generals who seemed to be dragging their feet. So was his Secretary of the Treasury, Salmon P. Chase, who was not much impressed by Stanton or Lincoln. Though the reports of the Committee no doubt inflamed public opinion, members of the public such as G. T. Strong were already disposed to share their restless inquisitorial attitudes. After the defeat at Fredericksburg Strong expressed his fear that "Franklin and many of his brethren are, like the late General Fitz-John Porter, bad cases of blood poisoning and paralysis from hypertrophied McClellanism." As late as November 1864, Strong was still an enthusiastic admirer of Benjamin Butler. Butler might not have won brilliant victories: the important thing was that he was a true Union man, a "terrier" well able to deal with Copperhead "rats."

The Committee, in other words, typified a fairly widespread Northern viewpoint. To see this as a contest between Republican zealots or intriguers and hapless West Pointers is to distort and oversimplify. Not all "political" generals were upheld: though the loyalty of N. P. Banks was not considered doubtful, he became as unpopular with the Committee on military grounds as were certain of the regulars. Nor were the regulars uniformly castigated. The Committee, in common with many American civilians, refused to accept the claim that professional training was an essential prerequisite for generalship. But at various times it eagerly urged the claims of regulars deemed to be of the right stamp: William T. Rosecrans in the West, McDowell, Pope and Hooker in the East.

Possibly the regulars were contaminated by the political

atmosphere. One may argue that they were forced into partisanship by the realization that the only chance of promotion, and sometimes of survival, lay in a real or apparent conversion to radicalism. Similarly, one may contend that as in the Mexican War, the more prominent generals were forced into political awareness by being openly discussed as presidential timber. This could be seen as McClellan's fate, when he became the somewhat reluctant Democratic nominee in 1864. Certainly political strategists knew that any general who achieved conspicuous success in an important command, especially in the East, was automatically entered for the presidential stakes. Lincoln's famous letter to Hooker of January 1863, appointing him commander of the Army of the Potomac, may be interpreted in this light. Lincoln praised Hooker as one who did not "mix politics with your profession." He went on:

> I have heard, in such a way as to believe it, of your recently saying that both the Army and the Government needed a Dictator . . . Only those generals who gain successes, can set up dictators. What I now ask of you is military success, and I will risk the dictatorship.

A letter full of the humorous sagacity for which Lincoln is justly admired. Yet it is also a sharp warning to Hooker *not* to meddle with president-making, on the assumption that he is very likely to be impelled to do so if he gains a victory. A few months later, when a successor to Hooker was being sought, the administration may have been stimulated to prefer Meade to John F. Reynolds on the ground that Meade, having been born abroad (his father was in the consular service), was thereby disqualified from becoming a presidential possibility. In 1864 Grant was being boosted for the White House; the *New York Herald* acclaimed him as "the man who knows how to tan leather, politicians and the hides of rebels." According to one account Lincoln delayed naming Grant to the command of the Union armies until he received an assurance—via J. Russell Jones, the U.S. marshal in Chicago and a confidant of Grant's—that the general had no intention of trying for the presidency, despite the encouraging chorus from Democratic newspapers.

Grant, and Sherman, were unusual among Union commanders in their distaste for political intrigue. This is not to say that they had no awareness of political nuances. Grant was after all only renouncing his chance of nomination for the coming election of 1864. The next time round, 1868, he was in fact the Republican candidate. Even in 1864 he could hardly fail to realize how much was at stake in Lincoln's campaign for re-election. He and other generals responded readily to the administration's appeal to send soldiers home on leave to sway the vote in doubtful states. Some states allowed their soldiers to vote in the field. Whether or not generals acquiesced, there is evidence that these votes were rigged to ensure Republican victory. Grant despatched a telegram to Lincoln the day after polling to inform him that the Sixth Corps had turned in a Republican majority of over twenty thousand. One biographer of Grant, citing the telegram, adds: "he was practically Jim Farley." [3] Not quite; still, the point is worth making.

Most Union generals, through whatever mixture of conviction and self-interest, displayed rather than disguised their political leanings. Burnside, Halleck, Hooker, McClellan, Rosecrans, Sherman, Stone and Grant were among the regulars who had left the army before the war. Some of them—including McClellan, a railroad executive and a Douglas Democrat—had quite well-defined political opinions. Ambrose Burnside, who resigned his commission in 1853, had run unsuccessfully as a Democratic candidate for Congress in Rhode Island before joining his friend McClellan in the Illinois Central. In the growing sectional crisis they could not help but form "views"—views which as civilians they were perfectly entitled to hold and express. Hooker, who also resigned in 1853, had particular reason to regard himself as a civilian. He had taken Pillow's side in the Pillow-Scott controversy during the Mexican War.

When he first offered his services to the army in 1861 he was snubbed by the War Department. The most plausible explanation was that he was being victimized by General Scott's

[3] Postmaster-general in Franklin D. Roosevelt's cabinet, and a totally professional politician.

regular subordinates. A number of serving regulars held or developed firm political convictions.

So while the Committee on the Conduct of the War may be blamed for forcing political alignments upon the Union generals, it cannot be said that the soldiers themselves were utterly apolitical. Their first appointments to the Military Academy were determined by Congressional, i. e. political, nominations. Their places in the army as commissioned officers were often secured by lobbying friends in Congress. Those who graduated high on the list at West Point went into the Corps of Engineers and were commonly employed on government construction schemes. Several officers actually worked for long periods in Washington on these semi-civilian tasks, and developed close links with Senators and Representatives. During the Civil War they bombarded Congressmen and the Administration with requests for promotion, for leave, for special consideration of every kind.

As we have noted, McDowell, Pope, Hooker, David Hunter and others declared themselves to be radical. McClellan insisted in his memoirs that he was innocent of political ambition. No doubt this was true at the outset. Yet despite himself he followed the path of Winfield Scott. He was a hero; he began to believe what he was told by his admirers, or by people who shared his resentment at the Republican administration—that he was a genius whose country needed him at the head of its counsels. Once he was sufficiently famous he was automatically a candidate for the presidency. As with Scott, his very fall from favor not only spurred his ambition and rancor but also made him the more attractive to the opposition party.

The most balanced assessment of the situation is that of Jacob Dolson Cox. This Ohio politician, who became a major-general and a corps commander, was a former brigadier-general of militia. Though he had never worn uniform in peacetime he claims to have long been interested in tactics and strategy. The volunteer battalions had, he concedes, many defects; they often went wrong, for example, in their initial choice of officers. But the worst errors were remedied, and the mass of young volunteer officers showed both ability and adaptability. As for the so-called "political generals," he wisely remarks:

> In an armed struggle which grew out of a great political contest, it was inevitable that eager political partisans should be among the most active in the new volunteer organizations. They called meetings, addressed the people to arouse their enthusiasm, urged enlistments, and often set the example by enrolling their own names first . . . It was a foregone conclusion that popular leaders of all grades must largely officer the new troops . . . It was the application of the old Yankee story, "If the Lord *will* have a church in Paxton, he must take *sech as ther' be* for deacons.

Cox admits that in a sense "the whole organization of the volunteer force might be said to be political," but that "we heard more of 'political generals' than we did of political captains or lieutenants." The infusion of politics at all levels, from the narrow matter of party patronage to the broadest and highest matters of Union policy, was thus not merely inevitable but even desirable.

On the question of patronage appointments, the West Point complaint was that senior commands were entrusted to men of no military talent, some of whom had got in by the door marked "push" and some by the door marked "pull." Could *anything* be said in praise of a Banks or a Butler, a McClernand, a Daniel Sickles, a Franz Sigel, or (on the Confederate side) a Gideon Pillow, a Howell Cobb or a Felix Zollicoffer? The most obvious answer is that Lincoln (and Davis, to a lesser extent) were obliged to appoint such men, or to accept them on pressing recommendation. There were not enough West Pointers to go round. Lincoln needed Sigel because Sigel was German-born and a leader in the St. Louis community. As such he was a valuable bellwether for German-Americans: "I fights mit Sigel" was said to be their slogan. Moreover, Sigel was a graduate of a military academy and had served in the army of his native Baden. He had been active in the militia since he arrived in the United States. It was reasonable until events proved otherwise to assume that Sigel might be another Steuben or de Kalb. Benjamin Butler's pre-war militia experience, his energy and confidence, and his standing as a War Democrat, made him too important to be brushed aside. Banks, a former Congressman and governor of Massachusetts, sounded like a politico and had a somewhat unimpressive war record, culminating in his resignation after the Red River fiasco in 1864. But he was a man of courage who held a series of thankless commands, and who had some grounds (like General John A. Logan, the former Democratic Congressman from Illinois) for believing that he was discriminated against by a West Point coterie. James S. Wadsworth was a radical Republican who interrupted his military service to run unsuccessfully for the governorship of New York: he was also a gallant leader who returned to the army, commanded a division at Chancellorsville and Gettysburg, and was mortally wounded in the Wilderness in 1864. The overriding fact, as Butler and Logan were to insist in later years, was that long before the end of the war every important command was in the hands of a regular soldier. The most that "political" or "civilian" soldiers could hope for was a subordinate role, or command of an unpromising sideshow like the Red River campaign. In other words, the professionals had no more reason to complain of this political feature of the war than of radical efforts to determine strategy.

The Committee on the Conduct of the War did behave arbitrarily. But insofar as there *was a* "West Point mentality," the Committee and its supporters were not entirely wrong to equate this with sluggishness. Though the wrong men—Buell, Porter—may have been hounded, there was a case for punishing a few commanders *pour encourager les autres.* Insofar as the West Pointers shared the same uncertainties and prejudices—including political ones—as the rest of their countrymen, the Committee was not entirely wrong in treating them accordingly.

While there was therefore a kind of *esprit du corps* among regulars, before and during the Civil War, its effects were limited. The professionals sometimes thought of themselves as an entity when they were threatened *as an entity* by outsiders, or believed they were. Their chief complaint was against politics and politicians because these were convenient shorthand terms. "Politics" covered a multitude of actual or fancied forms of neglect, ingratitude, injustice, disappointment. Like soldiers in other armies, who have looked forward to peacetime in order "to get back to real soldiering," they attributed to the military sphere everything that was simple, clear, honest and heroic, and to the political sphere everything that was tangled, discordant, frustrating and treacherous.

They were in fact, of course, far from united on most issues. In the Civil War the Union seemed at moments to be more at war with itself than with the Confederacy. They bickered over minor points, they split wide apart on the major issues of the war. Their factious quarrels spilled out in courts of inquiry, courts martial and even occasional duels. They were following the confused tradition of American civil-military relations.

The regular officers were then not a caste apart, absorbed in their craft and unaware of political contexts. It must be added though that their behavior was as a whole healthily strident. As a series of articles in the *Army & Navy Chronicle* of 1836–37 had revealed, there were at least two sides to the problem of the involvement of soldiers in politics. The pure, apolitical professional was apt to be too much cut off from the life of his country. He could degenerate into the outlook of a mercenary. Or, through disdain and conceit, he could conceive of himself as a privileged and powerful janissary. At the other extreme, the too-thoroughly civilianized soldier was equally dangerous: non-military factors played too large a part in his thinking.

Both of these extreme tendencies could be seen in other countries. The United States has not had "men on horseback" though it has had a number of generals in the White House. Among presidential aspirants, only the semi-civilian soldiers have carried the day. Those with vainglorious, proconsular temperaments have failed to satisfy the electorate. The public has, to use a distinction drawn by T. Harry Williams, preferred the "Ikes" to the "Macs"—Taylor to Scott, Grant to McClellan. Bearing in mind the deficiencies of Scott and McClellan, we may be glad that Democratic intrigue ruined the chances of the one, and Republican intrigue the chances of the other. If Polk and Lincoln, and their henchmen, had acted with high-minded generosity toward these contenders, it is conceivable that both might have gained the presidency. It is almost certain that they would have made bad presidents. It is however also almost certain that neither would have indulged his grandiose egotism to the extent of subverting the Constitution. Though their heads were turned by ambition and flattery, they were still sane. In the 1860s there was a great deal of talk in the North, among soldiers and civilians alike, of the need for a strong man, a leader, a Cromwell to save the Union. The need remained a matter of talk. None of the putative Napoleons took any positive step to assume control. When challenged the men on horseback were quick to dismount. There was no real threat of a *coup d'etat*. None went even as far toward power as France's abortive hero of the 1870s, General Boulanger.

Neither before nor during Civil War did America solve the problem of how to steer neatly between the extremes of civilianness and militarism. But then, no other country has discovered the exact range of appropriate compromises. This is a problem without a perfect solution. The American answer leaned toward civilianness. In the words of "Alcibiades," writing in the *Army & Navy Chronicle* in January 1836:

> If a military officer feels no interest in the important political struggles of the day, . . . he acknowledges himself at once to be . . . a hireling . . . who would serve the *Russian Autocrat* the British King, or even Louis Philippe, provided the pay and rank were sufficient temptation.
>
> Nearly every officer of any distinction, at the commencement of the American Revolution, was a politician . . . Politics filled our early councils with those who had . . . wielded the sword against the enemies of liberty . . . Look to the late war with England! Were not many of the most distinguished officers of that period politicians, most of whom still live to prove the truth of the assertion?

The West Pointers were professional to the extent that they thought themselves better than amateurs, and gave preference to their own kind where they had the opportunity, as Sherman did in picking O. O. Howard rather than John A. Logan to command the Army of the Tennessee after the death in action of James B. McPherson. Otherwise they were quite deeply immersed in civilianness. If they had not been, perhaps fewer would have abandoned the Union and gone over to the Confederacy. But their critics were inconsistent in reproaching them simultaneously for being an aristocratic coterie *and* for responding so representatively to the emotions that swayed their fellow-countrymen. Many of the professional politicians were amateur soldiers. Many of the professional soldiers were amateur politicians. The interfusion made things chaotic: it helped to prevent them from becoming catastrophic.

THE AMERICAN IDEOLOGY

Robert G. McCloskey

The Problem of Definition

The title of this essay presents certain obvious difficulties that must be faced at the outset. The first is the problem of definition, and it will be solved in the Humpty-Dumpty tradition by an autocratic act of will. What I mean by "ideology" is an explicit body of political conviction rising to some reasonably advanced level of generality and abstraction. An "ideologue" then, to borrow an ugly but useful term, is a man whose political choices are influenced to some degree by such a body of doctrine. He need not be a political philosopher: the level of abstraction in question is far more modest than that. Concretely, one man may oppose federal medical care for the aged because he feels that his taxes are too high and that he does not want to pay new ones; another may oppose it because he feels it is bad for individual initiative to augment

Source: Robert G. McCloskey, "The American Ideology," in Marian D. Irish, ed., Continuing Crisis in American Politics (Englewood Cliffs, N. J.: Prentice-Hall), pp. 10–24. Copyright © 1963 by Prentice-Hall, Inc. Reprinted by permission of the publisher.

Robert G. McCloskey (1916–1969), was educated at the universities of Wisconsin, Michigan, and Harvard, where he taught as professor of government from 1948 until his death. The problem of contradictory tendencies in American political life provides the central theme of all his published works, which include American Conservatism in the Age of Enterprise: A Study of William Graham Sumner, Stephen J. Field, and Andrew Carnegie (1951), The American Supreme Court (1960), Essays in Constitutional Law (1957), and The Works of James Wilson, 2 vols (1967).

such governmental activities further. The latter is thinking ideologically, the former is not. The latter is not necessarily superior. He is simply different, whether for better or for worse.

The second difficulty is a graver one and cannot be handled so cavalierly: there may be some reason to doubt that the title refers to a real thing, even if the above definition is accepted, and even if we apply the rather generous standards of reality that normally prevail in the social sciences. The doubt can be expressed in two rhetorical questions: do Americans in significant number and degree think ideologically? And if they do, do they agree enough about what they think to justify the definite article in the title. In short, is there any warrant for using either the word "ideology" or the word "the" in conjunction with it?

Unfortunately these are not the conventional, perfunctory misgivings expressed by the essayist as a ritual observance before he reaches what he regards as the meaty part of his discourse. They are palpable doubts that might threaten to prevent the discourse altogether. A few short years ago they could perhaps have been waived, or overridden by a dogmatic, intuitive assertion. One man's belief that there was a widely shared ideology underlying American politics was just as good as the next man's conviction that there was not: neither had much hard data to use against the other, and the discussion could proceed comfortably on the basis of either assumption. The student of political thought was blessedly free to talk, as he traditionally had, about the "political values of America" and about "agreement on fundamentals" as the indispensable condition of American democracy.

But today that freedom has been, if not lost, at least considerably attenuated and modified. The students of public opinion have begun to ask questions and find answers that render impossible the easy assumptions of yesterday. For example, Campbell et al. in The American Voter [1] have presented evidence to suggest that only a very small proportion of Americans cherish ideas about politics that are coherent enough to be called "ideology." For another example, Profes-

[1] Angus Campbell et al., The American Voter (New York: John Wiley and Sons, Inc., 1960).

sors Prothro and Grigg in their study of Ann Arbor and Tallahassee were unable to confirm the hoary hypothesis that there
is a consensus on fundamental democratic values among
Americans, and in fact their evidence suggested pretty
strongly that disagreement rather than agreement was the
American mode.[2] V. O. Key, in his magisterial treatment of
Public Opinion and American Democracy,[3] further develops
both of these insights with his usual combination of caution,
reliability, and charm. I concur with Robert Dahl [4] that no
would-be analyst of "the American mind" can hereafter reckon
without this accumulating evidence. The analyst may be able
to get around it; he may be able to explain it away and somehow restore the old axioms to their ancient status. But he cannot ignore it unless he simply prefers the never-never-land of
his own imagining to any real world that might impair the shin-
ing image. And as the evidence piles up further, the possibility
of retrieving the old canons of faith may become thinner and
thinner.

Meanwhile however, it seems that at least one escape
hatch has been left partly ajar. There is some reason to believe, or at any rate to hypothesize, that there is a small group
in the population whose members can be identified as "ideologues." This group includes, as Key says, politicians, lobby-
ists, officials, party leaders, and influentials"—in short the
"political activists of the society." This group, he suggests,
constitutes a kind of "political subculture" and "perhaps
within this group are to be found in high degree those beliefs,
values, habits of action, and modes of political belief that give
the political system its distinctive characteristics." [5] The idea
is that this "elite" (I use the term with neither pejorative nor
complimentary intentions) contains the "carriers" of the political culture and that the mass of the people thus engage in
"ideology by proxy." Perhaps ideology does play an important

[2] J. W. Prothro and C. M. Grigg, "Fundamental Principles of Democracy:
Bases of Agreement and Disagreement," *Journal of Politics,* XXII (1960),
276–94.

[3] (New York: Alfred A. Knopf, Inc., 1961).

[4] "The Behavioral Approach in Political Science: Epitaph for a Monument
to a Successful Protest," *American Political Science Review* LV (1961), 771.

[5] *Op. cit.,* p. 51.

part in determining the character of American government, but it is the ideology of this leadership group that plays the part, not the broad political convictions of people in general.

This hypothesis is in some ways more satisfactory to the student of intellectual history than the traditional assumptions about democratic principles and the mass mind. Both Campbell and Key have collected illustrations of the mass mind in action on questions of political ideology: for example, the college graduate who "when asked what she meant by calling herself a 'liberalist' replied that she liked *both* of the parties." [6] But most of us could draw similar anecdotes from our own experience, and it has always been hard to reconcile such scraps of data with the contention that "the American mind" as a whole has a coherent view about abstract questions of political value. If we hypothesize, with Key, that Americans in general have habits and attitudes of political significance and that the explicit ideology is "carried" by an influential minority, this difficulty is diminished. Moreover, the traditional materials of American political thought may then begin to have a more plausible relevance to American political behavior. It is most doubtful that the "liberalist" coed just cited could have been greatly affected in her thinking by Jefferson's First Inaugural Address or South Carolina's Ordinance of Nullification. But it is within belief that some of those in the circles of leadership may have a dim understanding of those pronouncements and have been influenced by them. The effect of these modern investigations of the popular mind may be to make it easier than before to talk relevantly about the nature of American ideology.

Suppose then we do narrow our field of discussion to that minority of the American population who can be called ideologues. By assumption and definition we have now disposed of the problem of whether the word "ideology" is permissible. We are talking now only about those to whom the term *does* fairly apply. But there remains the other problem: whether we can speak of "the" American ideology even among this restricted group, and whether we can find in the group the consensus on fundamental political values that political theorists

[6] Campbell *et al., op. cit.,* p. 232.

so hunger for. The evidence on this point is very scanty. Prothro and Grigg did find a somewhat higher degree of agreement on some supposedly democratic values as they moved up the educational scale in Ann Arbor and Tallahassee, but the trend was not consistent and on most issues the replies fell far short of unanimity. Herbert McClosky et al.[7] seemed to find smaller agreement among leaders than among followers, but their questions were directed to more or less current political issues, not to underlying ideological premises; questions of the latter sort might have changed the picture. Stouffer found "civic leaders" more attached than people in general to such a traditional democratic value as freedom of expression, but some of the answers even from these leaders were intolerant enough to leave doubt that any firm consensus exists.[8] Key offers an educated guess that political activists may share something resembling a common understanding about the rules of the game, but warns that more evidence is necessary before we can be confident even about this.

Both the data that we do have and the data we do not have could provide an opening for this essay. On the one hand the evidence permits (without, of course, proving) the assumption that the American ideology is limited to and carried by a subculture of leaders. This makes it possible to indulge the further assumption that ideas expressed in the literature of American political thought bear some resemblance to the American ideology, as we have now defined it. Congressman Doe and Senator Roe may be intellectually inferior to John Adams and James Madison, but in their tendencies of thought they represent a lower form, not a wholly different species. We cannot impute Hamilton's specific thoughts to them, but we can believe that they have thoughts about the ideological matters that engaged Hamilton, that there may be some kinship between their ways of thought and the ways of other articulate Americans past and present. In short, the uncertain state of

[7] "Issue Conflict and Consensus Among Party Leaders and Followers," American Political Science Review, LIV (1960), 406–27.

[8] Samuel A. Stouffer, Communism, Conformity, and Civil Liberties (New York: Doubleday and Co., Inc., 1955).

the evidence about this leadership group allows us some freedom to speculate about its character, using the literature as one of the clues, but also drawing on any other resource that may seem plausibly relevant. These speculations may be modified or displaced in the fullness of the years by the weight of contrary data. But one who is grateful for an opportunity when he sees it will waste no time in slipping through the breach.

The Nature of American Ideology

I would like therefore to offer a conjecture (I hesitate to call it a hypothesis) about the nature of the ideology of this group, whose convictions and habits of mind may play a decisive part in setting the tone of American government. The key word, I suggest, is "ambivalence." That is to say, it is characteristic of the American mind, insofar as this group represents it, to hold contradictory ideas simultaneously without bothering to resolve the potential conflict between them. I do not simply mean that Madison meant in the 10th Federalist—that there are some who believe in one principle and some who believe in another, and that the conflict between these persons of varying belief is often either compromised or left undecided. This may often be true, but it is not the heart of the matter. Many—perhaps most—of the persons in this group maintain a set of dualistic political values, and the ideology of the typical American "ideologue" is not therefore a consistent body of dogmas tending in the same direction, but a conglomerate of ideas which may be and often are logically inconsistent. Such a state of irresolution about the most fundamental and important articles of political faith would be intolerable to the dogmatic rationalist—to the "logical Frenchman" of folklore, for example. No doubt there have been and are Americans who also are vexed by incertitude and feel driven to seek out and dissipate the potential contradictions in their minds— John Calhoun was one of these. But most Americans, even those who are relatively thoughtful and articulate, seem to feel no such compulsion. They are able to believe both in majority rule and minority rights, both in conformity and in freedom, both in federalism and in centralization. Logically, they should either choose between these values or seek the basis for an accommodation between them. It may be rational to believe in both majority rule and minority rights and to a qualified view of each idea—majority rule with *these* reservations, minority rights with *those* reservations. But this is not the way Americans have approached such matters. We have tended instead to hold the two ideas in suspension and have largely ignored the logical difficulties inherent in such doublethink.

This conjecture has an obvious bearing on that traditional question about an American ideological consensus. There may be in fact, among the leadership group we are considering, some tacitly shared understandings about the rules of the game, a pattern of behavior that reflects wide agreement on procedures. But beyond that it may be meaningless to ask whether the members of the group agree with each other about fundamental political values, because they may not even agree with themselves about such values, much less with one another. Perhaps this helps explain the otherwise curious tendency of people to contradict themselves when subjected to public opinion surveys—those who want taxes cut even if it means putting off some important things that need to be done but who also support various kinds of foreign involvement that would obviously make tax cuts quite impossible; or the large number in the Prothro-Grigg sample who professed a belief in majority rule, but also believed that only the well-informed should be allowed to vote in a city referendum. To speak of agreement on fundamental political values among people with such ambivalent propensities may be to indulge the prepossessions of the viewer. Quite possibly the leadership group would display a lower rate of self-contradiction, especially on specific issue questions, because of a greater alertness to the implications of a given answer. But on questions involving root political values, the incidence of irresolution would probably still be very high.

By way of supporting this generalization about the nature of American ideology, let us examine three categories of American political phenomena: the political literature, institutions, and behavior of America. All are in part a reflection of its ideology. Such phenomena as institutions and behavior may be influenced by other factors: an institution may develop a life of its own and may, in fact, be the cause of ideology as well as its effect; behavior, even among the articulate minority, may be a function of habit or interests rather than ideological premises. The question of what weights should be assigned to these various causal elements is a very important one, but for the moment I leave it aside. It is enough if we can assume that ideology plays some inceptive part in our governmental arrangements and our political behavior. Insofar as that is the case, a doubly-explanatory relationship can be discerned: the institutions and the behavior provide us with a key to the nature of the ideology, and the ideology thus understood helps to account for the institutions and the behavior.

The Literature of American Political Thought

The literature of American political thought is thickly strewn with evidence of ambivalence about fundamental values that may be attributed to the American mind. Jefferson is such a perfect case that it is almost unfair to cite him, but his stature and his impact on our politics have been so great that it would be quite impossible to leave him out of account. As Merrill Peterson has recently reminded us,[9] he has been invoked on each side of almost every question that American politics has been concerned with. His admirers as well as his critics have endlessly sought the "real" Jefferson in the welter of pronouncements and actions that he bequeathed to us, only to be confounded by the protean quality of the man. His first inaugural address is the text of a mind divided within itself.[10] "The will of the majority," he tells us, "is in all cases to prevail" *but* "the minority possess their equal rights which equal law must protect"; "the support of the state governments in all their rights" *but* "the preservation of the general government in its whole constitutional vigor"; and so on. He is of course aware that these generalities are, on the face, contradictory, so he informs us that he is in each instance "stating the gen-

[9] Merrill D. Peterson, *The Jefferson Image in the American Mind* (New York: Oxford University Press, Inc., 1960).
[10] Henry S. Commager, ed., *Documents of American History* (New York: Appleton-Century-Crofts, 1949).

eral principle, but not all its limitations." The listener is to infer that Jefferson could resolve the paradoxes if he had time to do so, but the truth is that he never did have the time to spare. The vast body of his writings and the long record of his political career seem to compound the paradoxes rather than dispose of them. Did he believe in absolute majority rule or in minority rights? In state autonomy or in national authority? Jefferson's answer seems to be that in both cases he believed in both values, and similar dualisms are encountered almost everywhere we turn as we try to assess his essential quality.

But Jefferson, it might be said, has always been a special case, a man of such extraordinary qualities that no general insights about *homo Americanus* can be drawn from observing him. On the contrary, he has been enshrined in our political pantheon precisely because he so faithfully mirrored the various and conflicting wills-to-believe that we recognize in ourselves. However, it is true that one swallow, even such a swallow as this, will not make a summer. So let us consider his rival and sometime friend, John Adams. Parrington put him "midway between Hamilton and Jefferson," [11] and there is some validity in this categorization. There are differences in emphasis among the trio—these dualistic values are not always kept in perfect balance. Yet the dualisms are there in the mind of Adams, too. Did he believe in rule by the wise, rich, and well-born, or in rule by the many? Both, he tells us in the *Defence*,[12] and he offers us an executive who will stand between these contending forces, preventing both from triumphing, preventing in short the resolution of the contradiction between them. Parrington thought him a turncoat because as a youth he had espoused the rights of man, while as an old man he defended the rights of property, but this is to misconceive the nature of his thought. For Adams, young or old, both values had a place in his ethic, neither was displaced by the other.

With Hamilton, to round out that troika, the case becomes

---

[11] Vernon L. Parrington, *Main Currents in American Thought,* Vol. 1 (New York: Harcourt, Brace & World, Inc., 1930), 307.

[12] *The Defence of the Constitutions of Government of the United States of America (1787–1788),* in Charles F. Adams, ed., *The Life and Works of John Adams* (Boston: Little, Brown & Co., 1851), Vol. VI.

a little harder; one might escape making it by arguing that he was in fact atypical. He had a lawyer-like tendency in political disputation to state the position he took as strongly as possible so that the ambivalences he might feel were often overborne in the heat of the moment. His statement, in such a moment, that the people "is a great beast" has frequently been cited as the outcry of an antirepublican dogmatist. But in the famous letter to Edward Carrington he says on his "private faith and honor as a man" that he is "affectionately attached to the republican theory"; then in the next breath admits to some misgivings as to whether that theory is "consistent with that stability and order in government which are essential to public strength and to private security and happiness." If we believe him when he tells Carrington that he is speaking "the real language of [his] heart," [13] we must accept a Hamilton who, like Jefferson and Adams, held conflicting political values and who had left the basic conflicts unresolved.

I do not contend that such dualisms are never resolved, that the typical American leader perversely continues to hold them in suspension in the face of circumstances that call imperatively for a choice. On the contrary, we have been able to maintain this ambivalence about fundamental values largely because the pressure of circumstance has seldom been so stringent, because we have usually enjoyed a measure of leeway granted to few other nations in world history. In our comparatively rare moments of great crisis, some choices have become mandatory and then they have been made. Lincoln's insistence on the preservation of the Union at all costs became in his mind such a fundamental principle, allowing for no modification or exception. But it is worth noting that even this idea emerged slowly in his thinking and became fully explicit only when secession forced the decision upon him. Before that and even for a time afterward, the primacy of this value was not apparent in what he did and said, any more than it was apparent among Northerners in general. Before that he was the very prototype of the American political leader, con-

[13] Benjamin F. Wright, ed., *A Source Book of American Political Theory* (New York: The Macmillan Company, 1929), pp. 303–04.

tent to live with contradictory values in the hope that the logical dilemma need never be faced.

The so-called reactionary enlightenment among some
Southern thinkers in the pre-Civil War years did involve some
dogmatic choices between hitherto incompatible beliefs.
George Fitzhugh was not ambivalent about such questions as
the equality of man; Calhoun made his decision between majority rule and minority rights in unequivocal favor of the latter.
But again we have a case of extraordinary circumstances
producing an atypical result among men of a very special temper. It is significant that the intellectual movement in which
they participated established no tradition: Fitzhugh had been
almost forgotten until comparatively recent times when he was
rediscovered by scholarly antiquarians; Calhoun's reputation
as a statesman was so great that he himself could never be
forgotten, but his concept of absolute minority rights has not
been viable, even in the South, except with respect to one
issue. And surely it is noteworthy that the issues of the war itself became in time so blurred in the national memory that the
conflict could become, by a rather wonderful paradox, a symbol of national unity. To quote Oscar Handlin:

> The war was transmuted from the bitter conflict it had been
> into an episode of high adventure. Every base element van-
> ished; only nobility remained, as if those who survived could
> thus banish the guilt of having failed those who died. Above all,
> if the war were to bind Americans in national unity, both sides
> had to seem right. There could be no villains, only heroes.[14]

That is the heart of the matter. Not that there was some
right and some wrong on both sides, but that both sides were
right. That characteristic American illogicality was untenable
for a brief time while the cannons were still firing and during
the bitterness of reconstruction. But it could reassert itself
later when Confederates and Yankees began to celebrate
Decoration Day together.

As I run down the list of articulate Americans who have

[14] "The Civil War as Symbol and as Actuality," *The Massachusetts Review*, III (1961), 135.

been influential in political affairs, I find ambivalence wherever I turn. What of Theodore Roosevelt, for example? He is conventionally thought of as the exponent of regulated bigness as against Wilson's preference for restoring small-unit competition. But even on this matter Roosevelt was equivocal. And on what might be thought of as the more fundamental questions of democratic value, he was also firmly on record in support of both sides "exploding," as Richard Hofstadter has said, "in every direction at once." [15] He sometimes professed to fear the influence of the soulless, irresponsible plutocrats, yet he assailed the muckrakers for their exposés of business-government alliances. He was chronically worried about the dangers of populistic radicalism, yet, in his Bull Moose "Confession of Faith" in 1912, he came out for the unqualified right of the people to rule, even to overrule judicial decisions that were contrary to the popular will. These dizzy leaps from one trapeze to another might be set down to mere opportunism, rather than to inner conflict of beliefs; and opportunism may indeed have played its part. But he was, I think, too moral a person to assume consciously a position at odds with his fundamental values. The point—a convenient one for him—was that he had two sets of fundamental values, so that in a given political context he could choose either one. And the fact that so many of our articulate leaders have been likewise richly endowed lends color to my conjecture that ambivalence is characteristic of the American political temper.

American Political Institutions

The coloring is reinforced when we turn away from what American political activists have said and consider the political institutions they have helped to shape and have lived with. Take the presidency, for example. Certain of the Founding Fathers—James Wilson, Gouverneur Morris, and perhaps Hamilton—hoped to establish an executive with broad powers resembling those described by John Locke under the heading of the "prerogative." However, the nation had recently under-

[15] Richard Hofstadter, *The American Political Tradition and the Men Who Made It* (New York: Alfred A. Knopf, Inc., 1948), p. 225.

gone some vivid experiences involving the royal governors and George III himself, experiences that fostered a deep suspicion of executive authority. Nor was this conflict of opinion resolved by the enactment of Article II of the Constitution. A political power play put the Constitution over and Article II along with it, but no clearcut image of democratic leadership was embodied either in the Constitutional language or in the thinking of those who influenced the development of the office.

In truth no such image has developed in the years that have followed. Is the presidency meant to be a position of creative leadership such as that described by James Burns in his evaluation of Franklin Roosevelt? [16] Does our ideology presuppose that the President will, like Jackson, mold the environment of public opinion, and "lead" in the literal sense of the word? Or is it expected that he will, like Eisenhower, follow public opinion and embody it, rather than try to control it? Either conception of the Presidency may be defensible in terms of one facet or another of the American tradition. As Myrdal has remarked, Americans seem to believe in leadership on the one hand and to resist it on the other. [17] We are prone to use the word "leadership" like an incantation. The impression is that any problem—slum clearance, juvenile delinquency, or the atom bomb—will be solved if we can only get the right leadership to go to work on it. But we are equally quick to condemn as "dictatorship" (once it would have been "monarchy") any attempt to step in and provide the leadership we seemed to be calling for. In short, the passivity of a Coolidge or the activism of Franklin Roosevelt in his first hundred days are both consonant with the institution that history has shaped; for that institution reflects the divided political mind of America.

Or take the Congress, which must surely be one of the most curious repositories of paradox that ingenious political man has yet devised. This was an agency set up to express the will of American democracy, and we might legitimately ex-

[16] James M. Burns, *Roosevelt: The Lion and the Fox* (New York: Harcourt, Brace & World, Inc., 1956).

[17] Gunnar Myrdal, *An American Dilemma* (New York: Harper & Row, Publishers, 1944), p. 709.

pect that the institution would reflect the nation's answer to the eternal democratic question about majority rule versus minority rights. But it gives us no such answer, unless the failure to provide one is a kind of answer in itself. In the first place, as everyone knows, the very creation of the two houses involved a contradiction: the House was dedicated to the proposition that the majority must rule; the Senate, to the idea that minority rights are sacrosanct. But it goes far beyond that. Within each of the two houses we find the same contradiction embodied. Consider, for example, the Senate's famous filibuster tradition. Under the present rule, the vote of two-thirds of the Senators present is necessary to halt debate and no limit at all can be imposed on debate on a motion to change the rules. Thus the minority enjoys, theoretically, an absolute power to frustrate the will of the majority. But on the other hand, there is no real doubt that a majority vote of the Senate could kill the filibuster rule tomorrow—including the rule that purportedly forbids cloture on a rules change. The Constitution gives each house the right to determine its own rules and that right is lodged in the majority of the Senate. So what we have here is not a choice between majority rule and minority rights, not even (in theory) a compromise between them, but an absolute representation of both ideas.

A similar paradox is mirrored in the procedures of the House. We hear much nowadays about the Rules Committee and its power to prevent the majority from expressing itself, a power analogous to that of a filibustering minority in the Senate. Yet a discharge petition signed by a majority of the House can at any time wrest a bill from the Committee's grasp and thus override the minority. Again we see the idea of majority rule and the idea of minority rights existing side by side. In practice, of course, in both Senate and House the two ideas are often compromised. The minority refrains from exercising its theoretically absolute veto unless the issue seems really vital to minority interests; in return for such self-restraint the majority does not invoke its own absolute power to override. But apparently there is symbolic value in maintaining the formal existence of the essential paradox. It comforts those who believe in both majority rule and minority rights and have never bothered to choose between them.

Or take finally the Constitution itself. The more one ponders the ancient cliché that the Constitution was a "bundle of compromises," the less satisfactory that seems as a description of what happened in 1787. Rather, the Constitution can be understood as a bundle of unresolved contradictions. The contradictions led, of course, to ultimate compromises in practice. But that is very different from saying that they were written into the Constitution. Does the Supreme Court, for example, have the power to say the last word about the validity of a legislative act, the power of judicial review? Certainly it does, and our constitutional history resounds with declarations that this is the case. Yet Congress has the impeachment power and the power over appellate jurisdiction, either one of which is enough to destroy the authority of the Court at a single stroke. So it would appear that the judiciary is both omnipotent and subservient to the legislative will. Did the Constitution seek to create a unified national government, or a league of sovereign states? Professor Crosskey on the one hand and Senator Thurmond on the other, the answer is again "both," or at any rate both ideas are tolerably plain in the document. Does the Constitution ordain the separation of powers? Surely the Framers thought it did. Yet the powers are also mingled in a variety of ways as every schoolboy knows, and the Congress can, if it really wants to, impinge on both the executive and judiciary unmercifully.

In short, the institutions of American government, like the spokesmen previously discussed, display a pervasive ambivalence about the most fundamental questions of political value. It seems reasonable then to suppose that the very existence of such self-contradictory governmental forms is further testimony to the thought processes of the men who have fostered them. Indeed, the institutions may be a more reliable clue to underlying ideology than the explicit statements about it. For institutions are a form of action, and there is truth in the old saw that actions speak louder than words. Senator Roe may say he believes in majority rule; Congressman Doe may say he believes in the indefeasible rights of the minority. But when we see the former accept an institutional arrangement that qualifies the majority principle; and the latter agree to an arrangement that involves majority control—we may wonder whether their statements reflect the truth of the matter after all.

American Political Behavior

These observations are also relevant to my final body of evidence to support the conjecture I have advanced. I suggest that the essential ambivalence of the American political mind is further reflected in certain peculiarities of American political behavior. Here, as before, my choice of illustration will have to be selective, but the examples are not chosen tendentiously.

The phenomenon of behavior that I am specifically interested in is a recent one, commonly called "McCarthyism." We have had a tendency in our political history to indulge in brief frenzies of anger, intolerance, or reform, those frenzies being followed almost invariably by a cooling of tempers and a return to the status quo. Instances of this tendency abound in American history; one thinks of the Alien and Sedition Acts period, of the Progressive Era, of the Red Scare following the first World War. In each case the initial excitement was considerable; in each case the excitement died down almost as suddenly as it had arisen. I choose McCarthyism because it is the most recent complete example of such a phenomenon, and because none of the explanations of its rise and fall that I have seen appears wholly satisfactory.

The basic explanation may be found in the propensity of the American political mind that I have been urging. McCarthyism directly or indirectly involved some of the primary-value dualisms of the American tradition. Take, for example, the question of the rule of law. In one sense Americans seem to be almost intoxicated with the wine of legalism. No other country has ever assigned courts the power we have assigned them. The public opinion polls regularly reveal that the judge is the most respected of our fellow citizens. We venerate the Constitution. Yet at the same time, one of the most striking things to foreigners who come here is the strain of lawlessness in our character. Every crisis in American history—some of them very mild crises—has seen demands that the rule of law be abrogated, has revealed a certain impatience with legal forms. No other civilized nation has had a record of lynching and mob violence comparable to ours.

Or take our attitude toward learning, toward education. Since the time of Jefferson, we have had a faith in the beneficence of education that is almost touching. We have dreamed of education for all; we have multiplied colleges and universities as no other nation has. Every other hamlet in the Midwestern states boasts a college, a monument to our national belief that, to put it in Platonic terms, knowledge is virtue. Yet on the other hand there is a parallel tradition that distrusts book-learning, that exalts the school of hard knocks. The comic, halfwitted professor of Hollywood's imagining is the symbol of our counter image. The state legislature of any state is at once proud of its great public university yet suspicious that it is a hotbed of subversives and impractical dreamers.

Or take, for one further dualism, the twin values of respectability and rebelliousness. Most of us are impressed by the spectacle of solid, affluent, silk-hat respectability. But at the same time there is a streak of the derisive in most of us. We take a certain pleasure in seeing the silk hat knocked off with a snowball, in seeing respectability challenged and defied.

The initial success of McCarthy and his movement may be explained by his appeal to one side of ideology. His evident contempt for the rule of law, his assault on education and especially on the ivy-covered institutions of the Eastern seaboard, his raffish irreverence toward such symbols of respectability as Dean Acheson, *The New York Times,* and the Army —all this struck a responsive chord in American breasts. The observer recognized one side of his own value system in these qualities and was drawn to the movement thereby.

That was the initial reaction. But as the Senator ran his course, something else began to be apparent. This man was not, like most of us, ambivalent about these values. He really meant it. His contempt for the rule of law was not matched by a parallel regard for it. His hostility toward education and related values was single-minded. He was interested not merely in knocking off the silk hat of respectability, but the head as well. And at that point his support, especially among political activists,[18] began to recede. Their regard for the rule of law, for education, for the ikons of respectability asserted itself and neutralized their initial attraction to his standard. He was a man with his mind made up who was trying vainly to appeal to an audience which had not made up its mind and felt no compulsion to do so.

No doubt other examples of the rise and decline of political enthusiasms in America can also be explained in these terms. This hypothesis about the character of American ideology might illuminate other common incidents of our political behavior. The apparent ease with which statesmen like Burton Wheeler or Tom Watson move from progressivism to the extremes of reaction, for example, may suggest that an ambivalence in basic values has been present from the first.

Space is too short to permit exploration of these possibilities and others that a further consideration of our political behavior might suggest. Suffice it to argue that our reaction to such phenomena as McCarthyism is consistent with the thesis I have advanced. The literature of American political thought, our political institutions, and our political behavior all indicate that our ideology may be a conglomerate of mutually inconsistent beliefs. If so, it may be idle to seek for "the" American tradition, for a "consensus" in any usual sense of the word. Perhaps our only really basic quality of mind is the pragmatic spirit that can tolerate such a state of affairs and build an enduring polity upon it.

[18] Unhappily, the citizenry in general seem to have been largely unaffected by such misgivings. See G. D. Wiebe, "The Army McCarthy Hearings and the Public Conscience," *Public Opinion Quarterly*, XXII (1958–59), 490.

AMERICAN CHARACTER AND FOREIGN POLICY

Gabriel A. Almond

Attitudes and opinions toward foreign policy questions are not only to be understood as responses to objective problems and situations, but as conditioned by culturally imposed qualities of character. These largely unconscious patterns of reaction and behavior strongly influence the perception, selection, and evaluation of political reality. At the level of mass opinion these "psycho-cultural" characteristics condition patterns of thought and mood on foreign policy problems. At the elite level they affect patterns of policy-making.

In order to speculate intelligently about the influence of these basic traits on foreign policy, it is first necessary to examine and analyze the most important interpretations of the "American character." Before specific judgment about the effect of these qualities on American foreign policy attitudes becomes possible, it is first necessary to discover what qualities Americans are alleged to have.

Source: Gabriel A. Almond, *The American People and Foreign Policy* (New York: Harcourt, Brace & World, 1950), pp. 29–46, 54–68. Copyright © 1950 by Harcourt, Brace & World. Reprinted by permission of Harcourt Brace Jovanovich, Inc.

Gabriel A. Almond (1911–   ), is professor of political science at Stanford University. He was educated at the University of Chicago, and has taught at Yale, Princeton, and the University of Tokyo. In addition to *The American People and Foreign Policy* (1950), he has written *The Appeals of Communism* (1954), and co-authored *The Struggle for Democracy in Germany* (1949), *The Politics of the Developing Areas* (1960), *The Civic Culture: Political Attitudes and Democracy in Five Nations* (1963), and *Comparative Politics: A Developmental Approach* (1966).

In the present state of knowledge all generalizations about "national character" are hypothetical in nature. All that we can say about the observations of historians, journalists, anthropologists, and philosophers who have contributed the bulk of these observations is that they are the reflections of more or less disciplined observers, possessing to a greater or lesser degree the kind of intuition and empathy so essential to this type of speculation. Perhaps a greater validity will attach to those judgments and observations which frequently recur in the literature. The main aim of this investigation is to isolate these persistent themes and set them up as hypotheses which may help us to speculate intelligently about American attitudes toward foreign policy.

Perhaps the most sensitive and accurate observer of American political behavior and institutions was the French aristocrat and historian Alexis de Tocqueville. He wrote of the America of the early 1830's but with a prophetic perception of potentialities which makes much of what he wrote still applicable today. To de Tocqueville, America was the great political experiment of his time, the experiment of political and social equalitarianism. He attributed the distinctively American behavior tendencies to social equality and the social mobility which resulted from it.

In the traditional regions of the Old World, de Tocqueville remarked, the people are ignorant, poor, and oppressed, ". . . yet their countenances are generally placid, and their spirits light. In America I saw the freest and most enlightened men, placed in the happiest circumstances which the world affords: it seemed to me as if a cloud habitually hangs upon their brows, and I thought them serious and almost sad even in their pleasures." [1]

De Tocqueville associated this restlessness and dissatisfaction with two patterns of behavior which he described as peculiar to democratic America. The first of these is an extraordinary emphasis on worldly and private values and gratifications at the expense of public and spiritual values. The sec-

[1] Alexis de Tocqueville, *Democracy in America*, tr. by Phillips Bradley (New York: Knopf, 1945), Vol. II, p. 136.

ond is an extraordinary competitiveness. Of the first tendency de Tocqueville remarks:

> In their intense and exclusive anxiety to make a fortune, they lose sight of the close connection which exists between the private fortune of each of them and the prosperity of all. . . . The discharge of political duties appears to them to be a troublesome impediment, which diverts them from their occupation and business. . . . These people think they are following the principle of self-interest, but the idea they entertain of that principle is a very crude one; and the better to look after what they call their business they neglect their chief business, which is to remain their own masters.[2]

With regard to American competitiveness de Tocqueville writes:

> It is strange to see with what feverish ardor the Americans pursue their own welfare, and to watch the vague dread that constantly torments them lest they should not have chosen the shortest path which may lead to it. . . . They have swept away the privileges of some of their fellow-creatures which stood in their way; but they have opened the door to universal competition; the barrier has changed its shape rather than its position. When men are nearly alike and all follow the same track, it is very difficult for any one individual to walk quickly and cleave a way through the dense throng that surrounds and presses on him. This constant strife between the inclination springing from the equality of conditions and the means it supplies to satisfy them, harasses and wearies the mind.[3]

At the same time he recognized a tendency toward periodic outbursts of evangelism, when the souls of the American people

> . . . seem suddenly to burst the bonds of matter by which they are restrained, and to soar impetuously to Heaven. . . . If their social condition, their present circumstances, and their laws did not confine the minds of the Americans so closely to the pursuit of worldly welfare, it is probable that they would display more reserve and more experience whenever their attention is

[2] *Ibid.,* p. 141.
[3] *Ibid.,* pp. 136–38.

turned to things immaterial, and that they would check themselves without difficulty. But they feel imprisoned within bounds, which they will apparently never be allowed to pass. As soon as they have passed these bounds, their minds know not where to fix themselves and they often rush unrestrained beyond the range of common sense.[4]

De Tocqueville thus detects a moral dualism in American character. Coupled with the intense concern for private, material welfare is a propensity for periodic moral and religious enthusiasm. And further, de Tocqueville with shrewd psychological insight points out that the anxiety and the futility of unrestrained competitiveness creates just this susceptibility to bursts of unworldly evangelism and enthusiasm. He foresaw a threat to American democracy resulting from this alternation of moods of intense, private self-interest and passionate enthusiasm. While in domestic policy common sense and an intimate knowledge of the issues mitigated the influence of these tendencies, in foreign policy the remoteness and complexity of the issues created a special danger. Here the instability of moods, "the propensity that induces democracies to obey impulse rather than prudence, and to abandon a mature design for the gratification of a momentary passion"[5] could have a relatively freer sway. It was fortunate indeed for the interests of the United States, concluded de Tocqueville, that it did not need a foreign policy, that "it is called upon neither to repudiate nor to espouse them [passions of the Old World]; while the dissensions of the New World are still concealed within the bosom of the future."[6]

Other observers of the America of the pre-Civil War period confirm some of de Tocqueville's observations, although none presented so coherent and comprehensive a psychological characterization. Francis J. Grund, a German observer who lived in the United States in the early 1830's, commented on the great emphasis on material success in American culture and the discredit attaching to material failure and poverty.

[4] *Ibid.,* pp. 134–35.
[5] *Ibid.,* Vol. I, p. 235.
[6] *Ibid.,* Vol. 1, p. 234.

A man, in America, is not despised for being poor in the outset —three-fourths of all that are rich have begun in the same way; but every year which passes, without adding to his prosperity, is a reproach to his understanding or industry; and if he should become old without having acquired some property, or showing reasons which prevented his success . . . then I am afraid he will be doubly punished—by his own helpless situation and the want of sympathy in others. . . . Happiness and prosperity are so *popular* in the United States, that no one dares to show himself an exception to the rule. . . .[7]

Grund also comments on the exclusive addiction to "business" in the United States at the expense of leisure.

Active occupation is not only the principal source of their happiness and the foundation of their national greatness, but they are absolutely wretched without it, and instead of the *dolce far niente,* know but the horrors of idleness . . . the Americans pursue business with unabated vigor till the very hour of death . . . the term of *rentier* is entirely unknown.[8]

Charles Dickens, on the basis of his first tour of America, made a number of observations among which two are especially worthy of comment. First, he was strongly repelled by the "universal distrust" which he described as "a great blemish in the popular mind in America." According to Dickens, social relations in the United States were marred by excessive mutual hostility and lack of confidence. As an illustration of this tendency he pointed to the unwillingness of able men to engage in political careers because of fear of character assassination, a point later elaborated by James Bryce. Dickens made no effort to account for this hostility; but it would appear to be a trait closely associated with de Tocqueville's "universal competition." If each man is imperatively bent on his private success in competition with all his fellows, the stability and confidence of personal relations can hardly avoid impairment.

[7] Francis J. Grund, *The Americans,* Marsh, Capen and Lyon, 1837, pp. 173–74. For similar views see Alexander Mackay, "Every Amercan is an Apostle of The Democratic Creed" in *America in Perspective,* ed. by H. S. Commager, Random House, 1947, pp. 95 ff.

[8] Grund, *op. cit.,* pp. 202–06.

Dickens also remarked on the standard of secular morality in the United States and its divergence from the accepted
norms of Christianity. What especially troubled him was the
apparent public approval given to successful rogues. He cites
an imaginary conversation to illustrate the point.

> "He [a scoundrel who had gotten rich by questionable
> means] is a public nuisance, is he not?"
> "Yes, sir."
> "A convicted liar?"
> "Yes, sir."
> "He has been kicked, cuffed, and caned?"
> "Yes, sir."
> "And he is utterly dishonourable, debased, and profligate?"
> "Yes, sir."
> "In the name of wonder, then, what is his merit?"
> "Well, sir, he is a smart man." [9]

Both Herbert Spencer and Matthew Arnold were among
the host of English observers in the post-Civil War period who
offered analyses of the American character and spirit. The
main burden of Arnold's critique was the absence of esthetic
and spiritual distinction or "elevation" in American culture. He
also comments that American men and women were extremely
nervous because of excessive worry and overwork. The pace
of life was too active. There was too little provision for relaxation and creative leisure.[10]

Herbert Spencer's characterizations were remarkably out
of character for the philosopher of "Social Darwinism." [11] The
British sociologist complained in a public interview and lec-
ture in the United States of the "aggressiveness" of American
behavior and of the "disregard for the rights of others." American life was a high pressure life. "Exclusive devotion to work
has the result that amusements cease to please; and when relaxation becomes imperative, life becomes dreary from lack of

[9] Charles Dickens, *American Notes,* Dutton, 1934, pp. 242 ff.

[10] Cited in Allan Nevins, *Americans Through British Eyes,* Oxford University Press, 1948, pp. 360 ff.

[11] Richard Hofstadter, *Social Darwinism in American Thought 1860–1915,*
University of Pennsylvania Press, 1945, Chapter II.

its sole interest—the interest in business . . . the satisfaction of getting on devours nearly all other satisfactions." [12]

A few decades later James Bryce remarked on similar trends in American opinion. With respect to the tension, competitiveness, and nervousness of American life and its consequences for the level of political thinking in America, he observed: "The sense that there is no time to spare haunts an American even when he might find the time, and would do best for himself by finding it." [13] In a remarkable chapter entitled "The Fatalism of the Multitude" Bryce to an extent anticipated a hypothesis later developed by Erich Fromm and elaborated by David Riesman.[14] He describes the United States as a country

> . . . where complete political equality is strengthened and perfected by complete social equality, where the will of the majority is absolute, unquestioned, always invoked to decide every question, and where the numbers which decide are so vast that one comes to regard them as one regards the . . . forces of nature. . . . Out of the dogma that the views of the majority must prevail . . . grows up another which is less distinctly admitted, and indeed held rather implicitly than consciously, that the majority is right. And out of both of these there grows again the feeling, still less consciously held, but not less truly operative, that it is vain to oppose or censure the majority. . . . Thus, out of the mingled feelings that the multitude will prevail, and that the multitude, because it will prevail, must be right, there grows a self-distrust, a despondency, a disposition to fall into line, to acquiesce in the dominant opinion, to submit thought as well as action to the encompassing power of numbers.[15]

Bryce viewed this tendency toward "band wagon" psychology in democracies as a source of political instability and irrationality. After an election in which his candidate has suffered defeat "the average man will repeat his arguments with less faith, less zeal, more of a secret fear that he may be

[12] Nevins, *op. cit.,* p. 356.

[13] James Bryce, *American Commonwealth,* Commonwealth Publishing Co., 1908, Vol. II, p. 307.

[14] D. Riesman and N. Glazer, "Character Types and Political Apathy," *Research Project in Mass Communications,* Yale University, May 26, 1948.

[15] Bryce, *op. cit.,* pp. 360–63.

wrong, than he did while the majority was still doubtful; and after every reassertion by the majority of its judgment, his knees grow feebler till at last they refuse to carry him into the combat." [16] Stable attitudes and opinions rest on inner conviction, habit, or tradition. Movements of thought in older social structures are obstructed by the barriers of class and status, but when each man tends to adjust his opinion to the majority decision, or to the pressure of numbers around him, opinion tends to become volatile, subject to sudden changes in mood and shifts in focus of attention and interest.

> . . . they have what chemists call low specific heat; they grow warm suddenly and cool as suddenly; they are liable to swift and vehement outbursts of feeling which rush like wild fire across the country, gaining glow like the wheel of a railway car, by the accelerated motion. . . . They seem all to take flame at once, because what has told upon one, has told in the same way upon all the rest, and the obstructing barriers which exist in Europe scarcely exist here. Nowhere is the saying so applicable that nothing succeeds like success.[17]

Basing his observations on a painstaking analysis of American political parties, M. Y. Ostrogorski developed a number of themes about the American character, some of them original, some of them confirming the views of de Tocqueville and Bryce. He placed special emphasis on materialism, practicality, optimism, the preference for improvisation, and the hunger for fellowship. "In that new world which was a mine of untold riches for whoever cared to work it," wrote the Russian political theorist, "material preoccupations have engrossed the American's whole being." [18] The function of the state came to be viewed as solely that of assisting in the production of wealth. The enormous productiveness of the land and the availability of natural resources have created a pattern of materialistic improvisation. "Of all races in an advanced stage of civilization, the American is the least accessible to long views. . . . Always and everywhere in a hurry to

[16] *Ibid.,* p. 362.

[17] *Ibid.,* p. 310.

[18] M. Y. Ostrogorski, *Democracy and the Party System in the United States,* Macmillan, 1910, p. 399.

get rich, he does not give a thought to remote consequences; he sees only present advantages. He is preeminently the man of short views, views which are often 'big' in point of conception or of greed, but necessarily short." The riches of America coupled with equality of opportunity have produced a "boundless optimism." This faith in success, that "things will right themselves," "is not only a general tendency, but almost a national religion. Next to the 'unpractical man' there is no one held in such contempt as a 'pessimist.' " [19]

But the quality and mobility of American life produce a loneliness and individual isolation which is uniquely American. The citizen of the Old World, for all his disadvantages, is anchored in social space. He has "moral support," a sense of belonging. "The American lives morally in the vagueness of space; he is, as it were, suspended in the air; he has no fixed groove. The only traditional social groove which did exist, and which was supplied by the churches, has been almost worn down by the incessant action of material civilization and the advance of knowledge." To meet this need the American creates artificial associations—"all revealing the uneasiness of the American mind assailed by a sort of fear of solitude . . ." [20]

Among the more recent "intuitive" analysts of American character, the French conservative Lucien Romier comes closest to presenting a systematic interpretation comparable to those of de Tocqueville, Bryce, and Ostrogorski. Siegfried and Brogan suggest this approach but they have mainly been concerned with the description of institutions and the development of policies.[21] Romier, writing from the viewpoint of a conservative European, attracted by American enterprise and energy, and repelled by its mass culture and materialism, formulated his conclusion in terms of a struggle between the European and American spirit.[22]

[19] *Ibid.*, pp. 400–01.
[20] *Ibid.*, pp. 409–10.
[21] André Siegfried, *America Comes of Age,* Harcourt, Brace, 1927; D. W. Brogan, *Government of the People,* Harper, 1933; Brogan, *The American Problem,* London, 1944.
[22] *Who Will be Master, Europe or America?,* Macaulay, 1927.

Among the various qualities which he lists Romier gives greatest emphasis to the "pace" of American activity. The most distinctive quality of Americans in his judgment was their *élan,* youth, rapidity of movement. America is a youth- or child-centered culture; old age and death are pressed into the background. ". . . the American is a man who 'works fast,' who seldom shows finesse and blunders rather often into scrapes, which he is at any rate able to get out of with some spirit and much good humor. His devouring ambition is to get to the end of an affair quickly, and to make a lasting or profound effect is a lesser consideration with him." [23] Romier attributes to Americans a preference for action rather than reflection, speed or practical efficiency rather than depth, constant and lightning-like changes rather than enduring qualities.

He refers to the obligation to work and make money as socially and economically inescapable. The American is caught up in a system of incessant competition with efficiency and success as ultimate values. He points out that this "cult of practical activity" and "obligation to make money" is a matter of moral salvation rather than a product of hedonistic values.

Romier also attacked the American "mass market" orientation. The lack of American esthetic and intellectual subtlety, the superficiality and instability of American political opinion, he attributes to the pressure of the mass market, which rewards the sensational and well-packaged production and is indifferent to the more complex and profound creative effort.

More recent commentators have done little more than repeat and elaborate on points that had already been made by previous observers. What is especially interesting in this series of characterizations is the surprising consistency and agreement between the early and the later observers, suggesting, perhaps, that these patterns of behavior had asserted themselves at least as early as the beginning of the nineteenth century and had remained relatively stable up to the present time. Thus, Mary Agnes Hamilton in 1932 remarks on the tension of American competition and its negative effects on intellectual and political life.[24] Laski, in the years after World War

[23] *Ibid.,* p. 189.
[24] Cited in Allan Nevins, *op. cit.,* pp. 456 ff.

II speaks of the stress in America on practicality and immediacy and the anti-theoretical orientation even among American intellectuals. He refers to the "universal passion for physical prosperity," the prevalence of the "idea of the dynamic career," and the "zeal for individual accumulation" which has become a "whole-time job." [25]

Henry Steele Commager, after a much more exhaustive survey of the literature than that contained here, also was impressed by the consensus among foreign observers—coming from different backgrounds and writing at different times—as to American characteristics. It is of interest that his selection of recurring themes should coincide so closely with those discussed in the foregoing material.[26]

Psycho-Cultural Hypotheses About American Character

What distinguishes these earlier observations concerning American character from the hypotheses discussed below is that they proceeded largely from insight and intuition rather than from an explicit general theory of human behavior. The propositions presented by the psychologists and anthropologists are similarly untested observations, but they have the advantage of being derived from a considerable body of evidence as to the interrelationships between culture and personality. Thus de Tocqueville observed the tension involved in the American striving for success and attributed it to the absence of class barriers and the general equality of conditions. Mead and Gorer follow the process through, hypothetically, from social structure, to childhood experiences, to adult behavior. What would appear to a nineteenth century historian as discrete behavior patterns are seen by the "psycho-cultural school" as interdependent aspects of cultural values and structure and personality tendencies. Consequently, their observations have greater direction. If they isolate a behavior tendency they know where to look for its genesis; and from one behavior tendency they can formulate hypotheses as to

[25] Harold Laski, *The American Democracy*, Viking Press, 1948, Chapters I and XIV. See also Ralph Barton Perry, *Characteristically American*, Knopf, 1949, Chapter I.

[26] Commager, *op. cit.*, p. x ff.

what other behavior tendencies might be found in association with it. In the present state of knowledge this has both advantageous and dangerous aspects. To an intellectual a theory is a species of property and, in common with other property-owners, he is often somewhat careless as to the means used to defend it. The Marxist historians illustrate this propensity to mold and select reality to support propositions which have ceased to be hypotheses and have become sacred dispensations. The same criticism can be leveled against the Freudian interpreters of culture who have displayed remarkable, if unfortunate, ingenuity in pressing reality into a neat and preconceived frame. Consequently, while the psycho-cultural approach holds out the hope of a science of human behavior, its present production has to be taken with a great deal of caution.

Three anthropologists have recently offered interpretations of the American character—Margaret Mead, Geoffrey Gorer, and Clyde Kluckhohn.[27] Margaret Mead comments at great length on the success ethic of American culture. She ascribes its origins to the family pattern in which affection is accorded to or withheld from the growing child in the degree to which it fulfills achievement norms. Affection is not accorded to the child in principle but in relation to performance. As a consequence the American places an extraordinary premium on achievement; he measures his worthiness or unworthiness first by parental responses, and later by community responses.

Two things might therefore be said about the American success imperative: (1) the emotional force of the propulsion toward success is strongly compulsive since the stake involved is the individual's fundamental sense of self-esteem and worthiness; (2) the criterion of achievement is not located in the self but in the responses of others—parents and the

[27] Margaret Mead, *And Keep Your Powder Dry,* Morrow, 1943; Geoffrey Gorer, *The American People,* Norton, 1948; Clyde Kluckhohn and Florence R. Kluckhohn, "American Culture: Generalized Orientation and Class Patterns" in *Conflicts of Power in Modern Culture,* Seventh Symposium of Conference on Science, Philosophy and Religion, Harper, 1947, pp. 106–28; for a more general bibliography on psycho-cultural studies of national character see Nathan Leites, "Psycho-cultural Hypotheses About Political Acts," in *World Politics,* October, 1948, pp. 103 ff.

parent-surrogates of adult life. These hypotheses of Margaret
Mead are quite similar to Karen Horney's concepts of "compulsive competitiveness," and "the neurotic need for affection." [28] Horney argues that the competitiveness of modern
culture places the individual in a state of hostile tension
with his fellows which affects all personal relationships, those
between parents and children, between parent and parent, between siblings, and between adults in their business and social relationships. Self-esteem is dependent upon the evaluations of others according to a culturally defined success-
failure scale. ". . . under the pressure of the ideology, even
the most normal person is constrained to feel that he amounts
to something when successful, and is worthless if he is defeated." The emotional isolation consequent upon this pervasive hostility "provokes in the normal individual of our
time an intensified need for affection as a remedy." [29] This
theme is also developed by Erich Fromm in an historical and
ideological context.[30]

A second point made in Mead's analysis is the peculiar
attitude toward authority which she attributes to the predominantly immigrant origins of the majority of Americans. A large
proportion of Americans, she argues, have in the course of the
past few generations gone through the experience of rejecting
the cultural patterns of foreign parents. This common experience has tended on the one hand to undermine the strength of
tradition and to weaken authority, and on the other to produce
strong conformist tendencies. The particular processes which

[28] *The Neurotic Personality of Our Time,* Norton, 1937, pp. 281 ff.

[29] *Ibid.,* p. 286.

[30] *Escape from Freedom,* Farrar and Rinehart, 1941, pp. 270 ff.; *Man for
Himself,* Rinehart and Co., 1947, pp. 67 ff. Fromm's concept of the "Marketing Orientation" is quite similar to Horney's concept of "competitiveness."
Fromm similarly shows the connection between compulsive striving for external success and excessive demands for love and affection. See also the
elaboration of the "marketing character" in David Riesman and Nathan
Glazer's series of mimeographed memoranda on "Political Apathy and Character Structure" for the Committee on National Policy: *Research Project in
Mass Communications,* Yale University, January 19, 1948, March 17, 1948,
and May 26, 1948. Fromm's conception of the "marketing orientation" was
partly anticipated in C. Wright Mills, "The Competitive Personality," *Partisan
Review,* September-October, 1946, pp. 433 ff.

seem to be involved here are the following: the American rejects and discredits parental authority, and to some extent carries over this attitude toward all institutional and personal authority. Thus, in his competition with others for success and achievement he lacks stable traditional standards to which to conform. Similarly, his standards of achievement have no internal stability. He is dependent from childhood to adulthood on external reassurance. The American consequently is in a constant process of breaking with the past and conforming to transitory norms, fashions, and fads. He is an anti-traditionalist and a conformist at the same time, illustrating a type of ambivalence which possibly lies at the root of the hectic restlessness which troubled European observers from de Tocqueville to the writers of the present day. Mead places the immigrant origins of most Americans at the center of this iconoclastic-conformist dualism. De Tocqueville attributed it to competitiveness and the equality of conditions of the American people. It is, of course, both factors taken together. What Horney, Fromm and Mead have done is to trace this and other tendencies from aspects of the culture, to patterns of child rearing in the family, to adult behavior.

A third proposition of Mead's has to do with American optimism. The American is ready to tackle any problem with the expectation that he can bring it to a swift conclusion. In this, he places his trust in improvisation and tends to reject complicated planning. He has extraordinary faith in good will and effort in the solution of all kinds of problems—personal and political. Because of the simplicity of his assumptions, and the lack of appreciation of the difficulties involved in many problems, this type of American improvisation is open to frequent disappointment and frustration. American action has tremendous *élan* which often works wonders, but when it doesn't work and when secondary improvisations are similarly thwarted, the bubble of optimism often collapses and gives way to moods of defeatism and deflation. Americans tend to reject the kind of sober reflection and calculation which might protect them from these shifts of moods.

A fourth point of Margaret Mead's has to do with the American attitude toward violence and aggression. Aggressiveness in general, she argues, is positively valued in American culture. Americans, from childhood on, tend to be encouraged to forward themselves and their interests without equivocation. But resort to force is ringed round by restraints. In the American family bullying behavior is inhibited by shame, and arbitrary resort to force is negatively evaluated. Force becomes morally usable in the event of attack. This does not imply an absence of combativeness. On the contrary the "chip on the shoulder" psychology which Mead emphasizes very often reflects an attitude of spoiling for a fight. But there would appear to be strong inhibitions against being the first to engage in a violent action.

Gorer's analysis of American character admittedly incorporates some of the main ideas of Margaret Mead. In certain respects his analysis is extreme and distorted. Thus, he attributes a degree of anti-authoritarianism to Americans which does not seem to accord with reality. Americans certainly are distrustful of authority and are eager to limit it by checks and restrictions, but it can hardly be said that "Authority over people is looked on as a sin, and those who seek authority as sinners." [31] A case may be made out that arbitrary authority is viewed as evil, but it is difficult to believe that authority, in principle, has this connotation in America. At the same time Gorer has made some slight improvements on Mead's interpretation of the American pattern of authority. Mead lays extraordinary stress on the rejection of the immigrant father as a source of American anti-authoritarianism. Gorer probes more deeply into American political and social history and places the problem in the broader context of American political and social tradition.

Gorer stresses the moral dualism in American culture, the conflict between Christian ethical standards, and the ethics of the "market-place." In an ingenious and imaginative chapter entitled "Mother-land" he points out that American iconography includes two symbols—the shrewd, horse-trading Uncle Sam and the magnanimous Goddess of Liberty. "They represent in the shorthand of symbolism, a most important psychological truth. America in its benevolent, rich, idealistic aspects

[31] Gorer, *op. cit.,* p. 33.

is envisaged (by Americans) as feminine; it is masculine only in its grasping and demanding aspects." [32] Like so many of his shrewd intuitions Gorer fails to carry his analysis through in a consistent and convincing fashion. He attributes the American tendency to cover all actions by some kind of moral rationalization to this maternally inculcated "idealism." But, if the American mother, as he alleges, is the dominant factor in the character development of children, and if the main burden of her influence lies in this idealistic, magnanimous direction, why, as he points out himself, should this idealistic factor in the "American conscience" affect behavior only superficially and mainly by requiring moral rationalizations for conduct that is based on quite different, and even contradictory, motives? Actually, the "American conscience" is a good deal more complicated than Gorer recognizes. While the American mother may typically be the most important child-rearing agent, it would seem to make more sense to view her as the bearer of both the "idealistic" and the "competitive" ethic.

In his treatment of the American emphasis on success Gorer points out that while money-making is the main criterion of achievement, there is little stress on accumulation for its own sake. "Americans will give their money with the greatest generosity, and not merely out of their superfluity: in many cases such gifts are made at the expense of considerable personal sacrifice." [33] At the same time this generosity is balanced by a "fear of being played for a sucker." Consequently, any action involving American generosity will be affected by this ambivalence. An underlying suspicion will require frequent reassurance that American gifts and contributions are not going "down the drain," or down a "rat hole," and that American goodwill is not being cynically exploited.

In briefer and more systematic form Clyde and Florence Kluckhohn summarize many of the propositions which have been discussed above. They also propose a number of original suggestions and elaborations. Thus they stress the American tendency to reduce problems to naively rational terms. The as-

[32] *Ibid.*, p. 53.
[33] *Ibid.*, p. 179.

sumption tends to be made that any problem can be resolved by reasonable discussion and the "personal" or direct approach. Another element in this particular pattern is the belief in simple answers and the distrust and rejection of complex ones. The American tends to be anti-expert, anti-intellectual; there is faith in the simple rationalism of the "Average Man." [34]

This anti-intellectualism, according to Kluckhohn is mainly limited to ideas and problems pertaining to personal and group relations. There is no such inhibition to sustained thought and complicated reasoning in matters pertaining to material culture. Thus the enormous development of American technology, and the great stress on labor-saving gadgets. Indeed there appears to be a strong tendency to reduce more complex social and political problems to the simple dimensions of technical gadgetry. Americans often act as though political and cultural problems are capable of being mastered by ingenious schemes.[35]

.   .   .   .   .

The orientation of most Americans toward foreign policy is one of mood, and mood is essentially an unstable phenomenon. But this instability is not arbitrary and unpredictable. American moods are affected by two variables: (1) changes in the domestic and foreign political-economic situation involving the presence or absence of threat in varying degrees, (2) the characterological predispositions of the population. Our knowledge of American character tendencies, meager as it may be, makes it possible to suggest potential movements of opinion and mood which may have significant effects on foreign policy.

[34] C. and F. Kluckhohn, *loc. cit.* This paper also contains a running commentary by Martha Wolfenstein and Nathan Leites which elaborates some of the points made by the Kluckhohns, and suggests hypotheses as to child-rearing practices which might be associated with the various behavior tendencies described.

[35] Clyde Kluckhohn, *Mirror for Man,* McGraw-Hill, 1949, pp. 241 ff.

1. Withdrawal-Intervention

Given the intense involvement of most Americans with private interests and pursuits, the normal attitude toward a relatively stable world political situation is one of comparative indifference and withdrawal. This was the case throughout the greater part of the nineteenth century, in the period between World War I and II, and . . . in the period immediately following World War II. The existence of this cyclical withdrawal-intervention problem suggests at least two serious dangers for foreign policy decision-making: (1) possible overreactions to threat; (2) possible overreactions to temporary equilibria in world politics. Under ordinary circumstances American emotion and action are directed with considerable pressure in the normal orbits of private competition. However, when threats from abroad become grave and immediate, Americans tend to break out of their private orbits, and tremendous energies become available for foreign policy. Thus, we see the explosions of American energy in World Wars I and II when, after periods of indifference and withdrawal, exceptional feats of swift mobilization were achieved. There is some evidence to suggest that the Russian threat may, if carelessly handled, produce dangerous overreactions. Thus the press conference of Secretary of State Marshall in the spring of 1947, in which he urged the American people to "keep calm," produced what amounted to a war scare. The volatility and potential explosiveness of American opinion must be constantly kept in mind if panic reactions to threat are to be avoided.

The danger of overreaction to threat is only one aspect of this withdrawal-intervention tendency of American opinion. Equally serious is the prospect of overreaction to temporary stabilizations in the world crisis. Because of the superficial character of American attitudes toward world politics, American opinion tends to react to the external aspects of situations. A temporary Russian tactical withdrawal may produce strong tendencies toward demobilization and the reassertion of the primacy of private and domestic values. The pull of "privatism" in America creates a strong inclination to self-deception. And while this is less characteristic of the informed and policy-making levels, it undoubtedly plays an important role here as well. The great American demobilization of 1945, both in the military establishment and in the civilian bureaucracy, and the hasty dismantling of war agencies and controls reflected the overwhelming eagerness to withdraw to private values and normal conditions. This movement was not based on a sober evaluation of the foreign situation and what this might require in military and political terms, but was a response to the overwhelming urge to have done with alarms and external interruptions and get back to the essential and important values.

2. Mood-Simplification

Closely connected with the withdrawal-intervention pattern is a tendency which has to do with characteristic changes in the internal structure of American foreign policy moods. It has already been pointed out that under conditions of political equilibrium American attitudes toward world politics tend to be formless and lacking in intellectual structure. We define policy, as distinguished from mood, as consisting of a relatively stable intellectual structure including (1) explicit assumptions as to the values involved in domestic or international political conflict, (2) explicit evaluations of the relative costs and efficiency of alternative means of maximizing the value position of one's own country or political group. From the point of view of this criterion, American attitudes tend to range from unstructured moods in periods of equilibrium to simplification in periods of crisis. So long as there is no immediate, sharply defined threat, the attitude is vague and indefinite—e.g., apathetic, mildly apprehensive, euphoric, skeptical. When the crisis becomes sharpened American responses become more specific. Here American distrust of intellectualism and subtlety, the faith in "common sense," and the belief in simple answers lead to oversimplifications of the threat and the methods of coping with it.

While these tendencies are more characteristic of the "uninformed" general run of the population, they affect policy-makers as well. Thus during World War II, the Roosevelt shift from "Dr. New Deal" to "Dr. Win-the-War" reflected this need at the very highest level of policy-making to reduce the issues to simplified proportions. The "unconditional surrender" policy was a similarly oversimplified resolution of the moral and political problems of the war.[36] The journalists and writers who directed American propaganda efforts in World War II solved their complex policy problems by the slogan of "the strategy of truth," which left to the lower-level, competitive policy-making process practically all of the important decisions of propaganda policy during the war. The policy of "non-fraternization" with Germans which was imposed on the American army of occupation similarly was understandable as a gratification of a need for moral simplism, but it bore only a slight relation to the complex and uncomfortable realities on which it was imposed. The entire sequence of American policies toward Germany had this character of mixed moral-expediential improvisations. At first these improvisations were motivated primarily by anti-German reactions; more recently the tendency is toward more pro-German improvisations. At the present time this tendency to oversimplify seems to be taking the form of reducing all the problems of world politics to a simple "East-West" conflict. There is considerable pressure to take as an ally any country or movement which is anti-Communist and anti-Russian.

It would, of course, be an exaggeration to attribute the same degree of "simplism" to policy-makers as might be expected of the "man in the street." But there can be little doubt that the process of foreign policy making is strongly influenced by this common-sense, improvisational tendency. Faith in policy-planning (which means in simple terms, taking the "long view," acquiring sufficient reliable information on which

[36] See among others Wallace Carroll's book on American propaganda policy during the war, *Persuade or Perish,* Houghton Mifflin, 1948. Apparently Roosevelt had in mind Grant's rather benevolent treatment of Lee at the time of the Southern surrender. But Roosevelt apparently never got around to explaining this to top advisers and administrators. Robert Sherwood in *Roosevelt and Hopkins* (Harper, 1948, pp. 696 ff.) makes the same point in detail.

sound policy can be based, weighing and balancing the potential value of military, political, diplomatic, and psychological means in relation to proposed courses of action) has hardly taken root in the American policy-making process.

3. Optimism-Pessimism

The problem of shifts in mood from euphoric to dysphoric expectations is clearly related to those aspects of American opinion already described. The involvement in private concerns, coupled with an optimistic faith in good will, common sense, and simple answers, renders the American public vulnerable to failure. This reaction tends to result from the frustration of successive improvisations, none of which have been adapted to the complex character of the problem. Under these circumstances there are two possible dangers: (1) withdrawal reactions; (2) hasty measures motivated by irritation and impatience. The development of American attitudes toward Russia since the end of the war is an excellent illustration of this problem. During the war and in the period immediately following its termination there was a widely shared belief among Americans and among American policy-makers that the Russian problem could be readily solved by good will and the "man-to-man" approach. The continued thwarting of American overtures and concessions to the Russians now seems to have produced an attitude of hopeless pessimism. Pessimism certainly seems to be justifiable on the basis of the facts, but the negativism which has resulted may possibly constitute a danger if negotiation and bargaining with the Russians in principle is interdicted. The objective problem would seem to be one of choosing the time, the occasion, and the conditions when negotiation might lead to advantage. There is a similar danger of excessive pessimism in relation to potential allies. Perhaps there is a tendency toward a premature "writing off" of peoples whose social and political structures are unstable, countries which don't react with "American speed" to American proposals or which are not ready to commit themselves to the American "side" in as whole-hearted a fashion as we might desire.

4. Tolerance-Intolerance

The point has already been made that the American attitude toward authority, toward moral and ideological norms, contains conflicting elements. On the one hand, the American is not hemmed in by the mores and morals of "the horse and buggy days," and at the same time he is a conformist, a value-imitator. He is ready to try new things and new methods, but not if they make him look "different" or "peculiar." The truth of the matter would seem to be that, while he has loosened himself from the bonds of earlier moral standards and beliefs, he has not replaced these guides for conduct with any other set of principles. The autonomous conscience of Puritanism has been replaced by the "radar-directed" conduct of the "marketer." [37] He tends to take his judgments as to what is right and wrong, proper and improper, from the changing culture as it impinges on him through the various social institutions and media of communication. This makes for a certain flexibility in attitudes toward other cultures and ideologies. But the flexibility is negative rather than positive. That is, the American has moved away from older moral and traditional norms without acquiring new bases of judgment. His toleration of difference therefore is unstable, and there is a substratum of ideological fundamentalism which frequently breaks through the surface and has an important impact on foreign policy. Thus in our efforts to stabilize the weakened and chaotic areas of Western Europe we have been prepared to go a long way in aiding "Socialist Great Britain" and the left-inclined powers of Western Europe. But there is a continual sabotage of this tolerance, frequent efforts at ideological imperialism, even occasional interferences at the administrative level, which are motivated by ideological fundamentalism.

In general, this intolerance of difference is more clearly expressed in periods of normalcy. Thus, even though the possibility appears to be remote, the prospect of a recrudescence of isolationism cannot be excluded. A tactical cessation of Russian pressure might produce just this kind of demobiliza-

[37] Riesman and Glazer, *loc. cit.,* p. 9.

tion and withdrawal reaction and the reassertion of older principles of conduct. This is not to say that such a reaction would be decisive so far as policy is concerned; but it is a prospect which sound policy-planning should anticipate.

5. Idealism-Cynicism

In still another respect American moral predispositions may have consequences for foreign policy. The annoyance and irritation of the peoples of foreign countries over American self-righteousness is, on the whole, a relatively minor source of difficulty. Americans would appear to be happiest when they can cloak an action motivated by self-interest with an aura of New Testament selflessness, when an action which is "good business," or "good security" can be made to "look good" too. Similarly there is resistance among Americans over the straightforward expression of conscience-motivated behavior. What is "good" has to be represented as satisfying the criteria of self-interest. They are happiest when they can allay the Christian conscience at the same time that they satisfy self-interested criteria. In this regard the peoples of foreign countries are well protected, perhaps overprotected, by their own cynicism.

But there are a number of respects in which this moral dualism may produce more serious problems for the policymaker. There would appear to be a certain cyclical trend in American moral attitudes. The great wave of idealism in the first world war gave way to the cynicism about foreign countries of the 1920's. The friendliness for our British and French allies of World War I gave way to bitterness over their defaults on their indebtedness. A little more than a decade ago the little country of Finland had a place at the very center of the American heart because she had kept up her payments on her war debts, while the European powers which had defaulted, and on the fate of which our security rested, were prevented from borrowing money in the American capital market. The chiliastic faith in the reasonableness of the Russians has now been supplanted by deep resentment over their base ingratitude.

American generosity and humanitarianism is a tentative phenomenon. Along with impulses toward goodwill and generosity, there is a deep-seated suspicion that smart people don't act that way, that "only suckers are a soft touch." In this connection a recent study which appeared in a popular magazine is of considerable interest.[38] This investigation, claiming to have been based on "reliable sampling procedures," reflected a degree of religious piety among Americans considerably greater than had previously been estimated. Of greatest interest was its description of American attitudes toward ethics. It would appear that almost half of the sample was sharply aware of the conflict between what was "right" and the demands of secular life. A somewhat smaller proportion considered that religion influenced their activities in business, political and social life. Considerably more than half felt that their conduct toward neighbors was governed by the golden rule; but more than 80 per cent felt that their neighbors fell considerably short of the golden rule in their conduct toward their fellowmen.

Quite aside from the question of the full reliability of a study asking such "loaded" and personal questions, there seems to be confirmation here for the proposition regarding the moral dualism in the American character. The aspiration to conform to Christian ethical ideals is clearly present among most members of the culture, but there would appear to be a strong apprehension that such standards of conduct are inapplicable because the outside world does not behave that way. Hence any impulse toward ethically motivated generosity is impaired not only by the feeling that it will go unrequited, but that one's neighbors will ridicule it or attribute it to some concealed, self-interested motive.

It would appear to be a reasonable speculation from the foregoing findings that any action involving the giving or loaning of American wealth to foreign peoples, even though it be motivated by calculations of self-interest, activates this fear that "only a sucker is a soft touch." Under conditions of threat, such as those of the present, these doubts and suspicions

[38] Lincoln Barnett, "God and the American People," *Ladies' Home Journal,* November, 1948, pp. 37 ff.

about "giving things away" have been kept within manageable proportions. But in a period of temporary stabilization when the superficial aspect of the foreign situation encourages withdrawal reactions, these feelings may play a role of some significance.

6. Superiority-Inferiority

In a sense America is a nation of parvenus. A historically unique rate of immigration, social, and geographic mobility has produced a people which has not had an opportunity to "set," to acquire the security and stability which come from familiar ties, associations, rights, and obligations. It is perhaps not accidental that in the vulgarization of psychoanalytic hypotheses in America in the last decades one of the first to acquire popular currency was the "superiority-inferiority" complex. In more stably stratified societies the individual tends to have a greater sense of "location," a broader and deeper identification with his social surroundings. He has not *made* his own identity, while in America a large proportion of each generation is *self-made*. Being self-made produces a certain buoyancy, a sense of mastery, but it leaves the individual somewhat doubtful as to his social legitimacy. This sense of insecurity and uncertainty may add a strident note to American claims for recognition. This may explain the stereotype of the American abroad, confronted with complex and ancient cultures, taking alcoholic refuge in assertions of American moral, political, and technical virtue. It may also account for a feeling in the United States that American diplomats are no match for the wiliness and cunning of Old World negotiators. In other words, Americans typically overreact in their self-evaluations. They over- and under-estimate their skills and virtues, just as they over- and under-estimate the skills and virtues of other cultures and nations.

It is perhaps this quality among Americans—and among the American elites—which strongly militates against a balanced and empathic appreciation of cultural and national differences so essential to the development of an effective diplomacy. One may entertain the hypothesis that Americans tend to judge other nations and cultures according to a strictly American scoreboard, on the basis of which America is bound to win. It is difficult for Americans to accept a humane conception of cultural and national differences. Somehow, other cultural values must be transmuted into an American currency so that it becomes possible in a competition of national cultures to rate the United States as the "best all-around culture of the year."

There is a noticeable sensitivity among Americans on the score of cultural and intellectual inferiority. Only recently the American press cited the throngs of visitors to art museums exhibiting the Habsburg collection of paintings as effectively refuting European claims of American cultural inferiority. Feelings of crudeness and inferiority are not only expressed in the form of direct refutation by citing such evidence as the above; they also are frequently expressed in the tendency to equate esthetic and intellectual subtlety with lack of manliness—artists and intellectuals are "queers."

This superiority-inferiority ambivalence may manifest itself in policy-making in a number of ways. It may take the direct and perhaps more typical form of cultural arrogance—assertions of the superiority of the American way in politics, in economics, in social relations, in morality, or in the physical amenities of life. In this case the psychological mechanism involved is a reaction-formation; unconscious feelings of inferiority lead to the assertion of superiority. Or it may take the form of an admission of inferiority and an attribution of superiority to other cultures or elite groups. In either case there is an alienation from the real character and potentialities of the self. One either becomes an ideal and non-existent American—a *persona* American—or one rejects one's Americanism entirely and attempts to "pass," for example, into English or French culture. These formulations, of course, state the problem in the extreme for purposes of clarity.

These reactions have a selective appeal among the various elite groups. Thus American artists, writers, and intellectuals have historically tended to manifest inferiority feelings in the form of imitativeness, or in expatriation. It has been asserted that members of the American foreign service have tended to assimilate themselves too readily to foreign cultures and aristocratic "sets," perhaps at the expense of their American perspective. The tendency for American families of wealth and prestige to ape the English and Continental aristocracies is too well known to call for detailed comment. All of these groups have in common the quality of having differentiated themselves from the American pattern through extraordinary wealth, through artistic or intellectual deviation, or through long residence abroad. The more "representative" American —the Congressman for example—tends to manifest the simpler form of cultural arrogance.

Either inferiority or superiority feelings in relation to other cultures may have a negative effect on the national interest. Cultural arrogance may alienate other peoples, impair confidence in the United States among actual and potential allies, or aid in some measure in the mobilization of hostile sentiment among neutrals and potential enemies. Cultural subservience, particularly if manifested by American diplomats and negotiators, may result in real and unnecessary sacrifices of the national interest.

The hypothesis may also be advanced that there is a certain periodicity of national moods of confidence and lack of confidence. These have perhaps been associated in the United States with the fluctuations of the business cycle. One may speculate that not least among the catastrophic foreign policy consequences of a serious depression in the United States would be an impairment of national self-confidence, a sudden welling to the surface of underlying doubt, which might result in a weakening of foreign policy resolution, a feeling of being overextended, a need for contraction, for consolidation, for withdrawal.

Conclusion: The Many Faces of America

It would be unfortunate if the preceding analysis conveyed the impression of a neat periodicity of American foreign policy moods. Actually the American approach to foreign policy problems at any given time is a historically unique phenomenon. It is influenced not only by these (and other) ambivalences in the American character, but by the immediate historical background and the specific content of the foreign policy problem. While it is useful analytically to talk about the alternation of "normalcy" and "crisis" moods, it must be recognized that crises differ from one another, just as do periods of normalcy, and that the American character is undergoing continual change. Thus from one era to the next, both the subjective and objective components of foreign policy moods may greatly change.

In the period before World War II, the dominant and overt foreign policy mood was a composite of withdrawal impulses, cynicism about power politics, intolerance of foreign peoples and cultures, and pessimism about the prospects of idealistic internationalism. Many experiences had combined to produce this state of mind. The development of a power structure in Europe which did not immediately and overtly threaten the United States provided a plausible justification for isolationism. Disillusionment over the collapse of the high moral purposes of the Allies in World War I provoked a cynical and pessimistic reaction which strengthened the withdrawal trend. The default on Allied war debts contributed to American arrogance with regard to the inefficiency and lack of integrity of foreign governments.

The growing threat to American security began to undermine this withdrawal mood in the late 1930's. But it took the catastrophe of Pearl Harbor to produce a broad interventionist consensus. American intolerance of foreign countries and social systems was supplanted by a tolerance of actual and potential allies. Cynicism and pessimism about international power politics were supplanted by moderately idealistic aspirations and somewhat optimistic expectations of peace and international amity.

This mood pattern lasted through the latter years of the war and the brief period of Allied amity which followed it. But as specific conflicts with the Soviet Union broadened into the general impasse of the Cold War, the American foreign policy mood changed again. Optimism about the future of peace gave way to pessimism. Idealist internationalism faded into "security realism." Overtones of impatience and intolerance began to emerge in public reactions to our relations with the Soviet Union, England, China; but the continuance of threat precluded an unequivocal expression of these reactions.

There is some value for the purposes of foreign policy planning in recognizing that an overtly interventionist and "responsible" United States hides a covertly isolationist longing, that an overtly tolerant America is at the same time barely stifling intolerance reactions, that an idealistic America is muttering *sotto voce* cynicisms, that a surface optimism in America conceals a dread of the future. Understanding of these ambivalences might save statesmen periodic shocks at the sequences of American moods. One must always take into account the fact that Americans in this period of their development are both responsible and irresponsible. A momentary rift in the clouds brings the irresponsible trends to the surface; an intensification of threat brings out a sober readiness to sacrifice.

America's contemporary role in world politics is hardly more than a decade old. Other nations have had generations to assimilate their great political lessons. That America has begun to assimilate some of its political lessons is suggested by the widespread resolution that it can no longer tolerate the degree of economic instability which has characterized the past. This rejection of the inevitability of the severe shocks of the business cycle is matched in the political sphere by a growing acceptance of our foreign policy status and the sacrifices it imposes. But with regard to the foreign policy cycle, as well as the business cycle, a confident sense of self-mastery is still lacking.

Another impression which analysis of American moods may have conveyed is that these reactions are equally distributed among the entire population. We shall have the occasion to observe at a later point that there are substantially different mood susceptibilities at different points in the social and political structure. Social classes, age groups, men and women, and the various educational levels approach foreign policy problems from different emotional and intellectual starting points. The fact that there are so many different Americas is not only attributable to attitude instability *through time,* but also to the fact that *at any given time* there is a bewildering variety of moods and foreign policy proposals.

THE IRONIC ELEMENT IN THE AMERICAN SITUATION

Reinhold Niebuhr

1

Everybody understands the obvious meaning of the world struggle in which we are engaged. We are defending freedom against tyranny and are trying to preserve justice against a system which has, demonically, distilled injustice and cruelty out of its original promise of a higher justice. The obvious meaning is analyzed for us in every daily journal; and the various facets of this meaning are illumined for us in every banquet and commencement-day speech. The obvious meaning is not less true for having become trite. Nevertheless it is not the whole meaning.

Source: Reinhold Niebuhr *The Irony of American History* (New York: Charles Scribner's Sons, 1952), pp. 1–16. Copyright © 1952 by Charles Scribner's Sons. Reprinted by permission.

Reinhold Niebuhr (1892–   ), is professor of applied Christianity, emeritus, at the Union Theological Seminary. He was educated at Elmhurst College, Eden Theological Seminary, and Yale Divinity School. He was ordained in the ministry of the Evangelical Synod of North America, and served as a pastor in Detroit before coming to the Union Theological Seminary to teach in 1928. In addition to *The Irony of American History* (1952), he has written *Moral Man and Immoral Society* (1932), *Beyond Tragedy: Essays on the Christian Interpretation of History* (1937), *The Nature and Destiny of Man* (1941), *The Children of Light and the Children of Darkness: A Vindication of Democracy and a Critique of Its Traditional Defence* (1944), *Faith and History: A Comparison of Christian and Modern Views of History* (1949), *Christian Realism and Political Problems* (1953), *The Self and the Dramas of History* (1955), *Pious and Secular America* (1958), *The Structure of Nations and Empires* (1959), *Man's Nature and His Communities* (1965).

We also have some awareness of an element of tragedy in this struggle, which does not fit into the obvious pattern. Could there be a clearer tragic dilemma than that which faces our civilization? Though confident of its virtue, it must yet hold atomic bombs ready for use so as to prevent a possible world conflagration. It may actually make the conflict the more inevitable by this threat; and yet it cannot abandon the threat. Furthermore, if the conflict should break out, the non-communist world would be in danger of destroying itself as a moral culture in the process of defending itself physically. For no one can be sure that a war won by the use of the modern means of mass destruction would leave enough physical and social substance to rebuild a civilization among either victors or vanquished. The victors would also face the "imperial" problem of using power in global terms but from one particular center of authority, so preponderant and unchallenged that its world rule would almost certainly violate basic standards of justice.

Such a tragic dilemma is an impressive aspect of our contemporary situation. But tragic elements in present history are not as significant as the ironic ones. Pure tragedy elicits tears of admiration and pity for the hero who is willing to brave death or incur guilt for the sake of some great good. Irony however prompts some laughter and a nod of comprehension beyond the laughter; for irony involves comic absurdities which cease to be altogether absurd when fully understood. Our age is involved in irony because so many dreams of our nation have been so cruelly refuted by history. Our dreams of a pure virtue are dissolved in a situation in which it is possible to exercise the virtue of responsibility toward a community of nations only by courting the prospective guilt of the atomic bomb. And the irony is increased by the frantic efforts of some of our idealists to escape this hard reality by dreaming up schemes of an ideal world order which have no relevance to either our present dangers or our urgent duties.

Our dreams of bringing the whole of human history under the control of the human will are ironically refuted by the fact that no group of idealists can easily move the pattern of history toward the desired goal of peace and justice. The recalcitrant forces in the historical drama have a power and persistence beyond our reckoning. Our own nation, always a vivid symbol of the most characteristic attitudes of a bourgeois culture, is less potent to do what it wants in the hour of its greatest strength than it was in the days of its infancy. The infant is more secure in his world than the mature man is in his wider world. The pattern of the historical drama grows more quickly than the strength of even the most powerful man or nation.

Our situation of historic frustration becomes doubly ironic through the fact that the power of recalcitrance against our fondest hopes is furnished by a demonic religio-political creed which had even simpler notions than we of finding an escape from the ambiguity of man's strength and weakness. For communism believes that it is possible for man, at a particular moment in history, to take "the leap from the realm of necessity to the realm of freedom." The cruelty of communism is partly derived from the absurd pretension that the communist movement stands on the other side of this leap and has the whole of history in its grasp. Its cruelty is partly due to the frustration of the communist overlords of history when they discover that the "logic" of history does not conform to their delineation of it. One has an uneasy feeling that some of our dreams of managing history might have resulted in similar cruelties if they had flowered into action. But there was fortunately no program to endow our elite of prospective philosopher-scientist-kings with actual political power.

Modern man's confidence in his power over historical destiny prompted the rejection of every older conception of an overruling providence in history. Modern man's confidence in his virtue caused an equally unequivocal rejection of the Christian idea of the ambiguity of human virtue. In the liberal world the evils in human nature and history were ascribed to social institutions or to ignorance or to some other manageable defect in human nature or environment. Again the communist doctrine is more explicit and therefore more dangerous. It ascribes the origin of evil to the institution of property. The abolition of this institution by communism therefore prompts the ridiculous claim of innocency for one of the vastest concentrations of power in human history. This distillation of evil from the claims of innocency is ironic enough. But the irony is increased by the fact that the so-called free world must cover itself with guilt in order to ward off the peril of communism. The final height of irony is reached by the fact that the most powerful nation in the alliance of free peoples is the United States. For every illusion of a liberal culture has achieved a special emphasis in the United States, even while its power grew to phenomenal proportions.

We were not only innocent a half century ago with the innocency of irresponsibility; but we had a religious version of our national destiny which interpreted the meaning of our nationhood as God's effort to make a new beginning in the history of mankind. Now we are immersed in world-wide responsibilities; and our weakness has grown into strength. Our culture knows little of the use and the abuse of power; but we have to use power in global terms. Our idealists are divided between those who would renounce the responsibilities of power for the sake of preserving the purity of our soul and those who are ready to cover every ambiguity of good and evil in our actions by the frantic insistence that any measure taken in a good cause must be unequivocally virtuous. We take, and must continue to take, morally hazardous actions to preserve our civilization. We must exercise our power. But we ought neither to believe that a nation is capable of perfect disinterestedness in its exercise, nor become complacent about particular degrees of interest and passion which corrupt the justice by which the exercise of power is legitimatized. Communism is a vivid object lesson in the monstrous consequences of moral complacency about the relation of dubious means to supposedly good ends.

The ironic nature of our conflict with communism sometimes centers in the relation of power to justice and virtue. The communists use power without scruple because they are under the illusion that their conception of an unambiguously ideal end justifies such use. Our own culture is schizophrenic upon the subject of power. Sometimes it pretends that a liberal society is a purely rational harmony of interests. Sometimes it achieves a tolerable form of justice by a careful equilibration of the powers and vitalities of society, though it is without a conscious philosophy to justify these policies of statesmanship. Sometimes it verges on that curious combination of cynicism and idealism which characterizes communism, and is prepared to use any means without scruple to achieve its desired end.

The question of "materialism" leads to equally ironic consequences in our debate and contest with communism. The communists are consistent philosophical materialists who believe that mind is the fruit of matter; and that culture is the product of economic forces. Perhaps the communists are not as consistently materialistic in the philosophical sense as they pretend to be. For they are too Hegelian to be mechanistic materialists. They have the idea of a "dialectic" or "logic" running through both nature and history which means that a rational structure of meaning runs through the whole of reality. Despite the constant emphasis upon the "dignity of man" in our own liberal culture, its predominant naturalistic bias frequently results in views of human nature in which the dignity of man is not very clear.

It is frequently assumed that human nature can be manipulated by methods analogous to those used in physical nature. Furthermore it is generally taken for granted that the highest ends of life can be fulfilled in man's historic existence. This confidence makes for utopian visions of historical possibilities on the one hand and for rather materialistic conceptions of human ends on the other. All concepts of immortality are dismissed as the fruit of wishful thinking. This dismissal usually involves indifference toward the tension in human existence, created by the fact that "our reach is beyond our grasp," and that every sensitive individual has a relation to a structure of meaning which is never fulfilled in the vicissitudes of actual history.

The crowning irony in this debate about materialism lies in the tremendous preoccupation of our own technical culture with the problem of gaining physical security against the hazards of nature. Since our nation has carried this preoccupation to a higher degree of consistency than any other we are naturally more deeply involved in the irony. Our orators profess abhorrence of the communist creed of "materialism" but we are rather more successful practitioners of materialism as a working creed than the communists, who have failed so dismally in raising the general standards of well-being.

Meanwhile we are drawn into an historic situation in which the paradise of our domestic security is suspended in a hell of global insecurity; and the conviction of the perfect compatibility of virtue and prosperity which we have inherited from both our Calvinist and our Jeffersonian ancestors is challenged by the cruel facts of history. For our sense of responsibility to a world community beyond our own borders is a virtue, even though it is partly derived from the prudent understanding of our own interests. But this virtue does not guarantee our ease, comfort, or prosperity. We are the poorer for the global responsibilities which we bear. And the fulfillments of our desires are mixed with frustrations and vexations.

Sometimes the irony in our historic situation is derived from the extravagant emphasis in our culture upon the value and dignity of the individual and upon individual liberty as the final value of life. Our cherished values of individualism are real enough; and we are right in preferring death to their annulment. But our exaltation of the individual involves us in some very ironic contradictions. On the one hand, our culture does not really value the individual as much as it pretends; on the other hand, if justice is to be maintained and our survival assured, we cannot make individual liberty as unqualifiedly the end of life as our ideology asserts.

A culture which is so strongly influenced by both scientific concepts and technocratic illusions is constantly tempted to annul or to obscure the unique individual. Schemes for the management of human nature usually involve denials of the "dignity of man" by their neglect of the chief source of man's dignity, namely, his essential freedom and capacity for self-determination. This denial is the more inevitable because scientific analyses of human actions and events are bound to be preoccupied with the relations of previous causes to subsequent events. Every human action ostensibly can be explained by some efficient cause or complex of causes. The realm of freedom which allows the individual to make his decision within, above and beyond the pressure of causal sequences is beyond the realm of scientific analysis. Furthermore the acknowledgment of its reality introduces an unpredictable and incalculable element into the causal sequence. It is therefore embarrassing to any scientific scheme. Hence scientific cultures are bound to incline to determinism. The various sociological determinisms are reinforced by the general report which the psychologists make of the human psyche. For they bear witness to the fact that their scientific instruments are unable to discover that integral, self-transcendent center of personality, which is in and yet above the stream of nature and time and which religion and poetry take for granted.*

Furthermore it is difficult for a discipline, whether philosophical or scientific, operating, as it must, with general concepts, to do justice to the tang and flavor of individual uniqueness. The unique and irreplaceable individual, with his

> Thoughts hardly to be packed
> Into a narrow act,
> Fancies that broke through language and escaped.

> Browning

with his private history and his own peculiar mixture of hopes and fears, may be delineated by the poet. The artist-novelist may show that his personality is not only unique but subject to infinite variation in his various encounters with other individuals; but all this has no place in a strictly scientific account of human affairs. In such accounts the individual is an embarrassment.

---

* In his comprehensive empirical study of human personality Gardner Murphy nicely suggests the limits of empiricism in dealing with the self. He declares: "We do not wish to deny the possibility suggested by James Ward that all awareness is colored by selfhood. . . . Least of all do we wish to attempt to set aside the still unsolved philosophical question whether the process of experiencing necessitates the existence of a non-empirical experiencer. . . . Nothing could be gained by a Gordian-knot solution of such a tangled problem. We are concerned solely with the immediate question: Should the student of personality at the present stage of research postulate a non-empirical entity distinct from the organism and its perceptual responses? . . . To this limited question a negative answer seems advisable." Gardner Murphy, *Personality*, p. 491. There can of course be no "non-empirical entity." But there may be an entity which cannot be isolated by scientific techniques.

If the academic thought of a scientific culture tends to obscure the mystery of the individual's freedom and uniqueness, the social forms of a technical society frequently endanger the realities of his life. The mechanically contrived togetherness of our great urban centers is inimical to genuine community. For community is grounded in personal relations. In these the individual becomes most completely himself as his life enters organically into the lives of others. Thus our theory and our practice tend to stand in contradiction to our creed.

But if our academic thought frequently negates our individualistic creed, our social practice is frequently better than the creed. The justice which we have established in our society has been achieved, not by pure individualism, but by collective action. We have balanced collective social power with collective social power. In order to prevail against our communist foe we must continue to engage in vast collective ventures, subject ourselves to far-reaching national and international disciplines and we must moderate the extravagance of our theory by the soberness of our practice. Many young men, who have been assured that only the individual counts among us, have died upon foreign battlefields. We have been subjected to this ironic refutation of our cherished creed because the creed is too individualistic to measure the social dimension of human existence and too optimistic to gauge the hazards to justice which exist in every community, particularly in the international one.

It is necessary to be wiser than our creed if we would survive in the struggle against communism. But fortunately we have already been somewhat better in our practice than in our quasi-official dogma. If we had not been, we would not have as much genuine community and tolerable justice as we have actually attained. If the prevailing ethos of a bourgeois culture also gave itself to dangerous illusions about the possibilities of managing the whole of man's historical destiny, we were fortunately and ironically saved from the evil consequences of this illusion by various factors in our culture. The illusion was partly negated by the contradictory one that human history would bear us onward and upward forever by forces inherent in it. Therefore no human resolution or contrivance would be necessary to achieve the desired goal. We were partly saved by the very force of democracy. For the freedom of democracy makes for a fortunate confusion in defining the goal toward which history should move; and the distribution of power in a democracy prevents any group of world savers from grasping after a monopoly of power.

These ironic contrasts and contradictions must be analyzed with more care presently. Our immediate prefatory concern must be the double character of our ironic experience. Contemporary history not merely offers ironic refutation of some of our early hopes and present illusions about ourselves; but the experience which furnishes the refutation is occasioned by conflict with a foe who has transmuted ideals and hopes, which we most deeply cherish, into cruel realities which we most fervently abhor.

2

One of the great works of art in the western tradition, which helped to laugh the culture of chivalry and the ideals of medieval knight errantry out of court, was Cervantes' Don Quixote. Quixote's espousal of the ideals of knighthood was an absurd imitation of those ideals; and it convicted the ideals themselves of absurdity. The medieval knights had mixed Teutonic class pride and the love of adventure of a military caste with Christian conceptions of suffering love. In Quixote's imitation the love becomes genuine suffering love. Therefore, while we laugh at the illusions of this bogus knight, we finally find ourselves laughing with a profounder insight at the bogus character of knighthood itself.

Our modern civilization has similarities with the culture of medieval knighthood. But its sentimentalities and illusions are brought to judgment, not by a Christ-like but by a demonic fool; and not by an individual but a collective one. In each case a mixture of genuine idealism with worldliness is disclosed. The medieval knights mixed pride in their military prowess with pretenses of coming to the aid of the helpless. However, the helpless were not those who really needed help but some fair ladies in distress. Our modern commercial civilization mixes Christian ideals of personality, history and community with characteristic bourgeois concepts. Everything in the Christian faith which points to ultimate and transcendent possibilities is changed into simple historical achievements. The religious vision of a final realm of perfect love in which life is related to life without the coercion of power is changed into the pretension that a community, governed by prudence, using covert rather than overt forms of power, and attaining a certain harmony of balanced competitive forces, has achieved an ideal social harmony. A society in which the power factors are obscured is assumed to be a "rational" rather than coercive one. The knight of old knew about power. He sat on a horse, the symbol of military power. But the power of the modern commercial community is contained in the "counters" of stocks and bonds which are stored in the vaults of the bank. Such a community creates a culture in which nothing is officially known about power, however desperate may be the power struggles within it.

The Christian ideal of the equality of all men before God and of equality as a regulative principle of justice is made into a simple historical possibility. It is used by bourgeois man as a weapon against feudal inequality; but it is not taken seriously when the classes below him lay claim to it. Communism rediscovers the idea and gives it one further twist of consistency until it becomes a threat to society by challenging even necessary functional inequalities in the community. The Christian idea of the significance of each individual in God's sight becomes, in bourgeois civilization, the concept of a discrete individual who makes himself the final end of his own existence. The Christian idea of providence is rejected for the heady notion that man is the master of his fate and the captain of his soul.

Communism protests against the sentimentalities and illusions of the bourgeois world-view by trying a little more desperately to take them seriously and to carry them out; or by opposing them with equally absurd contradictory notions. The bourgeois world is accused of not taking the mastery of historical destiny seriously enough and of being content with the mastery of nature. To master history, declares Engels, requires a "revolutionary act." "When this act is accomplished," he insists, "—when man not only proposes but also disposes, only then will the last extraneous forces reflected in religion vanish away." That is to say, man will no longer have any sense of the mystery and meaning of the drama of history beyond the limits of his will and understanding; but he will be filled with illusions about his own power and wisdom.

For the bourgeois idea of a society in which the morally embarrassing factor of power has been pushed under the rug, communism substitutes the idea of one final, resolute and unscrupulous thrust of power in the revolution. This will establish a society in which no coercive power will be necessary and the state will "wither away." The notion of a society which achieves social harmony by prudence and a nice balance of competitive interests, is challenged by communism with the strategy of raising "class antagonisms" to a final climax of civil war. In this war the proletariat will "seize the state power" and thereby "put an end to itself as a proletariat" (Engels). This is to say, it will create a society in which all class distinctions and rivalries are eliminated.

For the liberal idea of the natural goodness of all men it substitutes the idea of the exclusive virtue of the proletariat, who, according to Lenin, are alone capable of courage and disinterestedness. Thus it changes a partially harmful illusion about human nature into a totally noxious one. As if to make sure that the illusion will bear every possible evil fruit, it proposes to invest this allegedly virtuous class with precisely that total monopoly of power which is bound to be destructive of every virtue.

Communism challenges the bourgeois notion of a discrete and self-sufficing individual with the concept of a society so perfect and frictionless that each individual will flower in it, and have no desires, ambitions and hopes beyond its realities. It thinks of this consummation as the real beginning of history and speaks of all previous time as "pre-history." Actually such a consummation would be the end of history; for history would lose its creative force if individuals were completely engulfed in the community. Needless to say the change of this dream into the nightmare of a coercive community, in which every form of individual initiative and conscience is suppressed, was an inevitable, rather than fortuitous, development. It proved that it is even more dangerous to understand the individual only in his social relations than to deny his social substance.

In every instance communism changes only partly dangerous sentimentalities and inconsistencies in the bourgeois ethos into consistent and totally harmful ones. Communism is thus a fierce and unscrupulous Don Quixote on a fiery horse, determined to destroy every knight and lady of civilization; and confident that this slaughter will purge the world of evil. Like Quixote, it imagines itself free of illusions; but it is actually driven by twofold ones. Here the similarity ends. In the Quixote of Cervantes the second illusion purges the first of its error and evil. In the case of the demonic Quixote the second illusion gives the first a satanic dimension.

Our own nation is both the participant and the victim of this double irony in a special way. Of all the "knights" of bourgeois culture, our castle is the most imposing and our horse the sleekest and most impressive. Our armor is the shiniest (if it is legitimate to compare atom bombs with a knight's armor); and the lady of our dreams is most opulent and desirable. The lady has been turned into "prosperity." We have furthermore been persuaded by our success to formulate the creed of our civilization so passionately that we have suppressed its inconsistencies with greater consistency than any of our allies. We stand before the enemy in the first line of battle but our ideological weapons are frequently as irrelevant as were the spears of the knights, when gunpowder challenged their reign.

Our unenviable position is made the more difficult because the heat of the battle gives us neither the leisure nor the inclination to detect the irony in our own history or to profit from the discovery of the double irony between ourselves and our foe. If only we could fully understand that the evils against which we contend are frequently the fruit of illusions which are similar to our own, we might be better prepared to save a vast uncommitted world, particularly in Asia, which lies between ourselves and communism, from being engulfed by this noxious creed.

THE NATION'S DILEMMAS: A CRITIQUE

Stanley Hoffman

As we have seen, the historical experience of the United States buttresses the nation's principles, and, together with the domestic consensus on those principles, it explains the United States' unique brand of pragmatism. The total result could be termed an unpolitical approach to foreign policy. Distance from history, dogmas instead of guidelines, an engineering technique that works best on technical problems—all combine to depoliticize world affairs. Just as domestic American politics provide no analytical model for the understanding of other political systems, American foreign policy, precisely because it reflects a polity that has no counterpart elsewhere, seems as if it misunderstood the political dimension of world affairs.

This explains why American foreign policy frequently oversimplifies the complexities, conflicts, and crises of other nations, translating them into a more familiar but less relevant

Source: Stanley Hoffman, *Gulliver's Troubles* (New York: McGraw-Hill, 1968), pp. 176–94. Copyright © 1968 by Council on Foreign Relations, Inc. Reprinted by permission of McGraw-Hill Book Company.

Stanley Hoffman (1928–   ), is professor of government at Harvard University. He was born in Vienna, educated at the Institute d'Etudes Politiques, the Paris Law School, and Harvard, and has taught at Harvard since 1955. In addition to *Gulliver's Troubles, Or the Setting of American Foreign Policy* (1968), he has written *Organisations Internationales et Pouvoirs Politiques des États* (1954), *Le Mouvement Poujade* (1956), *Contemporary Theory in International Relations* (1960), *In Search of France* (1963), and *The State of War* (1965).

language, maintaining a lofty distance from reality, and channeling the energies of its practitioners into rather predictable and narrow paths.

Second, American foreign policy is marked by what might be called over-expectations, or excessive optimism, or one-way contingency planning—planning for only the most favorable alternative, or the one over which one has most control, assuming that all will go well or that the success of what is being undertaken will *ipso facto* take care of all the harrowing problems that gave rise to the policy in the first place. Marshal Foch's famous edict, *"on s'engage et puis on voit,"* corresponds only too well to this procedure.

Third, whatever its fundamental continuity, American foreign policy shows, like a fever chart, the appearance of a jagged line. A national ethos of progress and "built-in obsolescence," a way of acting that constitutes a kind of full-fledged mobilization in response to challenges thrown down by others, a devotion to principles among which (as among Supreme Court precedents) one can select what one needs— all these explain why changes in emphasis are called revolutions, curves are deemed turning points, and mild waves christened brainstorms. Thus, a qualified reaction to ensure that there will be no Korean wars becomes "massive retaliation," a systematic re-evaluation of the consequences of nuclear stalemate becomes the new McNamara Doctrine; greater emphasis on reform in Latin America and a more favorable attitude toward neutralism are presented as almost sensational reversals in policy. Here, as in other respects, American institutions have a share in the responsibility.

A national style that neglects or distorts the political factors different from those of its own experience creates far more trouble than these familiar flaws. The chief problem within the American style is what I would call its dualism, a deep tension between two ways of dealing with political issues, and this, in turn, leads to two other sets of problems.

America's Dualism

Manifestations

Perhaps the primary manifestation of American dualism in foreign affairs concerns the "image" the United States likes to present to the other nations of the world. In a world of revolutionary challenges, Americans like to remind themselves and others that the United States was once the "first new nation," the product of a revolution which was the first act of colonial emancipation in history, and also the first in the "age of the democratic revolution." At the same time, the United States likes to emphasize that it stands for order and stability, for private enterprise, sound finances, balanced growth, constitutional procedures, the avoidance of revolution, the prevalence of legality—everything that, to listeners and observers, appears *not* compatible with revolutionary forces, whether of the new nationalism or of communism. Far from competing under a banner that says, "I can understand the former and am far more genuine than the latter," the United States seems to oppose those forces and to defend its privileged position as the well-endowed leader of the industrialized West.

Similarly, the United States likes to appear as the keystone of an arching, world-wide alliance engaged in a protracted conflict, the basic design of which (although variations may well give statesmen kaleidoscopic surprises) is monotonously unchanging—the containment of forces of evil bent on universal conquest and global turmoil. At the same time, it likes to proclaim the American faith in the Communists' capacity to understand their common interests with the West, and in the prospect of a diverse world in which everyone will have a place in the sun. One side of the argument stresses that *plus ça change, plus c'est la même chose;* the other suggests that *plus c'est la même chose,* the more things will actually change and improve.

The difficulties that come from this perfectly honest habit of dualism are familiar. The "first new nation" has, in some Latin American countries such as Venezuela, backed forces that appeared willing to do battle with traditional oligarchies; but in Brazil the champion of order and stability has supported a regime that, for all its financial orthodoxy, can hardly be called a force of social progress, not to mention rigorous legality. The "first new nation" saw in the Suez crisis the occasion for what one of its leaders called a "declaration of independence from Europe," but that crisis was provoked by an American decision made largely on Cold War considerations (punishing Egypt for dealing with the Soviet Union) and led in time to the United States' reassertion of its role as protector of the Western Alliance (when the Soviet Union resorted to blustering threats against Britain and France).

A second manifestation is a tendency to speak two different languages, neither of which is entirely convincing and which are difficult to reconcile. The first is the language of power. Here, American leaders "talk tough," they ask how many divisions the Pope has, and they explain to the European allies that power cannot really be shared effectively unless all the sharers can unite to reach a scale "commensurate with the requirements" of power, and unless all of them are willing to accept world-wide responsibilities; they warn their enemies that failure to desist from hostile acts will be met by the full weight of American might. The second is the language of community and harmony. There, American leaders protest their sincere dislike of imperialism; they stress that the United States is a disinterested nation that acts out of responsibility, not selfishness, a world power that for the first time in history leads by giving rather than taking; they explain that power is a tragic necessity but that peace, love, reason, bread, and friendship for all are the goals.

Of course, only a symbolic eagle can hold both the arrows and the olive branch easily at the same time. When other nations accuse us of playing a classical game of power politics, we protest, pointing to our community ideals and our aspirations for brotherhood; and we find the use by other nations of pure or traditional power plays to be nefarious and intolerable when they are our foes, disruptive and anachronistic when they are our friends. When other nations appeal to our sense of community and our ideal of human harmony, we are apt to point to our special burdens and to require an admission fee to our school.

Then too, a kind of double bookkeeping afflicts each of these languages. In essence, both the language of power and the language of harmony are universal; they can be used by whoever wants to act on the world stage, yet Americans seem to ask for special treatment. Thus, when we speak the language of force, we do not quite avoid implying that although we recognize power as a universal commodity and the necessary, amoral means for all nations, our power is somehow morally superior and deserves a privileged position; that we can trust ourselves but not others; and that others can trust us, but nobody else. Our policy of trying to stop the arms race, which often implies that the optimum would be a situation of equality between the opponents, leaves room for various more or less convincing rationalizations of why we should be allowed to maintain military superiority. Tough talk with our allies about power logically ends with an invitation to unite so as to be able to share power with us, and to develop their power so as to deserve being our partners. But if allies develop their power independently, we consider that their multiplicity is reason for not taking them too seriously. And our exhortation to them to unite does not go so far as to suggest that the resultant "shared power" would ever apply to the realm of nuclear control. We argue that there is no reason why the continental Europeans should trust a British nuclear deterrent or why the Germans should feel protected by a French one, but we are confident that the Germans, the French, or the British should have no doubt about the reliability of ours. In discussions with our allies, we hint that their criticisms would be more likely to be taken into account if they supported us in our policies elsewhere, if they defined world responsibility in the same way we do. In debate with our allies as with our opponents, we assume that our strategy is the only rational one, and that their failure to see this is due either to ignorance or to obstreperousness.

There is the same double bookkeeping in our talk about community. We stress reasonableness, the need to behave as equals willing to subordinate separate interests to the higher common good. But, at the same time, we suggest that our very disinterestedness and our world-wide responsibilities thrust upon us the role of interpreter and trustee of the common good; we are the only ones who see the whole picture and want nothing for ourselves; the others have a parochial vision. In defining the common good, we also see to it that our peculiar geographical position, or our special position as the most powerful nation on earth, is taken into account (for instance, our limited-war strategy in Europe just happens to correspond with the possibility, enjoyed only by a superpower situated on a separate continent, of waging war while keeping the home territory a sanctuary).

A third and last manifestation of American dualism is in the issue of the use of force. When the United States overtly or covertly resorts to force in the form of repressive moves against a foe, or deterrent build-ups, or advice and training for friendly soldiers of nations threatened from within or without, it does so with a remarkable technical efficiency, or at least self-assurance. It is as if a button had been pushed and a hidden spring of energy had been suddenly released. The strategic design may be confused, the relevance of the act to the objectives may be dubious, and yet there goes into the undertaking not merely a puritan sense of duty but an exuberant (albeit disciplined) sense of mission and aptitude—in a word, a calling—that can be a little overwhelming. What elicits such a response is the American quest for efficiency, the need for technical expertise, the comfort of self-reliance, the nonambiguity of ends, the pleasure of a morally simple and technically apt job done for a good cause. Restraints are often preserved, to be sure, but at the cost of a difficult exercise in self-discipline, for they do not come naturally. They are respected because the international system requires them; our own instinct does not. They are observed because we want to survive, i.e., because we want our foes to observe them too, not because we want to spare our foes. Significantly, the "internalization" of those restraints has consisted in developing ingenious theories which give to the art of proportioning means to ends the reassuring air of a science that can be learned as engineers learn their trade. But when other nations act as we do, often in quite similar circumstances, we frown, grumble, or condemn. The use of force, the threat of force, the preparations to use force by our opponents are evil; military operations or plans made by our friends (except at our request) provoke laments or sermons—war is too risky, the world is too dangerous for this, nothing is worth playing with fire.

Meanings

These contradictions require explanation. No light is to be shed on them by talking of hypocrisy or imposture. A hypocrite is a man who deceitfully pretends that he is what he is not; an impostor is a man who tries to pass for what he is not. The charge of hypocrisy, so often made, is a projection of the national style of those who proffer it. Diplomats and observers who come from a tradition of Machiavellian calculations and elaborate self-serving designs tend to interpret all diplomacies in this way, and to see in double standards or in the legions of principles nothing but a reflection of age-old cynicism, a shield behind which it is polite, profitable, and practical to advance. But things here are not so simple; they go deeper. Nor do the tensions I have described come from pretenses. They come from the fact that the nation's values (and leaders) point simultaneously in opposite directions.

There is, in the American style, a tension between the instinct of violence and the drive for harmony. The United States is a nation impatient with, intolerant of, unadjusted and unaccustomed to basic conflicts of ends. (It would be interesting to analyze the intellectual origins of this attitude, for instance in Puritanism. The *Federalist Papers* display the same hostility in their discussion of "factions.") The immigrants that founded and peopled the United States were exiles or refugees from societies where such conflicts were often inexpiable; indeed, these pilgrims and these huddled masses were often the victims of those conflicts. They wanted to build a society of concord and consensus. Moreover, the elements that made America were so diverse that this new Jerusalem could prosper only if the differences were sacrificed on the altar of harmony. Concord required the melting pot; for in any society threatened by deep conflict yet driven toward unity (from above, by charismatic leaders, or below, by popular messianic hopes), unanimity must be created or maintained as the only way of keeping the society together. The impulse of violence and the thrust toward harmony are both escapes from the unbearable reality of inevitable conflict.

When Americans *are* faced with a fundamental conflict of ends, their experience has been to resort to force—considered the most decisive and compelling of all ways to end such conflicts. In using force, they have sought not just the infliction of pain on the enemy, which Schelling rightly sees as a dirty bargaining process, but the elimination of the conflict through the elimination of the foe. "Coercive violence," being a process, requires rules and structures; it is part and parcel of societies to which conflicts of ends are inherent, it is a way not of eliminating the conflict but of managing it. In domestic affairs, the slightly hagiographic readings of American history have over-stressed harmony and community. Violence was used against Indians, Negroes, and among Americans, in a civil war that was the bloodiest conflict of the nineteenth century, and in labor conflicts that were anything but mild. What is unique about American history is not the absence of violence but the absence of permanent conflicts of ends, and the unwillingness to live with such protracted conflicts. As a result, violence plays the role of a great, cleansing purge. (After the Civil War, the issue of the Negro's civil rights remained, but the inexpiable conflict of ends was somehow appeased.) Whenever conflicts of purposes reappear, or when segments of the population feel threatened, the tendency to revert to violence reasserts itself both on the part of the majority and on the part of a minority that often has no other resort. Just as there is little middle ground in the "liberal society" between the nihilistic "alienation of the uncommitted" and the complacency of the great mass, there is little middle ground between the great consensus and violence in dissent. Arthur Schlesinger has written of President Kennedy's awareness "of the fragility of the membranes of civilization, stretched so thin over a nation so disparate in its composition, so tense in its interior relationships, so cunningly enmeshed in underground fears and antagonisms, so entrapped by history in the ethos of violence." [1] On the side of the committed majority, the "paranoid style in American politics," so well analyzed by Richard Hofstadter [2]—the witch hunts and extremism, the beatings and the lynchings—are the marks of a frustration that expresses itself in a kind of blind hitting out at evil rather than a forcing of the victims into "internal emigration" or permanent alignments, as in other societies marked by conflicts of ends. On the side of the dissenters, one small but significant symptom of violence can be seen in the record of assassinations of Presidents of the United States. In Europe, opposition to society or to the dominant politics has a way of being channeled through various institutions and competing ideologies or belief systems. But when there is a "tyranny of the majority," when the only avenues of dissent are narrow, a kind of desperado violence breaks out that expresses not only dissent but also the hopelessness and helplessness of the isolated, rejected, and unharnessed outsider. When a minority group is organized as a political or social force, it becomes part of the great consensus and no longer challenges fundamentals. As long as it does, it is condemned to the frustrations of quasi-clandestinity.

The United States' external experience has corroborated this internal one: conflicts of ends between the United States and other nations have again and again led to the simple and drastic test of arms: with Mexico, Spain, in World War I, in World War II. Thus, to use Ernest May's useful term, the resort to force has been the "axiomatic response" [3] of a nation whose initial harmony within and protected insulation without meant that human obstacles or contrarieties were resented as intrusions, like the sudden burst of a nightmare into a dream. Moreover in such conflicts, a long tradition of successes and pride in one's principles and in one's pragmatic skills foster a

[1] *A Thousand Days: John F. Kennedy in the White House* (Boston: Houghton Mifflin, 1965), p. 725.

[2] Richard Hofstadter, *The Paranoid Style in American Politics and Other Essays* (New York: Alfred A. Knopf, 1965).

[3] "The Nature of Foreign Policy: The Calculated vs. the Axiomatic," *Daedalus*, Fall 1962, pp. 653–67.

fierce competitiveness that clamors for nothing less than victory.

Yet at heart, America—proud of its unique harmony, its lack of ideological trenches, its capacity to absorb and fuse diverse experiences and peoples, its repudiation of power politics—dislikes the very violence that is its spontaneous response: horrendous proof of the fragility of the dream it likes to think it lives. Americans believe that violence is evil, perhaps because of their admirable, if slightly startling, conviction that tragic conflicts of ends are not a necessary part of life, and because force gives to clashes that ought not to exist a sharper reality, a kind of gory blessing and christening in blood. The presence of the damned spot makes it impossible to deny the nightmare. The only way of reconciling one's ideal of life to that presence and to that stench is to spread as much incense as possible into the air: if the means are deeply felt to be repulsive, they can be justified only by a holy end. And it is this lingering awareness of the evils of violence that lessens the role of force in American history. So the only excuse for violence is provided by high principles, but these in turn release in full the passion for unbridled violence. In the last analysis, violence is justified by only one ideal, which subsumes all those principles: not merely the final elimination of force from history,[4] but the final ironing out of conflicts of ends.

It is also part of the American experience and ethos to expect harmony as the norm—at the cost, sometimes, of a national repression of issues on which there is no consensus and no division deep enough to justify violence (civil rights).[5] When the division does go too deep, the will to restore the norm inspires the use of force. The impatience for harmony makes violence a curse and a necessity. It is because of a basic consensus on values and on structures, on institutions and on directions, that American society can afford to display many conflicts (and American social scientists take as a model a

[4] On this point, see Robert W. Tucker, *The Just War* (Baltimore: The Johns Hopkins Press, 1960).

[5] See Kenneth Keniston, *The Uncommitted* (New York: Harcourt, Brace 1965), especially pp. 375 ff.

group theory that conceives of politics as a contest of interests for the distribution of resources). For those conflicts are channeled, tamed, and ultimately resolved by the basic consensus; they keep the consensus vigorous by nourishing it (and, in the utilitarian universe of group theory, the absence of "conflicts of gods" reduces political contests to a competition of measurable interests, leading to equilibrium). This is the sophisticated translation of a national experience without ideological differences and without profound class differences, in which political parties merely compete for the management of the basic order, and social classes are little more than the shifting products of income differences, having no metaphysical subjective connotations. In such a society, accommodation can be reached by purely technical means—*ad hoc* procedures of arbitration, mediation, compromise. "Reasoning together" is fruitful because the momentary clash on immediate objectives fails to erase a fundamental agreement on assumptions and purposes. The "engineering of consent" is a phrase that could gain currency only in a nation in which consent is a matter of engineering.

In other countries, differences in ideological outlook (which color, magnify, and distort clashes of interests), class oppositions, and the needed accommodations are infinitely more complex, more laborious, more creative. They require the painful consideration and reconsideration of questions that do not have to be asked here, where the answers are known and shared by all. When accommodation succeeds (as it has, on the whole, in Great Britain), the two extremes of force and "consensual engineering" are avoided. When accommodation breaks down, force is the remedy, but, given the nature of the society, it is more a political instrument, less a moral cataclysm; it is recognized as an inevitable last resort rather than a necessary calling. Since harmony was not a norm, violence entails less shame.

If politics, in Bertrand de Jouvenel's phrase, is what remains insoluble, then the United States is an unpolitical nation. Political systems avert force through the more or less dirty, more or less civilized bargaining processes of disciplined violence; they aim less to resolve issues than to manage the unsolvable. In the United States, the bargaining processes aim to solve problems; the unsolvable brings forth the flash of force and the exorcising spell.

In foreign policy also, proneness to force and a pining for harmony are the two sides of the same coin. It would be a mistake to identify each side with a particular school of thought; for although force as the reflex of frustration is characteristic of radical nationalists in American history—from the days of the Spanish-American War to the days of Barry Goldwater— the "hawks" are not found in that one sector only. Even among radical internationalists, one may find the desire to brandish the shiny sword for causes supposedly of concern to whole mankind. On issues like Vietnam, or even the elimination of Tshombe's Katanga independence movement, recent memoirs and events show "evidence of a desire by the peace-lovers to show their belief in military solutions, too" [6] (and unconditional surrender was not an invention of radical nationalists). Conversely, the international harmony of good will is not the preserve of the internationalists. But both sides overestimate America's aptitude to influence the world, both "postulate a world responsive to our will." [7]

However, the tension between the two aspects is not easy to resolve. The nasty crack someone made about John Foster Dulles, that he brandished the Bible in one hand and the atomic bomb in the other, has a caricatural value that goes beyond the late Secretary of State. There is always the pole of force and the pole of friendship, the offer of nectar and the threat of napalm—sometimes in alternation, sometimes in startling juxtaposition (as in President Johnson's speech on Vietnam at the Johns Hopkins University in April 1965).

Toward force, even in the nuclear age, the basic attitude is a crusading one. But the crusader must be cautious; there are all those rungs on the ladder of escalation; and he must master the art of climbing without a fall into nuclear hell. The only justification for this disagreeable task is, still, the cause

[6] Theodore C. Sorensen, *Kennedy* (New York: Harper & Row, 1965), p. 638.

[7] Charles Burton Marshall, *The Exercise of Sovereignty* (Baltimore: The Johns Hopkins Press, 1965), p. 88.

for which he must climb the ladder. Bad conscience, which explains the crusading attitude, now demands self-restraint, which does not come easily but which is rightly seen as the only way to prevent the use of force from abolishing history and man, instead of conflicts among men and force in history. Bad conscience thus turns into its opposite—excessively good conscience—by the satisfaction derived from following a clean, cool, cautious, and controlled strategy of limited brute force and graduated infliction of pain. Bad conscience also explains why the crusader must paint a gruesome picture of the enemy that makes him more diabolical, more effective, more powerful, more insidious than he is. For were the foe anything less, the shame of violence could not be removed; yet if the foe is a monster, guilt can be turned into pride. Bad conscience explains why there remains a strong and sincere dislike of the United States' own use of force for "possession goals." Bad conscience explains why there remains a damning dislike of the use of force by others; they usually seek possession goals and are resigned, nay, sometimes even dedicated to, the perpetuation of conflicts of ends in an imperfect world. Bad conscience explains why America trusts only America with force, for what it has faith in is not its sword but its principles, with which the sword is oiled. Overwhelming foes with our power thus becomes the necessary prelude to the healing victory of our vision of harmony. So strong an insistence on central control for nuclear weapons, on undivided commands in military operations cannot be explained by technical reasons alone; the unwillingness to entrust the sword to others has deeper reasons. There is no deceit in the American way of telling other nations, with a straight and suffering face, that they ought to leave to us the horrors and the burdens and the ironies of nuclear responsibility. Nor is there hypocrisy in the shrillness with which we assert, whenever we are locked in battle abroad, that none "of our political or economic interests [is] involved," [8] since indeed "we have few national interests in the narrow sense, outside our own territory." [9]

[8] Dwight D. Eisenhower, *The White House Years: Mandate for Change* (New York: Doubleday, 1963), p. 364.

[9] George Ball in Karl H. Cerny and Henry W. Briefs, eds., *NATO in Quest of Cohesion* (New York: Frederick A. Praeger, 1963), p. 18.

Beyond the excessively somber universe of force, there is only the excessively light universe of friendship and consensus: a world in which alliances are interpreted as incipient communities, localized rehearsals for a general world order, laboratories of the common good; a world in which personal contacts, functional assistance, cultural exchanges, and increasing cooperation are expected to grow into order and stability; a world in which legal texts are supposed to turn moral aspirations (deemed sacred to all) into the universal rule of law, and to exorcise evil practices by calling them illegal; a world that is just an enlarged and idealized version of home.

Those realms—force and friendship—are combined, not in any organic way, but only at the level of disembodied or contradictory principles and at the level of operational pragmatism. "You are advancing in the night bearing torches toward which mankind would be glad to turn, but you leave them enveloped in the fog of a merely experimental approach." [10] Hence the jarring juxtaposition of the Sermon on the Mount and of the variations on Clausewitz.

The same men, with the same good faith, invoke at one moment their experience as members of the beehive of the Atlantic Alliance in the late 1940s, when differences among nations in power or outlook somehow did not matter (with good reason); in the next, their contempt for world public opinion and their conviction that only power matters. At one moment, they explain their deep distrust of other countries' intentions and habits, in the next they proclaim their faith in a universal rule of law. To be sure, there is a kind of reconciliation in their minds, but it is too extreme to be explicit: given American principles, a world in which American power was supreme and unchallenged would be one of harmony, and the rule of American principles backed by American force would be the rule of law. Unfortunately, we are not ready for such a day; and in the meantime the elements coexist as well as they can, which often means not well at all. Thus, in Latin America, the United States simultaneously makes efforts toward development and progress which cannot succeed unless they shake oligarchies and dislodge vested interests, and efforts to prevent subver-

[10] Jacques Maritain, *Reflections on America* (New York: Scribner's, 1958), p. 118.

sion and insurgency which consist of rushing to the threatened gates and which therefore strengthen the *status quo*. In Europe, where we stress the virtues of federation, we tend to forget how few federations have been achieved or preserved without the use of force; and, when we insist that our allies must trust us with the supreme burdens of the common defense, we tend to forget that the community of purposes that would allow for such a mandate, has not yet been established.

A cynic could argue that a ruthless use of force for purely selfish purposes, but for such purposes only, is in the end more effective than resort to force on behalf of principles that alternately make one go too far for one's own good and make one stop half-way: the Soviet Union in Hungary, the French in Madagascar, gained more than the United States in Vietnam or, in all likelihood, the Dominican Republic. The American resort to force, somewhat uninhibited militarily because of the principles that promote it and the pragmatism that propels it, is often inhibited politically both by bad conscience and by the dream of brotherhood: hence a strange pattern, in which the sword is brandished but then once the dragon is wounded or is slain, one is at a loss. In Santo Domingo, the sudden realization that the use of force led down a blind alley and that the juntas or cliques the American intervention was serving were flawed (to use a polite word) led to a startling desire for a "coalition." In Cuba, only the fiasco of the Bay of Pigs saved the United States from the discovery that the replacement of the regime it wanted to destroy would perhaps have created more headaches than the Castro regime itself. In Vietnam, the contrast could not be greater between a spectacular military build-up and a pathetic political timidity which converts daily victories into glowing ashes.

There is another difficulty: both elements of the American dualism are (for different reasons) ill fitted for political realities. The side of force, by virtue of its heaviness, sinks deep into the mud of the road, whereas the millennial side, by virtue of its weightlessness, fails even to make contact. The sword clinks and swishes and cuts; the words dazzle and vanish. The military efforts leave marks, even if the result is not politically effective, even if the consequence is to divert energies in the wrong direction. Assumptions of harmony and consensus all too often have no result at all, except frustration, for efforts toward reform which lack instruments for reform remain in limbo. The pictures of John F. Kennedy will not hang forever in the huts of the Southern Hemisphere [11] if no deeds follow his ringing words. In Europe, calls for harmony leave the main issues in suspense and perpetuate the disarray in NATO; but in the meantime, American preponderance is preserved, and this too feeds that disarray. In Vietnam, the formidable difficulty of making American principles apply to a people apparently devoid of the capacity to govern themselves in any way we would like should American forces be removed, and the formidable difficulty of convincing a beleaguered opponent of a "sincere" desire to restore a dialogue, give the United States' peace proposals and offensives a singular woolliness, but there is nothing fuzzy about the cutting edge of its military operations. In such a quandary, Americans view their militant fist in an apologetic light: what really matters is the outstretched hand; and it is the contrariness of those who would deny harmony that obliges us to keep using our fist. Others, to whom disharmony is normal and who discount ideals that have no grip but who notice the fist that smashes, respond with regret or rage.

We thus are caught in a vicious circle. The brutality of force, even used for lofty principles, often suffices to corrupt or destroy our goals or to drive them underground. Marines are not the best agents of good neighborly relations; napalm (or the black market and prostitution that a huge military force brings in its wake) is not the surest agent of a dream of "an end to war . . . a world where all are fed and charged with hope." [12] The great society for all mankind must wait until the military costs of the war in Vietnam give way to programs instead of words. But the more unreachable the ends, the greater the "apotheosis of means." As a substitution for the faded vision, we offer what we know best—the by now familiar

[11] George Lodge, "Revolution in Latin America," *Foreign Affairs*, January 1966, p. 174.

[12] President Johnson, speech at the Johns Hopkins University, April 1965, quoted in Marvin Gettleman, ed., *Vietnam* (Greenwich: Fawcett Publishers, 1965), p. 329.

combination of force and economic aid. (What these really are is a substitute for political experience.) But "situations of strength" do not automatically convert our might into settlements negotiated on our terms, despite our rather mechanical expectations. They do not bring us closer to our vision; and, since only that vision justifies the force, we feel guilty, and we seek to exorcise that guilt with a purely negative incantation —that of anti-Communism. "The escalation of force" requires "an escalation of theory," to bring "the cost and the return into somewhat better balance." [13] It is the evils of communism that force us to use violence, we say; it is the wiles of communism that prevent us from establishing harmony. The concentration of our energies against the foe diverts us from, and gives us an excuse for giving up, trying to break down the deeper obstacles to harmony. When dissent racks our own alliances, we accuse the dissenters of playing into the enemy's hands.

When only the threat of this hydra-like enemy justifies our action, then we must interpret Marshal Lin Piao's celebrated manifesto, *Long Live the Victory of the People's War!,* as a new *Mein Kampf* (rather than as a devious way of telling future liberation movements to rely primarily on themselves). When harmony is the norm, we perforce see our foes as monsters, since their hostility is abnormal. A nation that recoils before the moral complexities of most political issues yet finds that it is not always possible to behave according to one's principles in international affairs tends to apply to its necessary acts the cosmetics of a higher cause. But others see through the make-up.

The trouble is that others judge us as we judge them: on acts, not on intentions. Nations always act as they are, rather than as what they think they are; or rather, in the eyes of other nations, our acts define what we are. Power talks loudly, even if the holders of powers speak softly, using loud words only to protest about the agonies of power. However much we may be convinced that we approach other nations as equals

[13] Theodore Draper, "The American Crisis," *Commentary,* January 1967, p. 41.

and as potential members of a community, they cannot help seeing the enormous reservoir of power behind us. When President Eisenhower tells Latin American students: "We know we make mistakes, but our heart is in the right place," [14] he may think he has straightened out the record, but they care little about the heart and find the mistakes more tangible than the motives. Aware of the frequent discrepancy between acts and intentions, we try to correct the situation by throwing our "sincerity" into the balance (as in our Vietnam "peace offensives"). But we do not sufficiently realize that the only proof of sincerity in international affairs is, as it were, to pay cash—even though we ourselves have a habit of asking for cash, not credit, deeds, not words. Indeed, we fail to realize that since our goals are often beyond reach or without substance, we tend in practice and for the short term to make anticommunism and pro-Americanism the criterion for our choices and substance of our goals—as when officials of the Agency for International Development define political development as "anti-Communist, pro-American political stability," or when our ambassador's advice to President Bosch, whenever the latter was under fire from the Dominican right, was for Bosch to take tough anti-Communist measures.[15]

Quietism and Activism in American Foreign Policy

The experience of a nation that built its strength through its ability to control nature and eliminate obstacles, principles that appear to have a built-in guarantee of self-evidence and universality, a method at its best in the assembly-line array of technical means—these do not prepare the nation and its statesmen for the complexities of sharing responsibilities and dealing effectively with other countries. The tension between the realms of force and harmony is compounded by a tension between what one might call the two *tempi* of America's foreign relations.

[14] Ibid., p. 29.
[15] John Bartlow Martin, *Overtaken by Events* (New York: Doubleday, 1966), pp. 471, 562.

The Wilsonian Syndrome

I take Woodrow Wilson as a symbol of a characteristic tendency in the whole nation's approach to foreign affairs. For years, he did his best to keep the United States out of those entanglements President Washington had denounced; America was "too proud to fight"; she was, in one observer's words, "to save the world through what she did at home . . . a model to be emulated rather than a pattern to be imposed." [16] In 1917, Wilson nevertheless decided that the United States must enter the war, or rather—again in characteristically American fashion—he was gradually pushed into it by the combined pressure of foreign misdeeds and the United States' image of itself. Here, indeed, is the thread of continuity: concern for the purity and vigor of the American message. When clouds on the horizon are thick enough to threaten the clear sky of America and obfuscate the world's vision by removing the American "model" from sight, the clouds must be dispersed and the sky made clear all over the globe.

The chief feature of the Wilsonian syndrome is an oscillation from quietism to activism. It is close to the "cycles" described by Dexter Perkins,[17] from phases of withdrawal (or, when complete withdrawal is impossible, priority to domestic concerns) to phases of dynamic, almost messianic romping on the world stage. When complacency brings crisis, quietism breeds activism. But the world resists and resents America's zeal; hence the United States withdraws, disappointed, from the world. The golden mean eludes. Foreigners are never sure whether they are going to be left to their own devices, with nothing from Washington except the advice to take whatever initiatives may be required, or whether they are going to be told in no uncertain terms what their fate is to be. But the world of international relations is a world of interdependence. Even the United States depends on its dependents. Both quiet-

[16] Roger H. Brown in Gene Lyons, ed., *America: Purpose and Power* (Chicago: Quadrangle Books, 1965), pp. 19–49.

[17] *The American Approach to Foreign Policy* (Cambridge, Mass.: Harvard University Press, 1952), Ch. 7.

ism and activism are "compensatory assertions of total independence" [18] and, as such, virulent accesses of nostalgia.

Even in the postwar era, which has nailed the United States to the cross of commitment, the quietistic impulse has not disappeared. It is expressed often enough on the left by men who have a lingering nostalgia for isolationist days, when domestic reform could be made the chief political issue, and who look forward to the day when the United States can practice neutralism. It is shared on the right by many who would like the United States to look after its own business behind a nuclear shield, which could be brandished to ward off foes but which would obviate actual entanglements. To some extent, the doctrine of massive retaliation functioned as a shield in this way, for the basic motive behind it was the avoidance of costly limited wars. Dirk Stikker has noted his impression of General Eisenhower's desire to get American boys home from NATO's Europe, as soon as possible after the recovery of Europe.[19] As in the great reversal of 1920, quietism has a way of following the frustrations of overactivism: the Eisenhower-Dulles doctrine of massive retaliation expressed the United States' revulsion over Korea. President Johnson's prolonged retreat from leadership in Europe follows the disappointments of the Grand Design. Even the very activist involvements in South Vietnam and Santo Domingo are accompanied by a desire to create a situation that would make a quietistic disengagement possible. Moreover, overcommitment in one part of the world may well lead, for institutional as well as for psychological reasons, to passivity and "abdication of power" elsewhere.[20]

There is a world of difference between a policy of self-restraint, which aims at influencing men and events and

[18] Keniston, cited, p. 304.

[19] *Men of Responsibility* (New York: Harper & Row, 1965), pp. 303 ff.

[20] For a critique of American "abdication" in the Middle East crisis of 1967, see Theodore Draper, "Israel and World Politics," *Commentary,* August 1967, pp. 41—42. A case could be made to show that in the days that preceded the outbreak of the war on June 5, a stronger American stand against Egypt, backed by *limited* military means, might have made the bloody "third round" between Middle Eastern neighbors unnecessary.

calculates that the best results will be achieved by vigilant un-
obtrusiveness, and an impulse to get off and get out. The
former is a policy; the latter is not. By its weight alone, a great
power influences and acts whether it wants to or not; self-restraint may (or may not, depending on circumstances) be the
most productive way of keeping control of men and events.
But the quietistic impulse simply gives up the attempt to control and stops worrying about where things will fall. Self-restraint is a way of collaborating with others, the quietistic
impulse is a way of repudiating them. Self-restraint is responsible, withdrawal is neglect. The trouble with quietism is that
a superpower cannot afford it, especially if its overactivism
has previously deprived its associates of the aptitude to act
responsibly.

For it is true that the United States' periods of activism
are marked by a kind of missionary busy-ness that makes
effective collaboration difficult. Sorensen said of President
Kennedy, but it is true of American statecraft as a whole, that
"he was at his best when his responsibilities did not have to
be shared." [21] To shake itself out of quietism, the United
States has to feel that it is in control—whether as dominant
head of a coalition, enjoying the privileges of "multilater-
alizing" its point of view, as in the days of President Truman;
or, when others are too reluctant, slow, or divided to follow,
through unilateral actions, as was often Dulles' tendency [22]
(despite all his pacts), and increasingly President Kennedy's
and Johnson's. It is significant that when the United States
awoke to the challenge of the postwar world, its program of
aid to Greece and Turkey was put "in a world perspective," in
the terms of a need to lead the fight against communism all
over the globe (despite George Kennan's objections). When
the United States intervenes, it is with the belief in the normal-
ity of its total leadership. This is true not only of the United
States government. American business abroad also can be un-
sharing in its own way—in the choice of investment, in the
organization of management, in the attitude toward local so-

[21] Cited, p. 563.

[22] See Victor Bator, *Vietnam—A Diplomatic Tragedy* (New York: Oceana,
1965), Ch. 14, on the "elbowing out" of France and Great Britain after Geneva.

cial customs and legislation, or in the distribution of benefits.

Another difficulty is that Americans express their activist selves by a proliferation of interventions and proposals. Just as the American car industry seems unable to let its yearly models alone, even when the changes are perfunctory, American foreign policy in its activist phases assumes that the national interest is involved in every corner of the globe and showers other nations with proposals and blueprints, as if "doing something" were the only logical way of "getting things done." [23]

The activist assumption that the United States leads the world is responsible for America's familiar overoptimism—the rosy expectations that make one wonder why, if circumstances are so favorable, there is any need for activism in the first place. External circumstances must yield to American techniques, foreigners (whose cooperation is needed) are seen as part of the team, and hostile foreigners are held susceptible to one's control. Unfortunately, this postulate of control leads all too easily to an erroneous assessment of the resources and trouble-making capacities of a friend or foe, as we have discovered, for instance, in dealing with de Gaulle's foreign policy and with North Vietnam.

[23] Since the fall of 1966, a shower of suggestions has been advanced by American foreign-policy-makers for "building bridges" to the U.S.S.R. and Eastern Europe—a worthy objective but one that could lead to trouble if our activist enthusism should be either exploited by the U.S.S.R. for its own political purposes, or misconstrued by our allies, always suspicious of direct U.S.–Soviet deals.

SUGGESTIONS
FOR FURTHER READING

Students and scholars intrigued by the concept of a contrapuntal civilization may wish to explore its complexities more deeply. The pertinent literature is virtually limitless, and no attempt is made here at comprehensiveness—merely suggestiveness within the loose framework of diverse possibilities.

Gregory Bateson first proposed the use of a "bipolar continuum" in identifying and distinguishing national characteristics in "Morale and National Character," an essay found in Goodwin Watson, ed., *Civilian Morale* (New York, 1942), 71–91. Two provocative applications of the concept of polarity in areas related to American history have been made by J. H. Hexter and Nikolaus Pevsner. See Hexter, "Factors in Modern History," in *Reappraisals in History* (New York, 1963), 26–44; and Pevsner, "The Geography of Art," in *The Englishness of English Art* (London, 1956), 11–19.

One of the best bibliographies on the subject of American national character appears in Michael McGiffert, ed., *The Character of Americans: A Book of Readings* (Homewood, Illinois, 1964), 361–77. A useful supplement is Burl Noggle's "Variety and Ambiguity: The Recent Approach to Southern History," *Mississippi Quarterly,* 17 (Winter 1963): 21–35.

The American Paradox, by Helene S. Zahler (New York, 1964), provides an interpretive synthesis of American history. It is simplistic and sketchy in spots, but often quite thoughtful.

Daniel J. Boorstin has criticized the elusiveness of a

"polar framework" for the study of national character in "America and the Image of Europe," reprinted in his collection of essays with the same title (Cleveland, 1960), 19–39. Allen Guttmann, *The Conservative Tradition in America* (New York, 1967), perceptively locates dilemmas and contradictions in some of our major thinkers, especially in "The Paradox of Southern Liberalism," pp. 32–46. Eric F. Goldman discusses individualism and populism in "Democratic Bifocalism," found in George Boas, ed., *Romanticism in America: Papers Contributed to a Symposium Held at the Baltimore Museum of Art* (Baltimore, 1940), 1–11.

Ambivalence has been characteristic of American assumptions about the past, about religious institutions, about the life of the mind, and about the landscape. See, for example, Arthur P. Dudden, "Nostalgia and the American," *Journal of the History of Ideas,* 22 (October 1961): 515–30; Robert N. Bellah, "Civil Religion in America," in William G. McLoughlin and Robert N. Bellah, eds., *Religion in America* (Boston, 1968), 3–23; Merle E. Curti, *American Paradox: The Conflict of Thought and Action* (New Brunswick, N.J., 1956); Leo Marx, *The Machine in the Garden: Technology and the Pastoral Ideal in America* (New York, 1964); and Roderick Nash, *Wilderness and the American Mind* (New Haven, 1967).

The development of pragmatic idealism emerges as a theme in Bernard Bailyn, *The Ideological Origins of the American Revolution* (Cambridge, Mass., 1967). Edward P. Alexander describes *A Revolutionary Conservative: James Duane of New York* (New York, 1938), while Timothy H. Breen sees John Adams as a conservative revolutionary in "John Adams' Fight Against Innovation in the New England Constitution: 1776," *The New England Quarterly,* 40 (December 1967): 501–20. John C. Miller's *Alexander Hamilton: Portrait in Paradox* (New York, 1959) is a thorough examination of Hamilton's career and writings, and emphasizes the contradictions and incongruities in a man who loved his adopted country but not its people, who undertook to run a farmers' republic for the immediate benefit of businessmen, who was a republican yet took the British monarchical constitution as his political model, and whose virtues were never far from his vices.

Arthur O. Lovejoy, "The Theory of Human Nature in the American Constitution and the Method of Counterpoise," in *Reflections on Human Nature* (Baltimore, 1961), 37–65, provides a profound analysis of *Federalist* Number 10 and shows that the Founders' cynicism about individual behavior caused them to seek counterpoise among political institutions as a means of restraining the men who controlled them. Paul Eidelberg, *The Philosophy of the American Constitution: A Reinterpretation of the Intentions of the Founding Fathers* (New York, 1968) offers a dualistic and controversial interpretation. David Tyack, "Forming the National Character: Paradox in the Educational Thought of the Revolutionary Generation," *Harvard Education Review,* 36 (Winter 1966): 29–41, touches upon the quest for cultural unity in the young republic.

William W. Freehling explores some of the contradictions in the political ideas of John C. Calhoun in "Spoilsmen and Interests in the Thought and Career of John C. Calhoun," *Journal of American History,* 52 (June 1965): 25–42. William R. Taylor's *Cavalier and Yankee: The Old South and American National Character* (New York, 1961) is rich in insight and subtlety, as is Fred Somkin's beautifully written *Unquiet Eagle: Memory and Desire in the Idea of American Freedom, 1815–1860* (Ithaca, 1967). Rex S. Burns extends Marvin Meyers' dualistic Jacksonian to village blacksmiths and forgemen in "The Yeoman Mechanic: 'Venturous Conservative,'" *Rocky Mountain Social Science Journal,* 4 (October 1967): 8–21, while Cushing Strout extends Meyers' analysis of Tocqueville in "Tocqueville's Duality: Describing America and Thinking of Europe," *American Quarterly,* 21 (Spring 1969): 87–99.

For the later nineteenth century there are a number of relevant works, such as Philip Gleason, *The Conservative Reformers: German-American Catholics and the Social Order* (Notre Dame, 1968) and Frederic C. Jaher, *Doubters and Dissenters: Cataclysmic Thought in America, 1885–1918* (New York, 1964). The biographical approach is also fruitful for this period. See Mark M. Krug, *Lyman Trumbull: Conservative Radical* (New York, 1965); Michael Wreszin, "Albert Jay Nock and the Anarchist Elitist Tradition in America," *American Quarterly,* 21 (Summer 1969): 165–89; and Naomi W. Cohen, *A Dual*

Heritage: The Public Career of Oscar S. Straus (Philadelphia, 1969).

In *The Paradox of Progressive Thought* (Minneapolis, 1958), David W. Noble suggests that Veblen, Becker, Croly, Patten, Ely and their generation believed simultaneously in such polar opposites as liberty and uniformity, freedom and authority, savagery and civilization, science and faith. See also Morton White's chapter on Veblen, "The Amoral Moralist," in *Social Thought in America: The Revolt Against Formalism* (Boston, 1957), 76–93. As a pertinent case study in Progressive sensibility, see Walter Lippmann's *Drift and Mastery: An Attempt to Diagnose the Current Unrest* (New York, 1914). By the later 1920s American intellectuals were trying seriously to come to terms with some of these contradictory tendencies. See, for example, Benjamin N. Cardozo, *The Paradoxes of Legal Science* (New York, 1928); Arthur O. Lovejoy, *The Revolt Against Dualism: An Inquiry Concerning the Existence of Ideas* (London, 1930); and especially Cynthia Eagle Russett, *The Concept of Equilibrium in American Social Thought* (New Haven, 1966), which examines developments in political science, sociology, and anthropology.

Daniel Walden, ed., *American Reform: The Ambiguous Legacy* (Yellow Springs, Ohio, 1967), contains some disparate essays, some unsatisfactory ones, and some thoughtful ones. Carle C. Zimmerman, "The Evolution of the American Community," *The American Journal of Sociology,* 46 (May 1941): 809–17, provides a semi-historical approach. Zimmerman distinguishes between nominal and real types of community organization, and discerns a process of "play and counterplay [which] has continued through the whole history of the American community."

The concept of hyphenated Americanism may very well be symptomatic of the dual allegiances felt by many immigrant groups in this country. Explorations of this social and emotional biformity appear in Louis L. Gerson, *The Hyphenate in Recent American Politics and Diplomacy* (Lawrence, Kansas, 1964) and in Alexander Alland, *American Counterpoint* (New York, 1943), a photographic essay in praise of pluralism.

Lionel Trilling was the first critic to call for analysis of

American literary traditions in terms of debate, struggle, and dialectic. See "Reality in America," in *The Liberal Imagination: Essays on Literature and Society* (New York, 1950), 3–21. Stephen E. Whicher has brilliantly dissected the "double consciousness" of Emerson in *Freedom and Fate: An Inner Life of Ralph Waldo Emerson* (Philadelphia, 1953); and Joel Porte widens the connection in "Emerson, Thoreau, and the Double Consciousness," *The New England Quarterly,* 41 (March 1968): 40–50, wherein the dualistic problem of reconciling the Soul with Nature is discussed. Edward Wagenknecht, *John Greenleaf Whittier: A Portrait in Paradox* (New York, 1967) makes the militant Quaker appear appealingly ambivalent—a mystical realist.

Herman Melville's novels are filled with psychological and philosophical tensions. Perhaps the best introduction from the perspective of this anthology is Henry A. Murray's brilliant editorial essay in *Pierre; or, The Ambiguities* (1852: New York, 1949). For two of Melville's later contemporaries, see Richard Wilbur, "Sumptuous Destitution," in *Emily Dickinson: Three Views* (Amherst, 1960), 35–46, and Edmund Wilson, "The Ambiguity of Henry James," in *The Question of Henry James. A Collection of Critical Essays,* F. W. Dupee, ed. (New York, 1945), 160–90. Charles C. Walcutt, *American Literary Naturalism: A Divided Stream* (Minneapolis, 1956) contends that the main stream of Transcendentalism divided toward the end of the nineteenth century and produced two lines of thought: the approach to Spirit through intuition, nourishing idealism, progressivism, and social radicalism; and the approach to Nature through science, nourishing mechanistic determinism. The dualistic cast of John Crowe Ransom's mind is probed by Robert Buffington in *The Equilibrist: A Study of John Crowe Ransom's Poems, 1916–1963* (Nashville, 1967). The "polar imagination" of Faulkner is examined in *Quest for Failure: A Study of William Faulkner* (Ithaca, 1960) by Walter J. Slatoff.

Various studies of American popular culture confront the problem of contradiction, notably in the areas of art, leisure, sport, and role identity. Among the more interesting studies are Barry Ulanov, *The Two Worlds of American Art: The Private and the Popular* (New York, 1965); Russell Lynes, *A Sur-*

feit of Honey (New York, 1957); Gregory P. Stone, "American Sports: Play and Dis-Play," *Chicago Review,* 9 (Fall 1955): 83–100; and Patricia Cayo Sexton, *The Feminized Male: Classrooms, White Collars and the Decline of Manliness* (New York, 1969).

Deriving his title from a remark by Thomas Jefferson, Jack Bell has written *The Splendid Misery: The Story of the Presidency and Power Politics at Close Range* (New York, 1960). One of the most symptomatic campaign documents to appear in recent years was written by Robert H. Finch and Richard C. Cornvelle, entitled *The New Conservative-Liberal Manifesto* (San Diego, 1968). John H. Bunzel has captured the essence of an important recent phenomenon in *Anti-Politics in America: Reflections on the Anti-Political Temper and Its Distortions of the Democratic Process* (New York, 1967).

Paradoxically, authors of diverse ideological persuasions all seem to recognize major paradoxes in the nature and operation of American capitalism. Speaking for the conservatives, Richard S. Morrison has written *The Paradox of Capitalism: A Discussion of Certain of the Inner Contradictions of Our System of Free Capitalism and How They May be Resolved* (New York, 1964); and speaking for the left, Sidney Lens has written *Poverty: America's Enduring Paradox: A History of the Richest Nation's Unwon War* (New York, 1969).

The racial problem in America has had its anomalous aspects also. Witness Nathan Glazer, "America's Race Paradox: The Gap Between Social Progress and Political Despair," *Encounter,* 31 (October 1968): 9–18; Martin Kilson, "Black Power: Anatomy of a Paradox," *Harvard Journal of Negro Affairs,* 2 (1968): 30–34; Nathan Hare, *The Black Anglo-Saxons* (New York, 1965); J. Kirk Sale, "The Amsterdam News: Black is Beautiful/Ugly, Comfortable/Sensational, Moderate/Militant," *The New York Times Magazine,* February 9, 1969.

In writing *The Lonely Crowd: A Study of the Changing American Character* (New Haven, 1950), David Riesman turned Ralph Barton Perry's "collective individualism" on its head. What had once been regarded as a positive good came to be viewed with pejorative pity. *The Americans: A Conflict of*

Creed and Reality (New York, 1969), by Ronald Segal presents a critically compassionate view intended especially for non-American readers. Thomas J. J. Altizer, leading American exponent of the "God is dead" theology, entitled his major treatise *The Gospel of Christian Atheism* (Philadelphia, 1966). And René Dubos has written "The Despairing Optimist," an appreciation of the late Joseph Wood Krutch, *The American Scholar* 40 (Winter 1970–71):16–20.

In *Bullet Park,* (New York, 1969) John Cheever's latest novel, the author divides the American psyche between his two main characters: Eliot Nailles and Paul Hammer. Nailles is conventional, upper middle class, stable, and hypocritical. Hammer is unconventional, illegitimate, unstable, and brutally honest. Nailles is oversexed, provincial, respectable, and fond of the status quo, while Hammer is under-sexed, cosmopolitan, shady, and searching for change. Nailles is first and foremost a father, raises an overprotected child, loves his son, and finds friendship an important part of his life, whereas Hammer is essentially a neglected child, unloved by his parents, and incapable of friendship. Nailles has too much ancestry, his existence is too routine, but ultimately he affirms life. Hammer has no ancestry he can claim, is incapable of permanency, and finally suffers from a death wish. *Bullet Park* stands as the latest and one of the better attempts by a contemporary novelist to see the American personality whole by dividing it in half.